50 HIKES
IN THE BERKSHIRE HILLS

OTHER 50 HIKES BOOKS OF INTEREST

50 Hikes in Vermont

50 Hikes in Massachusetts

50 Hikes in Connecticut

50 Hikes in the Maine Mountains

50 Hikes in Coastal and Inland Maine

50 More Hikes in New Hampshire

50 Hikes in the White Mountains

50 Hikes in the Adirondacks

50 Hikes in the Lower Hudson Valley

50 Best Hikes in New England

50 HIKES
IN THE BERKSHIRE HILLS

Lauren R. Stevens

THE COUNTRYMAN PRESS

A division of W. W. Norton & Company

Independent Publishers Since 1923

Manufacturing by Versa Press
Book design by Chris Welch

The Countryman Press
www.countrymanpress.com

A division of W. W. Norton & Company
500 Fifth Avenue, New York, NY 10110
www.wwnorton.com

978-1-58157-356-5 (pbk.)

10 9 8 7 6 5 4 3 2

To my children and grandchildren

"They, hand in hand, with wandering steps and slow,

Through Eden took their solitary way."

John Milton, *Paradise Lost*

Although Eden is changing, it can still be enjoyed.

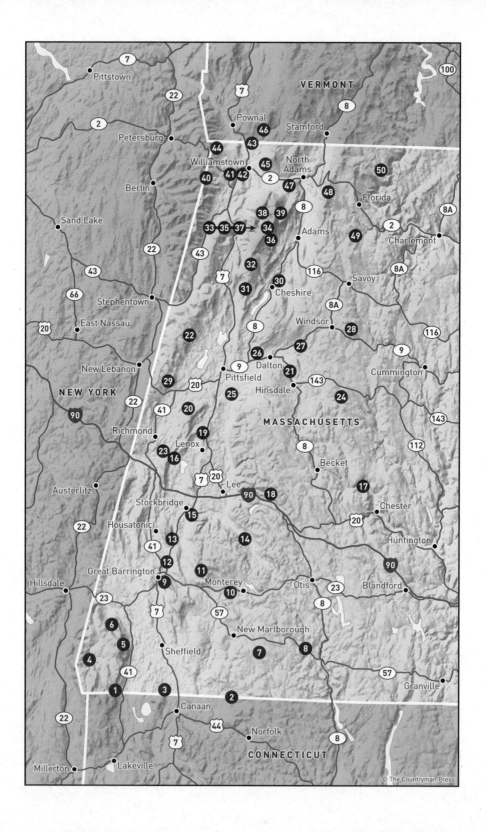

Contents

III. NORTHERN BERKSHIRES | 149

Foreword

To the imaginative mind, every one of our beautiful Berkshire mountains invites the question of what lies beyond. The US Census Bureau declared the American frontier closed in 1890, but our personal frontiers remain countless. Thanks to foot trails—and to the fine book you're holding—you can expand your horizons without spoiling the experience of discovery for those who follow.

Every trail will move you from here to there. The better ones will please you as you walk. The best will tell a story from start to finish, rich in detail, structured for tension and reward, packed with emotional power.

Peter S. Jensen, one of our country's leading designers and builders of natural trails, began his practice in the Berkshires. You'll see his work at the Great Barrington Housatonic River Walk. You'll notice Jensen's craft on portions of the trail up Monument Mountain. Walk his paths around Olivia's Overlook and at Stevens Glen. Enjoy some of his finest work at Basin Pond in Lee, on the Old Mill Trail in Hinsdale, and high on the Hoosac Range up north.

Jensen is to trails in our time as Frederick Law Olmsted was to parks in his. Make yourself a connoisseur. Locate his trails, here in the Berkshires and farther afield, and make them part of your life.

But don't forget that Jensen and his fellow builders would have nowhere to work without their predecessors. From the late 19th century onward, visionary men and women saw that Berkshire County would need to protect its most essential natural lands if people, plants, and animals were to have a future worth living in.

These men and women saw this—and they did something about it. Thanks to them, at this writing, to wit 240,000 of Berkshire's 600,000 acres will remain forever free from residential and commercial development. Groups ranging from town land trusts to governmental agencies care for these lands, doing all they can to ensure that these lands deliver benefits to you and me.

It is impressive ... but it's not enough.

Our conservation lands are vast, but fragmented. You might walk to the horizon line, only to confront a fence or a No Trespassing sign that stops you from going farther. To honor and fulfill the work of the past, we must finish the job.

Berkshire Natural Resources Council has launched a campaign to create a continuous, uninterrupted trail network throughout the Berkshires.

We call this the High Road.

We envision loop upon loop, linking paths long and short to the towns, villages, and cities where most of us start our daily journeys.

Why travel to the Rockies for endless hikes? Why fly to Europe for an inn-to-inn walking holiday? Why not vacation here in the Berkshires?

This web of trails—the High Road—will connect our developed world to land set aside for clean air and water, wildlife, farming, forestry, flood control, scenic views, recreation, study, and adaptation to climate change.

Over time, we will work with families

and institutional partners at every level to identify and secure the most critical land and trail connections needed to put the whole puzzle together.

It may take longer than our lifetimes to complete the Berkshire High Road. But we hope that some future edition of this book will not list 50 distinct hikes, but 50 highlights along an unbroken chain of pathways, each with its own story, each offering a new frontier to the imaginative walker.

Tad Ames
President
Berkshire Natural Resources Council

Preface

Berkshire County is unique, as far as I know, for the number and variety of day hikes through property open to the public, regardless of ownership, on well-maintained trails that are the pride of many hard-working organizations. This book tempts you to enjoy these trails, rediscover your natural habitat, and find a personal sanctuary in the beauty of the Berkshire landscape.

Perhaps with that in mind, neighbors often present this book as a welcome gift to newcomers. Although Berkshire claims many attributes, cultural and otherwise, an introduction to its trails is a gracious gesture.

I hiked every trail in this book during a concentrated period in the spring of 2015, so information is current as of that time. Many trails described here are new to the book; I have altered virtually all descriptions of those picked up from previous editions. All major waterfalls in the area are included, as are some out-of-the-way swimming areas. *50 Hikes in the Berkshire Hills* offers a new perspective on the Berkshire hiking landscape.

—LRS

Acknowledgments

Special thanks to those people who provided information, to those who have been hiking and walking companions, and to those who have been both, including county residents Rebecca Barnes, Robert K. Buckwalter, Henry N. Flynt, Jr., Dustin Griffin, Paul Karabinos, Allison Lassoe, Mike Leavitt, Christopher Niebuhr, Bernice O'Brien, and George Osgood. Berkshire native Ed Alibozek and Mike Whalen provided company and technical support. Dennis Regan, Robert Spencer, Edgar and Piri Taft, George S. Wislocki, Reinhard A. Wobus, and Alice Sedgwick Wohl, plus many more casual encounters with people who offered suggestions, on-trail and off. Whit Griswold's *Berkshire Trails for Walking and Ski Touring*, long out of print, introduced me to several previously unknown venues. The publishers and I thank him for making his text available as a resource.

I spent a fine morning hiking Shaker Mountain with John Manners, who rediscovered the sites, researched their history, and led the Boy Scouts in laying out the trail. Deborah Burns made stylistic suggestions on early drafts of the first edition. Robert D. Hatton, Jr., former County Trail Coordinator for what is now the Massachusetts Department of Conservation and Recreation, reviewed the original material and provided technical support for this edition. If you spot an error, blame me—and please let me know about it or other improvements via my publisher, so we can correct the next edition.

Introduction

Whether you want to spend an afternoon ambling through an azalea grove or take a strenuous day hike with sweeping vistas of five states, it's tough to beat Berkshire County. For variety and tradition, few areas in the United States offer prospects as rich as those of western Massachusetts. Some of the routes described in this book move you inward, toward contemplation and quiet. As Henry David Thoreau said of the Bellows Pipe, his trail to the summit of Mt. Greylock: "It seemed a road for the pilgrim to enter upon who would climb to the gates of heaven." Furthermore, he testified that he found Heaven on the summit. Other routes, beside brooks dropping many feet or along rocky ridges fringed with firs, may inspire you to shout with joy. Through them all, you will absorb the rhythms with which previous generations have trod, and enjoy being at one with ancients known and unknown, famous and infamous. The old carting roads, stone walls, cellar holes, and apple trees in the forests all have their stories.

The number of public trails on protected land in Berkshire is the product of numerous factors, probably the greatest being furniture making. Nineteenth-century loggers who provided wood from western Massachusetts for chairs and tables made in central Massachusetts tended to abandon their cutover areas rather than reforest them. The Commonwealth, concerned that it would run out of marketable timber, acquired the properties. The exodus of farmers to the west left more land to be acquired by tax taking. In the 1930s, the Civilian Conservation Corps was assigned to plant trees and create recreational amenities. Hence, the western end of the Bay State became weighted toward state forests and parks, so much so that in several towns the state owns more than half the land. Various land protection groups, such as Massachusetts Audubon and the Trustees of Reservations, and local land trusts (most notably their granddaddy, Berkshire Natural Resources Council), colleges and schools, municipalities, and other entities have added to the mix.

Most trails may have begun as Indian paths, carting roads, or logging roads. Just about every Berkshire stream once had a road beside it. They have been marked and kept open for hiking over the years, with re-routing as required, because their river neighbors eroded them. More recently, the laying out and construction of trails has become more professional, with pathways following the topography rather than fighting it, and the heavy work done to move stone, create water bars, or cribbing almost invisible to most passers by. The result is to make the trail seem as natural—and manageable—as possible.

These descriptions overflow into neighboring states and counties because Berkshire's mountainous boundaries—the Taconics, Greens, Hoosacs, and Litchfield Hills—themselves offer prime areas to get out and enjoy the outdoors under your own locomotion. The Berkshire region can test the limbs and meet the curiosities of daily walkers in infinite ways. Though I certainly couldn't include all the trails, this little book lists 50 of the best.

A FEW DEFINITIONS AND LIMITATIONS

I occasionally identify a route as a "walk" rather than a "hike," not necessarily because it is shorter, but because it involves less up and down. Hike and walk descriptions are somewhat idiosyncratic. They will all get you there, but some linger longer on details of nature or culture.

Each description tells you the *length in miles* of the outing. Each hike description gives *elevation gain*, not just the height from base to summit, but the total distance upward. Each lists *elapsed time*, since you are more likely to wear a watch than a pedometer. This statement may soon become outdated as more and more hikers carry hand-held devices that allow them to check mileage, time, and elevation gain, not to mention GPS for the trailhead. A warning accompanies these figures, given in hours and minutes (1:37): you should add at least 20 minutes per hour, because **minutes in the book include only travel time**, not time to look at views or historic artifacts, for the best way to ford a brook, or for an obscure blaze. Or to take a breather. I resort to bold type because users of this book should understand that the pace is meant to be the minimum, not the optimum. Energetic folk, unencumbered by packs, papooses, or wandering puppies, measured the times.

Most of the hikes are in the woods or on mountain ridges, as are most of the walks. Many pass sites of cultural significance. Most trails are open to mountain bikes. The text hints at some cross-country skiing and road bicycling possibilities.

This book is not a guide to the extended hiking trails in and near the county, although sections that you pass over while following these routes are described. For further information, see the Appendix. The Appalachian Mountain Club and the Taconic Hiking Club publish guides to the Appalachian Trail and Taconic Crest Trail, respectively. See the Bibliography for these and other pertinent guides. The book includes suggestions for camping, covering state-owned properties only. Reservations for Massachusetts's state-owned campgrounds can be made through reserveamerica.com.

Trails in this book are marked by blazes. A blaze is a daub of paint or other bit of color, usually at about eye level, marked directly on a tree or rock—or on wood or metal attached to a tree, or to a post driven into the ground. A common route for two trails may be blazed with two colors. (Or it may be that maintainers have decided to change the color.) Two blazes, one above the other, signal a sharp turn or other unusual circumstance ahead. In this county the long distance trails are blazed white, including the Appalachian Trail, Taconic trails, and Mahican–Mohawk Trail; side trails are blazed blue; trails that don't connect to the long trails are blazed orange or red . . . although local exceptions may surpass the rule. Adjacent states have different marking systems. The maps referenced are standard USGS 7.5 minute series, 15′ quadrangle, available at bookstores or sporting goods stores, and at store.USGS.gov, or elsewhere online.

How to Use This Book

This book tries its best to be accurate and helpful. Neither the author nor the publisher can be responsible beyond that effort. Many things, both natural and man-made, are subject to change and out of the author's control. Despite the best intentions, errors are possible.

KEY TERMS, IMPORTANT NAMES, ABBREVIATIONS

The word "facilities," as used here, refers to man-made structures that could be convenient for hikers. For example, the descriptions differentiate between flush toilets and privies—what the state calls "pit toilets." Many properties now have privies powered by the sun. The initials "HQ" refer to headquarters for either state-owned or privately owned properties open to the public. The difference between "Hikes" and "Walks" is explained in the Introduction, as is the term "blazes," and how to read them.

"CCC" stands for the Civilian Conservation Corps—the New Deal employment of young men that improved forests and created recreational facilities. Their boot prints are all over Berkshire. "SCA" stands for Student Conservation Association, a more recent creation modeled after the CCC, that engages young people in environmental education and conservation, especially trail work. "AMC" refers to the Appalachian Mountain Club, the hiking and environmentally oriented not-for-profit organization that advocates for trails and hiking in the Northeast. It is related to, but not

the same as, the Appalachian Trail Conference, a group of local organizations that maintain the Appalachian National Scenic Trail ("AT"), the foot trail from Georgia to Maine that passes through Berkshire County. Some of the book's hikes and walks use parts of the footpath. While much of the AT runs across state land, as do most of the trails in this book, the National Park Service has purchased stretches of land to create an AT corridor to protect the trail.

Another not-for-profit environmental organization, the Massachusetts Audubon Society—a separate entity from the National Audubon Society—owns and maintains three sanctuaries in Berkshire, two of which are described here. Another major landowner, The Trustees of Reservations (TTOR), is also private. TTOR is a statewide group originally founded as analogous to a public library: a resource available to the public for beautiful and historic places. Five hikes or walks in this book take place on their land.

Though the land we walk on overwhelmingly belongs to the people of Massachusetts, the New England Forestry Foundation, another private group, owns the Dorothy Frances Rice Sanctuary. The Laurel Hill Wildlife Association, the Berkshire Natural Resources Council (five hikes), and the Williamstown Rural Lands Foundation own land over which the book walks and advocate for trails. Hikes and walks also cross the lands of Berkshire School in Sheffield, and Buxton School and the Clark Art Institute in Williamstown. Two hikes cross land belonging to Williams College. Walkers in the county owe a debt to many private landowners who willingly share these special places.

Walkers are indebted, as well, to numerous groups who lay out, maintain, and map trails, such as the Appalachian Trail Conference, Berkshire Natural Resources Council, Berkshire School, Massachusetts Department of Conservation and Recreation, the Green Mountain Club, the Williams (College) Outing Club, and the Taconic Hiking Club of New York—which is responsible for the Taconic Crest Trail (TCT).

ADDITIONAL MAPS

To find some of the less obvious corners of the county, a supplement to regular road maps is advisable. One is *Jimapco Map C12, Berkshire County, MA*. It is available in bookstores, drugstores, and newsstands or from Jimapco, 2095 Route 9, Round Lake, NY 12151: sales @jimapco.com, 1-800-MAPS 123. A lovely road map, originally drawn by Harry W. Heaphy, is available from the Register of Deeds, 44 Bank Row, Pittsfield, MA 01201. (Warning: the roads are coded by ownership, not present condition.) Our List of Maps indicates the U.S. Geological Survey quadrangle(s) for each hike and walk. These maps are available directly from the survey or at bookstores, sporting goods stores, and online. They provide the base for virtually all county maps.

ORGANIZATION

Following a generally accepted tradition, this book is organized into three parts: South, Central, and North County, as shown on the maps at the beginning of each section. The individual hikes are arranged loosely from south to north, as well. That system should help you locate the hikes and walks closest to you. Here is a plug, however; try some hikes or walks farther removed. They have interesting differences, which will help define the characteristics of the walks with which you are most familiar.

ACCESS

Using Tanglewood (on the Stockbridge-Lenox line) as the Berkshire reference point, here are distances to the following cities:

CITY	TIME	MILES
Albany	3/4 hr.	40
Boston	2½ hr.	135
Bridgeport	2 hr.	110
Danbury	1¾ hr.	85
Hartford	1½ hr.	70
Montreal	5 hr.	275
New Haven	2½ hr.	115
New York City	3 hr.	150
Philadelphia	4½ hr.	230
Providence	2½ hr.	125
Springfield	3/4 hr.	35
Washington, DC	7 hr.	350
Waterbury	1½ hr.	75
Worcester	1¾ hr.	90

Berkshire County is 56 miles south to north, from Sheffield to Williamstown. Depending on the season and the weather, a leisurely drive up Route 7 takes less than two hours. Route 8 takes a bit longer. Because of the mountain ranges that run along this route, east-west travel across the county remains more difficult, with all the county's east-west routes (2 in the north; 9, mid-county; 23 in the south; I-90, alias MassPike), these roads can be tricky drives in freezing or snowy weather.

Transportation

GETTING TO THE BERKSHIRES

From the south: Drive north on one of the most beautiful roadways in the world—the Taconic State Parkway. (I know, I know, it's narrow and slow, troopers hide behind every shrub, but open your eyes, people!) For southern Berkshire, exit the Taconic at "Hillsdale, Claverack, Route 23," and follow Route 23 east, toward Hillsdale and on to Great Barrington. For Stockbridge, Lee, and Lenox, proceed up Route 7. For Pittsfield and northern Berkshire, exit the Taconic at Route 295, to Route 22, following Route 22 north to Route 20 for Pittsfield, or to Route 43 through Hancock to Williamstown and North Adams.

Route 7 north was an early stagecoach thoroughfare to Berkshire, and you join the same trail at Danbury, via I-684 and I-84. To arrive in southeastern Berkshire, Route 8 is a scenic drive that follows the Farmington River north.

From Boston and east: The scenic Massachusetts Turnpike (MassPike, I-90) is the quickest, easiest route west to south Berkshire and Pittsfield. Most people exit at Lee or West Stockbridge. Farther to the north, eastern entry to Berkshire County can be gained by driving the Mohawk Trail, also known as Route 2.

From Manhattan, by bus (6.5 hours): Leaving from New York City's **Penn Station,** Bonanza (800-343-9999) stops in Great Barrington, Lee, Lenox, and Pittsfield on the way to Williamstown and Bennington, Vermont. Berkshire locales marked with an asterisk are Flag Stops, where you must wave to the driver in order to be picked up.

From Boston (3.5 hours): **Peter Pan** runs daily to Pittsfield and Lee-Lenox out of the Trailways Terminal at South Station. Transfers are required for North Adams-Williamstown. Contact 800-343-9999 or www.peterpanbus. com for prices and schedules. Peter Pan and Bonanza are really the same company.

In Pittsfield, an intermodal center brings local and long-distance buses together with Amtrak on Columbus Avenue between North and Center Streets.

By train, commuters ride at a fraction of the regular rate if they take **Metro North** out of Grand Central Station and get off at Wassaic, New York (on Route 22 near Sharon, Connecticut). You can do the same. Amtrak (800-USA-RAIL, 413-872-7245) can also get you to the Berkshires. Their Turboliner from Pennsylvania Station runs frequently and smoothly along the Hudson River, making for a splendid ride. For southern Berkshire, stay aboard till Hudson, a recently restored river town; for northern Berkshire, stay on to Rensselaer. For travel connections from Wassaic, Hudson, or Rensselaer to the Berkshires, you may require a taxi or limousine.

From Boston: **Amtrak** continues

to run a single train daily through the Berkshires, starting from Boston's South Station.

Once you're in Berkshire, the Berkshire Regional Transit Authority offers bus service to most of the towns six days a week, barring holidays: www .berkshirerta.com, 800-292-BRTA; 413-499-2782. The buses have bike racks.

Two aviation companies in Berkshire County operate air taxi service to just about any other northeastern airport: Berkshire Aviation, Great Barrington Airport, 413-528-1010, 528-1061; Lyon Aviation, Pittsfield Airport, 413-443-6700; Harriman & West Airport, North Adams Teamflys, scenic rides, 413-862-9359

Lodging and Dining

Berkshire offers a host of possibilities for lodging and dining, from the humble to the luxurious. The area's popularity as a tourist destination means that visitors in the summer and fall high seasons must plan ahead. Lodging reservations are particularly important. You can contact the Berkshire Visitors Bureau—lbeach@1berkshire.com; (p) 413-743-4500; (f) 413-743-4560; 66 Allen St., Pittsfield, MA 01201—to ask for their package of brochures about lodging and dining. The Visitors Bureau provides telephone numbers for chambers of commerce and other lodging reservations services.

Don't forget that one of the best dining possibilities for hikers and walkers is a well-planned picnic. Berkshire offers several traditional country general stores where you can buy provisions, or, if you like, order an elegant gourmet picnic-to-go from one of the area's upscale grocers or caterers.

Safety

W̲alking and hiking are two of the safest and healthiest activities you can engage in. Compared to driving a car, working in the kitchen, or cutting firewood, your chances of injury are extremely small. That is the way it should be: walking should be a worry-free, non-competitive, relaxing hobby. Walking doesn't even lead to pimples.

This section ought to stop right here, without borrowing trouble. Nevertheless, after exploring the county for several decades, I have acquired knowledge that could save you some discomfort.

A FEW BASIC RULES

I want to share some things you probably already know, but of which you may need to be reminded—as I do. They are all summed up in rule number one.

1. Take a few minutes before you go out to think through what you're going to do.
2. Carry water. You can't be certain of the purity of even the loveliest mountain brooks.
3. Wear comfortable, sturdy shoes or boots—not sandals, sneakers, or running shoes.
4. Remember that it may get warmer or cooler, especially on ridges.
5. If you are going solo, tell someone where you are going.
6. Signs and blazes are man-made and cannot always be trusted. Leave the cares of civilization behind, but bring a map (such as the ones in this book), a compass, and a watch.
7. Stay on the trail.
8. Do not leave any trash.

These rules and this book ought to get you where you want to go . . . and back.

A few special words for Berkshire newcomers: Welcome! Do any dangers lurk on the roadside or in the woods? Yes, a few. In the extreme southwestern part of the county, rattlesnakes live on the rock outcroppings. This book warns you on which trails they might be near. *They* warn you if you are getting too close. Should you get bitten, you have time to get to medical help from just about any of the locations described here, which you should do in an unhurried, but deliberate manner.

You might see a bear, which will usually move away from you, especially if you make some noise (they are nearsighted). Although these are normally mild-mannered black bears, some have been fed by humans, and are therefore unpredictable. Do not approach a bear or any other wild animal.

If you are allergic to bees, carry a bee sting kit. In 50 years of walking in Berkshire, I have never seen rattlers; I have been stung by bees only once in the woods.

Poison ivy exists in openings at lower elevations. Look for three-leaves: either on the ground or as a vine. The rash is caused by an allergic reaction to the urushiol oil on the plants. It is not contagious. In case of contact, wash with soap in cold water (warm water opens pores).

The greatest threat comes from the smallest creatures, such as mosquitoes, which may—very rarely—carry West Nile virus or eastern equine encephalitis. On the other hand, ticks that carry Lyme and other diseases—usually referred to as deer ticks although they are more likely to be carried by mice—are rife in Berkshire County. Use a mild spray, tuck your trousers into your socks, and inspect yourself after outings. Ticks are very small, but you can see them when they move.

Because of the terrain, storms can arrive without much warning—more of a potential problem in the winter than the summer. Bring extra clothes.

HUNTING

Hunting is allowed on most properties described here. Stay out of the woods and even off gravel roads during hunting season. Check at the local town hall for pertinent dates, because Massachusetts, Connecticut, New York, and Vermont each have different seasons, and each state has a variety of seasons for different animals and weapons. In general, be on the alert from mid-November through mid-December, especially during shotgun deer season, which attracts the most participants. There is no Sunday hunting in Massachusetts, however.

AUTOMOBILES

Walk against traffic on roads. Wear reflective clothing at dusk. When parking your car, be certain the shoulder is firm. Lock your car. If you don't like to carry your keys for fear of losing them, remember that losing your keys is ultimately less of a nuisance than losing your car.

WEATHER

Mark Twain, who summered in Tyringham, said of the local weather: if you don't like it, wait five minutes. He exaggerated. However, Berkshire weather does grow less predictable as you gain elevation, and summer thunderstorms or winter snow squalls can come out of nowhere. Normally you would expect county weather to be affected by its proximity (less than 150 miles) from the ocean. Because of the hills, however, this area is controlled more by the prevailing westerly wind. Thus, winters are colder and summers are cooler than either east or south of Berkshire.

Average Temperature	
October	49.3°F
January	21.2°F
April	44.3°F
July	68.3°F

Average Precipitation	
Snow	70"
Rain	36.14"
Total	43.14"

Both of these scales are increasing due to climate change.

CLOTHING

You don't need to invest in trendy clothing, though if you enjoy shopping, don't let me stop you. Since the weather will change on your walk, wear layers. If that means taking a small pack, well, that pack can also carry camera, snack, small first-aid kit, extra socks, and rain gear. A cap is a good idea. A pair of well-broken-in, comfortable boots or shoes is your single most important piece of equipment. These shoes are worth some extra time, applying neats-foot oil or other conditioning. Some hikers prefer to wear thicker socks over thin, so that friction occurs between the layers rather than between your heel and the sock.

TRAIL INDICATORS

Most of the county's trails are well-marked, which means that the next blaze is generally visible from the previous one. Don't keep going if you run out of blazes. Instead, double back to your last blaze sighting to look for the next. Dry creek beds look deceptively like paths. While a blow-down can disrupt a path and force a temporary detour, trails described here are kept in good shape thanks to the hard work of many volunteers. If what you're on doesn't seem like a trail anymore, turn back until you find hard evidence that you're going the right way.

USEFUL ITEMS IN THE WOODS

Carry water, map, compass, jackknife, matches, whistle, and a small flashlight. Many people like to carry a cell phone or similar device—this does not mean, however, that you should call for help on the slightest provocation. The concept of charging people for searches is becoming commonplace. As well as providing stability and a little extra push when needed, a walking stick is useful for fording streams. Bring a book to read while soaking up the ambiance at a leisurely pace.

FIRST AID

I am just as confused as you about which insect repellants really work. I prefer to stick with herbs and stay away from chemicals. What you don't wear—such as shampoos, perfume, or after-shave—can also be important. If you make yourself smell like a flower, you are likely to attract bugs. Your first-aid kit should include an antiseptic ointment and bandages large enough to cover a blister on your foot and a wrap for a strain. Benadryl or Zyrtec could ease the itches, as will bathing an area in oatmeal. The latest word on snakebite is to get to a hospital rather than trying to treat it in the field. No more trying to suck out the poison!

As the saying goes, "Leaves of three, leave them be." Again, avoid poison ivy, bees, deer ticks, rattlesnakes, and bears.

After reading all this, you will know as much as the natives.

Berkshire History

Natural history and social history in Berkshire are tales of ups and downs. Looking at both from the perspective of the 21st century, you may feel that the past was better than the present, but it ain't necessarily so. The county testifies that geography, for all our veneer of civilization, is still destiny. Today this county maintains a delicate balance of being close, but not too close, to the Boston-Washington megalopolis that holds down the East Coast. This is an accessible hinterland, with the position and resources to rise up into the future.

Six hundred million years ago, the area was deep below the ocean, which was at work forming the rocks. It was warm and wet, with sandy beaches and clear, shallow waters. The lapping waves built up beaches that turned to sandstone, which in turn metamorphosed into quartzite—the erosion-resistant backbone of many of the county's ridges. Shelled marine animals left their shells behind, which built coral reefs, which then calcified into limestone. The deposits of this alkaline agent, still mined on the side of Mt. Greylock in Adams, protect the area from the worst ravages of acid precipitation today. Some of that limestone was re-crystallized into marble, of which snowy chunks grace the hiking trails and can be inspected at the Natural Bridge in Clarksburg. Muddy offshore sediments settled to form shale and then schist (crystalline rocks that fracture cleanly). The bands of granite that run through the southern part of the county predate the metamorphic rock.

The continents began to shift in response to subterranean pressure. At a speed of about an inch a year over 150 million years, the landmasses that would become North America, Africa, and Europe moved towards each other, closing the proto-Atlantic Ocean. Several arcs of offshore volcanic islands were shoved onto the continent by a series of slow but cataclysmic collisions known as the Taconic Orogeny (mountain building). The entire continental shelf was squeezed into a series of folds—the monumental forerunners of the Appalachian Range. The bases of these mountains, some Alpine in height, must have just about filled Berkshire, when the county reached for the sky. Then the continents began to pull apart, as they continue to do.

As soon as mountains were stacked up, the process of erosion began. Rain fell, forming rivers that still drain these hills, but in those days more vigorously carving a landscape unrooted by vegetation. Water and wind sculpted the Berkshire hills, raging unbroken by trees and shrubs. The rugged landscape was tamed, waiting only for plants to soften it.

Less than two million years ago, the first of four ice sheets ground down in response to a cooling climate. These mile-high glaciers brought debris, gravel, and rocks, which were deposited around the nubbins of mountains that remained..Glacial lakes covered most of North County and a good portion of the south. Because the Hoosac Valley was pre-glacial, once the melt set in, the

Hoosic River returned to flowing across the path of the ice. It therefore stands as an anomaly in New England, where most of the rivers run north-to-south as a result of the glacial combing. Nor were the beds of the Housatonic or Westfield much altered. The Farmington River ran up against a load of glacial trash that turned its general southerly course in Connecticut.

The ice withdrew as recently as 10,000 years ago. Vegetation and wildlife followed its retreating edge. Perhaps a few of the earliest North American inhabitants, having boated or walked across the land bridge from Asia, were in Berkshire to bid farewell to the ice. The evergreen forest gradually moved away to the north, lingering only on the tops of the highest ridges, while the broad-leaved, deciduous forest moved in, characterized in North County by sugar maple and in the South by oak, with their associated pines, ash, beech, birch, and alder.

The rocky steepness of the county does not lend itself to leisurely flowing water and big lakes. With the exception of the southern reach of the Housatonic, which meanders through Sheffield, Berkshire rivers retain little water and rush to their destinations. What lakes the county has are partly due to the efforts of 19th-century industrialists who created heads or reservoirs to provide year-round water for power or manufacturing processes: Otis Reservoir, Cheshire Reservoir, Pontoosuc, Onota, and others.

Seen from above, the county presents the ridges that remain from the north-south running folds: the Taconics along the New York line; the lower end of the Green Mountains protruding over the Vermont line; the Hoosacs filling the northeast quadrant; the Southern Berkshire Plateau filling the southeast quadrant; and a line of river valleys, just to the left of center, made up of the Hoosic and Housatonic—albeit flowing in opposite directions—that meet in New Ashford.

The Greylock massif stands as a peninsula to the Taconics—as indeed it was when glacial Lake Bascom filled the Hoosac Valley up to the 1,300-ft. contour. Therefore it's appropriate that the summit of Greylock lifts a War Memorial Tower, its design influenced by lighthouses, bearing a beacon that can be seen by people navigating most of the county. If any man-made feature were needed to unite a geographical area so topographically well-defined, it would be that tower and the roads it guards (Routes 2, 7 and 8).

Getting in and out and around Berkshire initially presented a problem. The earliest Americans generally thought of the area as removed from their Hudson River homes—a hunting ground to visit in the summer. The Mahicans entered from the south or north, along the river valleys. Although the Bay Colony claimed the land early on, Bay Colony residents found it tough to surmount the Berkshire barrier to the east. Early European settlers found it easier to enter along the valleys, with a few Dutch infiltrating through the Taconics from New York. Residents from the area now known as Connecticut came up the Housatonic. Thus, the county was settled from the south to the north, with the earliest towns in the south dating to the first quarter of the 18th century. The main roads, railroads, and even sewer lines now follow the valleys.

The European settlers were primarily farmers, who typically worked the bottomlands and, as they filled up, moved up the sides of the hills. Remains of walls, cellar holes, and orchards remind you that these lofty ridges were once homes, especially for those who made their living grazing cattle or merino sheep. In Stockbridge, the English Society for the Propagation of the Gospel in Foreign Parts set up an Indian mission, which gradually acceded to the land hunger of the Europeans. By the time of the Revolution, virtually all of the earliest Americans had departed.

As a farmer installed a mill to grind his corn or saw his wood, and his neighbors came to have him do their milling, so industry followed the plow. Settlements that began as groupings to protect against French or Indian raids became trading centers. Depending on natural resources, specialty manufactures developed, such as glass, paper, charcoal, and textiles. Even education can be seen as a Berkshire industry, dependent on natural resources. After all, as Thoreau said of Williams College's position at the foot of Greylock: "It would be no small advantage if every college were thus located at the base of a mountain, as good at least as one well-endowed professorship . . . Some will remember, no doubt, not only that they went to college, but that they went to the mountain." The mountains continue to instruct. In Berkshire County, four colleges and many secondary schools are located at the base of mountains.

The opening of the Erie Canal in 1825 provided a practical way for younger residents to head west, where the thick topsoil had fewer glacial stones than Berkshire. As a result, the county was drained of human resources. One by one, lamps winked out on the sidehill farms. Meanwhile, by the middle of the century, three-quarters of the trees had been stripped for pasture, furniture manufacturing, charcoal, or to feed the insatiable maws of the railroad, the county has been simultaneously re-vegetating for 150 years. Today the earlier ratio is inverted. The county is now three-quarters wooded, which is why coyotes, bear, beaver, turkeys, and even moose are returning to join the populous deer and smaller animals.

The most important industrial event in the county's history took place in 1886, when William Stanley linked 25 shops along the main street of Great Barrington to form the world's first commercial electric system. That, in turn, drew the General Electric Company to Stanley's shop in Pittsfield. GE has been here ever since, although now much reduced. The second most important industrial event was the opening of the Hoosac Tunnel—at 4.75 miles, the longest bore in the world in 1875—which broke through the Berkshire barrier for direct train service in the North County, from Boston to Albany.

Even in the heady days when industry was king—the population of Pittsfield grew from 25,000 to 58,000 in the first 60 years of the 20th century—second homes, tourism, and culture were already crowned princes. In the Gilded Age that ended the 19th century, wealthy families collected great estates and built luxury palaces, known as "cottages," some 75 in Lenox and Stockbridge. Major literary figures toured the county: Emerson, Melville, Hawthorne, Holmes, Thoreau, Wharton, Twain. Some settled here. Actors, musicians, and artists followed, and they are still following.

As the county now, somewhat painfully, recognizes that industries will never again be what they were during World War II, it is coming to rely on a service economy to which it is no stranger. Filled with fine educational institutions (public and private), museums and musicians, and art and artifacts to grace nature's green walls, Berkshire's streams are cleaner and its woods thicker than when farms and industry first came to these garrison hills. In addition, the hills retain a plentiful supply of ground water, likely to become increasingly important to the future of this area.

Berkshire has now, as it has had since the ice left, a long-settled population that cares deeply for the land. Witness the many towns that have long had zoning, have established land trusts, and are considering land use countywide. Berkshire residents listen attentively at town meetings to discussions of protecting ridges and aquifers, saving farmland, and cleaning up hazardous waste. Little litter mars the many paths. Whether you drive its roads or walk its trails, you will soon understand that this land is cared for and cherished.

Hikes at a Glance

Hike Number/Name	Town/Mountain	Distance (in miles)	Difficulty
1. Bear Mountain	Sheffield	10.56	Strenuous
2. Campbell Falls	South Sandisfield	.16	Easy
3. Bartholomew's Cobble	Ashley Falls	Varies	Easy
4. Alander	Mount Washington	5	Moderate
5. Mount Everett	Mount Washington	5.5	Strenuous
6. Jug End	Egremont	4	Moderate
7. York Lake	South Sandisfield	2.2	Easy
8. Clam River	South Sandisfield	1.5	Easy
9. Housatonic River Walk	Great Barrington	2 short walks	Easy
10. Diane's Trail	Monterey	1.5	Easy
11. Benedict Pond	Great Barrington	1.7	Easy
12. Housatonic Flats Reserve	Great Barrington	.8	Easy
13. Monument Mountain	Great Barrington	2.8	Moderate
14. Tyringham Cobble	Tyringham	2	Moderate
15. Three Trails	Stockbridge	Varies	Moderate
16. Olivia's Overlook & Yokum Ridge South	Richmond	1.6	Moderate
17. Keystone Arch Bridges	Chester	3	Moderate
18. Basin Pond	Lee	3	Moderate
19. Kennedy Park	Lenox	Varies	Easy
20. Pleasant Valley & Lenox Mountain	Lenox	3	Moderate
21. Old Mill Trail	Dalton/Hinsdale	1.5	Easy
22. Berry Pond	Pittsfield/Hancock	5	Moderate
23. Stevens Glen	Richmond	2	Moderate
24. Rice Sanctuary	Peru	1.5	Easy

Rise (in feet)	Views	Water-falls	Good for Families/Kids	Notes
4,028	*	*	No	One of state's finest views, 2 peaks, camping
-100		*	*	2-state falls, 2 trails in
N/A	*		*	A top natural spot in the nation; historic house
840	*	*	*	Taconic ridge with 360-degree views; side trip to spectacular falls: camping
1,752	*		No	Fine views on AT; camping; handsome school
N/A	*		*	Contrasting habitats; former ski area
N/A	*		*	Views around CCC pond; excellent swimming
N/A	*		*	Tour of forest types, river frontage; excellent fishing
N/A	*		*	Inspiring citizens' river recovery
N/A			*	Meditation trail & bridge in wildlife sanctuary
N/A	*		*	Striking pond in mountain setting; excellent swimming, camping
N/A	*		*	River and wildlife views close to shopping/restaurants
720	*	*	No—steep cliffs	Storied climb on rocky outcrops; fine views
450	*		*	View of picturesque village from AT
600 to tower	*		*	From icy gulch to tower to bucolic walk
440	*		*	Views of Stockbridge Bowl, Tanglewood, wooded terrain
N/A	*		* but no guard rails	Engineering marvel on wooded trail by scenic stream
N/A	*		*	Dam stories of man's errors—resolved by beavers
N/A			*	Old hotel site reverted to deep woods
2,786	*		*	Through Audubon Sanctuary up mountain with fine views
N/A	*		*	Well-made trail along scenic river; industrial remains
1,217	*	*	*	Azaleas, views, old ski trails, swimming, camping
320	*	*	*	Cataract descends through hemlock forest; viewing platform
N/A			*	High elevation forest; wildlife

25. Canoe Meadows	Pittsfield	1.5	Easy
26. The Boulders	Pittsfield/Dalton/Lanesborough	Varies	Easy
27. Wahconah Falls	Dalton	Short	Easy
28. Notchview & Windsor Jambs	Windsor	5.5	Moderate
29. Shaker Mountain	Hancock	6.5	Moderate
30. Ashuwillticook Trail	Adams/Cheshire/Lanesborough	3.2	Easy
31. Bradley Farm Trail	Greylock	1.8	Easy
32. Rounds' Rock	Greylock	1.25	Easy
33. Campground Trails	Greylock	Varies	Easy, Moderate
34. Overlook Trail	Greylock	2.5	Moderate
35. Stony Ledge & Roaring Brook	Greylock	5.6	Moderate
36. Cheshire Harbor	Greylock	6.6	Moderate
37. The Hopper Trail	Greylock	8.8	Strenuous
38. Prospect & Money Brook Trails	Greylock	7.8	Strenuous
39. Bellows Pipe Trail	Greylock	9.5	Strenuous
40. Berlin Mountain	Williamstown	5.25	Strenuous
41. Sheep Hill & Fitch Trails	Williamstown	3.9	Moderate
42. Stone Hill	Williamstown	2	Moderate
43. Mountain Meadow	Williamstown/Pownal, Vermont	Varies	Easy
44. Snow Hole	Williamstown/Pownal, Vermont	7.6	Moderate
45. Pine Cobble	Williamstown	3.2	Moderate
46. The Dome	Pownal, Vermont	5.2	Moderate
47. The Cascades	North Adams	1	Easy
48. Hoosac Range Trail	North Adams	6	Moderate
49. Tannery Falls	Savoy	3	Easy
50. Dunbar Brook	Monroe	4.2	Moderate

N/A			*	Audubon Sanctuary, wildlife viewing, large trees
175	*		*	Old estate with views
N/A	*	*	*	Storied, major waterfall
300	*		*	Great estate turned cross-country ski heaven; side trip to cascade
1,165	*		*	Walk through Shaker industrial and 2 holy mounts; Shaker Village
N/A	*		*	Lake, "jungle" on rail line turned bike path
N/A	*		*	Well-designed nature trail with views from trailhead
N/A	*		*	Fine views and blueberries; plane wreck
N/A	*	*	*	Dramatic Hopper view, cataract, old growth, camping
691	*		*	Unique Hopper views; old carriage road; camping
1.460	*		*	Former ski trail leads to one of state's finest views; camping
1,691	*		*	Easiest climb to summit; fine views; camping
2,390	*		*	Historic trail to summit with fine views; colonial road, camping
1,790	*	*	No	Rigorous climb, including rocks, to one of state's finest views; camping
2,187	*		No	Follow Thoreau to the summit; colonial road and relics
1,600	*		No	Steep climb; 360-degree views, old stage road and tollhouse remains; berries
600	*		*	Former farm, views, secluded glen and brook
250	*		*	Town's favorite hike with views of Clark Art, town, and college campus
varies	*		*	Open meadows and wooded land with history of use and abuse
1,400	*		*	History, views, geology; maybe snow
1,000	*		*	Join generations of college students for climb to view town, campus
1,750	*		*	Boreal forest, views
N/A	*	*	*	The city's in-town waterfall
700	*		*	Well-constructed trail to spectacular views of North Adams, Hoosac Valley
200	*	*	*	Double/triple cascades; camping
700	*	*	*	Rippling brook through old growth forest; camping

I.

SOUTHERN
BERKSHIRES

UPPER HOUSATONIC VALLEY NATIONAL HERITAGE AREA

"The Upper Housatonic Valley National Heritage Area exists to illuminate the diverse, rich identity of the Upper Housatonic River Valley region and to preserve and promote its historical, cultural and natural resources," according to upperhousatonicheritage.org.

In October 2006, the U.S. Senate passed legislation designating 29 towns in the watershed of the Upper Housatonic River Valley—from Kent, Connecticut, to Dalton, Massachusetts—as a National Heritage Area, making it part of the National Park Service system. The act authorizes funding for a variety of activities that conserve significant natural, historical, cultural, and scenic resources, and that provide educational and recreational opportunities in the area.

A feasibility study determined that such a designation would be the most

Lauren R. Stevens

RACE BROOK FALLS

effective way to accomplish the region's goals for cultural and environmental preservation and education. The study acknowledged the region's significant national contributions through literary, artistic, musical, and architectural achievements; as the backdrop for important Revolutionary War-era events; as the cradle of the iron, paper, and electrical industries; and as a home to key figures and events in the abolitionist and civil rights movements. It includes five National Historic Landmarks and four National Natural Landmarks.

Included in the Heritage projects are: Heritage Walks, an Afro-American Heritage Trail, an Iron Heritage Trail, and heritage indoctrination for local teachers.

Its 36,000 acres of unfragmented forest make up one of the largest such blocks between Virginia and Maine. The Schenob Brook basin includes rare calcareous fens, since limestone and marble bedrock lie beneath it. This feature provides for a diversity of plants and protects the creatures from the acidic deposition from upwind sources. The topography yields high-energy cascades, many dropping 70 or 80 feet. Yet these scenic, natural, and cultural treasures are relatively easy to reach and concentrated.

Most of the sites where you will hike in the Housatonic Valley play a role in this designation. This is an area where forested ridges, working farms, and villages retain the flavor of old New England—the valley being listed as one of the Last Great Places by the Nature Conservancy. Alander, Bartholomew's Cobble, Mt. Everett, Jug End, River Walk in Great Barrington, Monument Mountain, Tyringham Cobble . . . the list goes on. One of the best places to take in this landscape is from the half mile of ridge climbing from Bear Mountain toward the summit of Race Mountain on the Appalachian National Scenic Trail.

Bear Mountain

SALISBURY, CT/SHEFFIELD	
HIKING DISTANCE: 10.56 miles	
WALKING TIME: 5 hours	
VERTICAL GAIN: 4,028 feet	
MAP: Bash Bish	

On this ambitious 10.5-mile hike, beginning in Salisbury, Connecticut, and ending in Sheffield, Massachusetts, you climb two peaks, losing much of the altitude gained on the first before climbing the steeper second. Five or more hours of hiking doesn't include a lunch stop or arranging for the automobile shuttle. This is really an all-day hike, the longest in this book. Aside from the ineffable pleasure of being on the trail, you'll be rewarded with remarkable views, among the finest in a book full of remarkable views. Pick a clear day for maximum reward, especially taking in the intimate views of the South Berkshire landscape from the ridge on Race Mountain.

CAMPING

There are campsites along the Appalachian Trail at Sages Ravine, Laurel Ridge, and Race Brook; a shelter is available just north of Mt. Everett at Glen Brook.

GETTING THERE

Best as a two-car trip: park the first car at Race Brook Falls trailhead, 2 miles south of Berkshire School on Route 41. To get to 41, turn west in Sheffield by the Police Station on Berkshire School Road, then south on 41. Drive the second car about 7.5 miles south, or 1.5 miles beyond the Connecticut border. Look sharp on the right for an opening into a parking area marked by a small, blue sign that reads: "Undermountain Trail." There is a kiosk and a privy. For a determined soloist: ride a bicycle from Race Brook to Undermountain and stash it there.

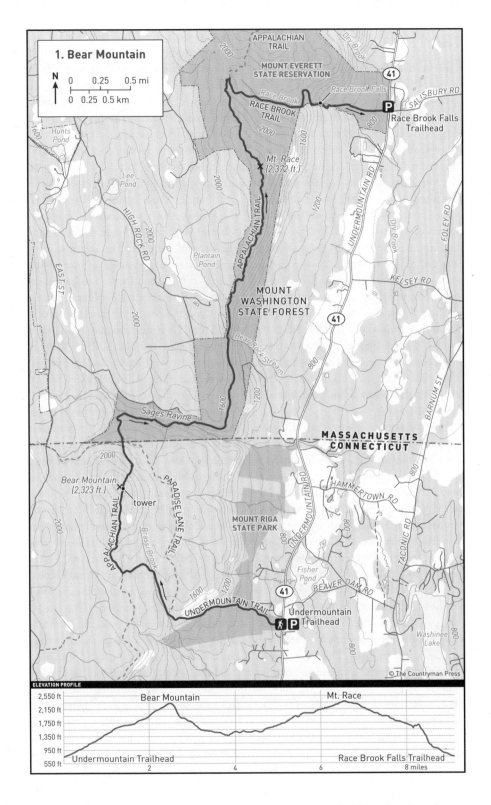

1. Bear Mountain

N

0   0.25   0.5 mi
0   0.25   0.5 km

APPALACHIAN
TRAIL

MOUNT EVERETT
STATE RESERVATION

Dry Brook

41

Race Brook Falls

Race Brook

SALISBURY RD

RACE BROOK
TRAIL

P
Race Brook Falls
Trailhead

Hunts
Pond

Lee
Pond

HIGH ROCK RD

2000

2000

2000

Plantain
Pond

2000

EAST ST

Mt. Race
(2,372 ft.)

2000

APPALACHIAN TRAIL

1600

1200

MOUNT
WASHINGTON
STATE FOREST

UNDERMOUNTAIN RD

41

Dry Brook

KELSEY RD

FOLEY RD

800

BARNUM ST

Bear Rock Stream

1600

1200

Sages Ravine

MASSACHUSETTS
CONNECTICUT

2000

Bear Mountain
(2,323 ft.)

tower

PARADISE LANE TRAIL

HAMMERTOWN RD

UNDERMOUNTAIN RD

800

TACONIC RD

2000

APPALACHIAN TRAIL

Brassi Brook

MOUNT RIGA
STATE PARK

Fisher
Pond

1600

1200

UNDERMOUNTAIN TRAIL

41

BEAVER DAM RD

800

Undermountain
Trailhead

P

Washinee
Lake

800

© The Countryman Press

ELEVATION PROFILE

2,550 ft	Bear Mountain	Mt. Race	
2,150 ft			
1,750 ft			
1,350 ft			
950 ft			
550 ft	Undermountain Trailhead		Race Brook Falls Trailhead
	2	4	6	8 miles

THE TRAIL

Hike from Connecticut into Massachu-setts so that you first experience the fine views from the grand and clear summit of Bear Mountain, and then those truly extraordinary views from the .5-mile ridge leading to the summit of Race Mountain. The extent of the panorama is unique in Berkshire County: the Housatonic Valley, in the two states, lies before you. This approach means going down the steeper side of Bear and Race mountains, however, which is a signifi-cant factor. If the trail is wet, you may want to take the Paradise Lane cutoff to avoid a possibly dangerous descent off Bear. Several lovely cascades and a gorgeous sight and smell of laurel (in June) also greet you. The access trails are each about 2 miles; plus 6.5 miles of the Appalachian National Scenic Trail (AT). Rattlesnakes have been seen in the area.

The Undermountain Trail (blazed blue) ascends in a determined, but mod-erate angle from the trailhead, which is wide and well-traveled (the most heavily used AT access trail in Connecticut). The oak forest is open. Although you cross streams, the route is predominantly dry. In 30 minutes, the Paradise Lane Trail exits right. (It continues to the AT avoiding Bear Mountain, making a sum-mit loop possible.) Pass over some bog bridges and through quantities of lau-rel. Turn north on the AT (blazed white) at 45 minutes. The campsite trail turns right 6 minutes later. The view opens up as you reach the pitch-pine-covered summit of Bear (2,351 feet) in 1:45. A plaque honors a stonemason whose labors yielded the monument that sig-nifies what was thought to be the highest peak in Connecticut. Climbing the stone

tower is best from the south side. (The highpoint of Mt. Frissell in Connecticut is higher, even though its summit is in Massachusetts.) Twin Lakes lie before you, as well as the curlicues of Schenob Brook, while the Housatonic River itself is obscured behind a low ridge.

The descent on the north is a steep scramble over rocks. Take care. In 20 minutes, reach Sages Ravine and the north end of Paradise Lane. Descend to the brook through a hemlock forest. In 5 minutes, a bridge leads to the camp-site, but follow along the south side—a precarious trail above the brook—for about 20 minutes. Cross the brook on stones, beginning a slow climb, partly on a woods road, with rock outcrops left. From the start, 2:30 takes you to the newly constructed Laurel Ridge Camp-sites and privy, substituting for the closed Bear Rock Falls Campsites, which were dangerously close to a precipice.

In 30 minutes, the view, especially on the east side, opens again as you con-tinue the slow approach to Race Moun-tain. (William Race was an early settler, killed in skirmishes with the Dutch who claimed ownership of the area.) The view extends from Mt. Greylock in the north to the Connecticut ridges. It is not so much a distance view as it is a compre-hensive look at what The Nature Conser-vancy calls one of the Last Great Places: a natural area of wetlands, water bodies, farmed fields, and wooded ridges. In 20 minutes arrive at the actual summit (2,365 feet) nestled in pitch pine that has been dwarfed by the wind and ice.

More laurel, oak, hemlock, and rock brings you in 40 minutes (about 3:45 from the start) to the Race Brook Falls Trail, where you turn right. Follow the brook, just forming, for 10 minutes until you cross the 2-log bridge and begin a

Lauren R. Stevens

TOWER BUILT WHEN BEAR THOUGHT TO BE TALLEST IN CONNECTICUT

LOOKING FROM THE APPALACHIAN TRAIL TOWARD RACE MOUNTAIN AND MOUNT GREYLOCK

Lauren R. Stevens

short climb; then walk down and across the stones below the upper cascades (23 minutes). The cascades are stunning and easier to view than the lower falls, to which a loop trail leads in 12 minutes. Your trail follows close, but above, the brook valley crosses the brook, and drops you in a field adjacent to the trailhead parking, 40 minutes from the "upper falls" (really a cascade), and 4:45 (call it 5) hours from the start.

Campbell Falls

This two-state park features a short walk down to the base of a nearly 100 foot waterfall, one of the major falls in the Berkshire region. More hiking is available on the Connecticut side.

NORFOLK, CT/SOUTH SANDISFIELD	
HIKING DISTANCE: .16 miles	
WALKING TIME: 20 minutes	
VERTICAL GAIN: 100 feet	
MAP: South Sandisfield	

GETTING THERE

Follow Southfield Road, south from New Marlborough to Southfield and the Norfolk Road south from there to Campbell Falls Road. The parking lot, somewhat obscure, is on the left. Or continue on Norfolk Road (Route 272) south into Connecticut, turning right on Tobey Hill Road to the park entrance on the right.

THE TRAIL

This little book introduces you to all the major waterfalls in Berkshire. Like the others, this is technically a cascade, with

CAMPBELL FALLS IN A TWO-STATE PARK
Lauren R. Stevens

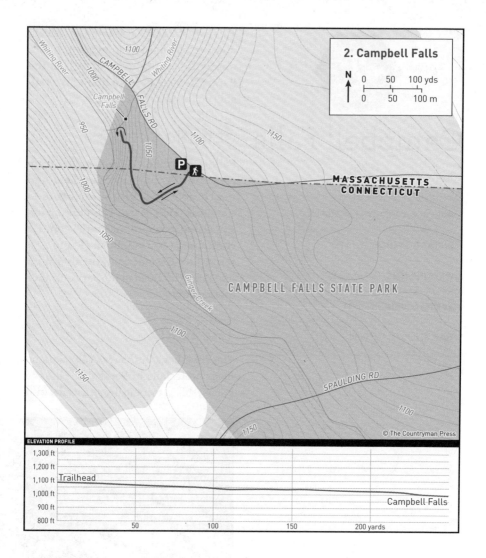

2. Campbell Falls

ELEVATION PROFILE

two pitches rather than one uninterrupted fall. Although the Massachusetts walk is short, it is steep. You pass the state boundary marker on the way. Those who want a longer walk should take the Connecticut option, about .5 miles in. Signs warn of dangerous swimming conditions.

Whiting Brook can be awe-inspiring as it drops, especially during heavy flow in the spring, or after storms. A setting of large hemlock adds to the majesty. The White Memorial Foundation of Litchfield, Connecticut, donated the property in 1923, and the two states passed special legislation the next year to cooperate in maintaining a two-state park. Massachusetts and New York cooperate to maintain a two-state park at Bash Bish and on the Taconic range at Petersburg Pass.

3

Bartholomew's Cobble

ASHLEY FALLS

HIKING DISTANCE: varies

WALKING TIME: varies

VERTICAL GAIN: N/A

MAP: Ashley Falls

The alkaline soil of this National Natural Landmark supports one of North America's greatest diversities of fern species (+/- 50) and their allies, as well as hundreds of woodland wildflowers. An optimum time to visit is in the spring, when the early flowers are out, but any season provides ample rewards. Furthermore, a pleasant walk next door takes you to the oldest house in Berkshire County: the Col. John Ashley House (1735), site of the Sheffield Declaration, which preceded the Declaration of Independence.

GETTING THERE

From Route 7 in Sheffield, turn west on 7-A, then shortly veer right over the railroad tracks onto Rannapo Road; continue right on Weatogue Road. Bartholomew's Cobble parking and visitors' center is on your left. The Ashley House is on Cooper Hill Road.

THE TRAILS

You are asked for a donation to support this property, and there is a fee to tour the Col. Ashley House. You have a choice of trails, which leave from the visitors' center. There is a self-guided tour of the Ledges Trail, a leisurely less-than-half mile, which has one of the most outstanding concentrations of native flora in the country. In some sections footing is rough as the trail winds down by the Housatonic River. Or you might like to hike up the Tractor Path (.75 miles) to the Connecticut line and take in a fine scenic vista of the Housatonic Valley. You pass through alternating woodlands and open fields rather than the special areas of ferns of native species. Backtracking, you could take a left on

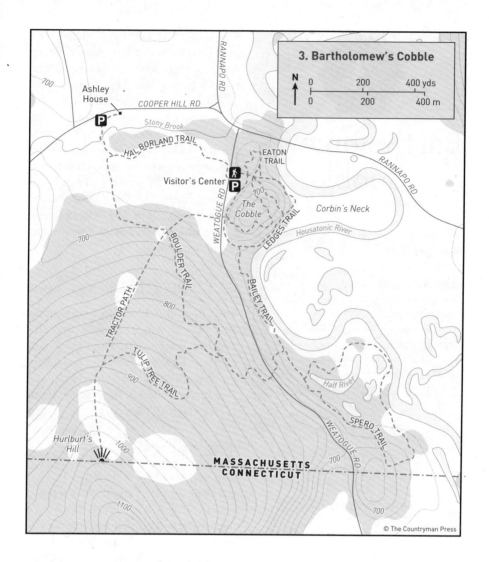

the Boulder Trail, crossing Stony Brook to the Ashley House. (The Col. Ashley House is described in the Culture section of this book.)

Col. Ashley led troops at the Battle of Bennington (1777). The Sheffield Declaration, written at the Ashley House, preceded the Declaration of Independence by three years. Theodore Sedgwick, originally of Sheffield but later of Stockbridge, successfully defended two of the Ashley slaves, Mumbet and Brom, who sought freedom under a "born free and equal" clause in the state's constitution. That decision led to the freedom of other slaves in the state. The house is open seasonally for guided tours. Note the remarkable collection of tools in the attic. The Borland Trail takes you back to Bartholomew's Cobble.

Lauren R. Stevens

SPRING FLOWERS AND FERNS AT BARTHOLOMEW'S COBBLE

THE VIEW FROM HURLBURT'S HILL

Lauren R. Stevens

Or, of course, you can join the various trails to spend a day on the 329-acre reservation. The Cobble, a name which refers to its rocky knoll, is a major migratory and nesting area for some 250 species of birds. Hurlburt's Hill is an excellent spot to watch for kettles of hawks from mid-September to mid-October. The area also contains one of the state's highest populations of bobolinks.

Alander

MT. WASHINGTON	
HIKING DISTANCE: 5 miles	
WALKING TIME: 3.5 hours	
VERTICAL GAIN: 840 feet	
MAP: Bash Bish	

Alander Mountain and Bash Bish Falls are remarkable by any set of criteria. (Pronounce it as you will, A-lander or Alan-der.) The open ridge of the mountain (2,250 feet) has a fine view west to the Catskills and, in clear weather, even to the taller buildings in Albany, New York, 50 miles northwest. The waters of Bash Bish Brook plunge 200 feet at the falls, the most spectacular in Berkshire, divided partway down by a pulpit-like granite outcropping before tumbling into a pool and then other riffles and pools downstream.

CAMPING

Part of the charm of Mt. Washington is the absence of any tourist facilities. There is a state-owned cabin on the trail between the two peaks of Alander that can be used on a first-come, first-serve basis. The primitive camping area on the Alander Trail is lovely for tenting (no facilities). Camping is available at the New York end of the two-state Bash Bish Park, with facilities. A cabin is available to AMC members (reserved in advance) off East Road near Sages Ravine.

GETTING THERE

Take Route 41 south from South Egremont Village, but turn right just past the pond, on Mt. Washington Road. (There is a state forest sign.) After 3 miles, the road swings southerly and begins to climb to a ridge. Signs help at the intersections, but you should essentially head straight to the Mount Washington State Forest Headquarters, on the right, 9 miles from the village. Park there and log in. There is a privy and a public telephone.

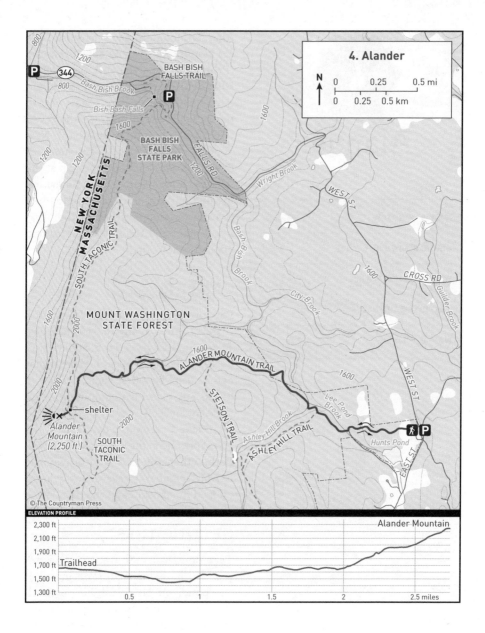

ELEVATION PROFILE

THE TRAIL

The Alander Trail is well worn from the Mount Washington State Forest Headquarters parking lot, where you can also register to use the campground. Follow the triangular blue blazes west, across a field, into woodland, and out into a blueberry field. At this point you are on what is virtually a road. At 9 minutes, cross a brook on a bridge and continue on the road, passing the Ashley Hill Trail, also a woods road, on your left (1 mile).

At 18 minutes, cross another bridge.

LOOKING WEST FROM ALANDER

Two brooks join here, with a mill foundation on the right. It's wise to wear hiking boots, rather than sneakers, on this somewhat wet trail. The trail rises moderately through hemlock forest, which gradually becomes a laurel grove, with a few birches and oaks. Old stone walls reflect the region's farming past. Pass the camping area to the left at 42 minutes. This oak/laurel forest is distinctly different from the northern hardwood forest you see farther up county, and characterized by a higher percentage of sugar maples. Similar spring ephemeral flowers are visible before the leaves come on the trees: mottled leaves of trout lily; hepatica with its blue-pink-white blossoms and oddly shaped

A CABIN NEAR THE SUMMIT

THE ALANDER SUMMIT

leaves; spring beauty, which has rose pink flowers with grass-like leaves; and distinctive Dutchman's breeches, with parsley-like leaves.

The woods road ends at a circle that marks as far as the warden could drive a jeep to get to the fire tower that once stood on Alander. Pass straight through, bearing left at a junction (both branches have blue blazes). Shortly, you will come to an ominous sign that says: "Last water during dry season," as the branch of the brook you are following begins to peter out. You are climbing more steeply through laurel now, including stone steps.

At 1:13, you'll see the state cabin in the notch between the south and north peaks of Alander. Just beyond is a bewildering nest of signs. Turn right, scrambling up the rocks to the western summit (3 miles from road). Note where you emerge on the cleared summit so that you can find your way back after exploring the area of the old fire tower footings for different views. The major highway on which you can see traffic is Route 22 in New York State. The white

between 200-foot rock walls. Although hiking to Bash Bish has fine views, this book recommends driving to Bash Bish or stationing a second car there. (You may have to go via New York State if Falls Road remains closed.) Follow the gravel road upstream from the parking lot to the falls. Stone steps lead down to the most dramatic view. Several people trying to climb the cliffs or dive into the pools have killed themselves. Rock climbing is only allowed with permission of the park ranger. The guardrails are intended to keep you on the trails. In addition to the danger of falling, rattlesnakes have been found in the vicinity.

Ten more minutes take you upstream to the upper parking lot, a good place to explore the lookouts. The gorge is colonnaded with large hemlocks, some of them clinging to what appears to be nothing but rock. Like every good county falls, Bash Bish has a myth of an Indian maiden connected to it. In this case, Bash Bish was unjustly accused of adultery and strapped into a canoe at the head of the falls as punishment. Just as the canoe was about to go over, the sun formed a halo about her head and butterflies gathered. Indians found the remains of the canoe in the pool at the bottom, but not her body. The falls still say her name, if you listen closely: bash, bish, bash, bish . . .

This Taconic ridge on the state's border is part of the Appalachians, pushed up when the continents collided and worn down by erosion ever since. The last glacier, 10,000 to 12,000 years ago, formed Bash Bish Brook when it melted. The quartz dike, halfway up the falls, was forced out of the earth 400 million years ago. As the sediment in the brook grows in the water, it will gradually destroy Bash Bish Falls. Enjoy it now!

blazes belong to the South Taconic Trail. There is a potential for rattlesnakes.

Massachusetts purchased the 400 acres around the falls in 1924, then purchased an additional 4,000 acres in the 1960s, to make up Mt. Washington State Forest. Since New York State owns land just downstream in Copake Falls and manages the camping area, this was the first case in which these two states jointly maintained a park (a second park is located at Petersburgh Pass, west of Williamstown). At the lower falls, two streams of water drop 80 feet

5

Mount Everett

MT. WASHINGTON

HIKING DISTANCE: 5.5 miles

WALKING TIME: 3.5 hours

VERTICAL GAIN: 1,752 feet

MAP: Bash Bish

Mt. Everett (2,602 feet) is the outstanding peak in Berkshire County south of the Greylock massif. Although the fire tower has been removed, views extend in most directions, especially as you approach the summit, as well as from the Appalachian Trail (AT) to the north and the south. The slopes are steep on this 5.5-mile hike, so wear good footgear for climbing over outcroppings of rock.

CAMPING

Numerous tenting sites exist in conjunction with the Appalachian Trail in this vicinity: sites just south of the summit of Bear Mountain, at Sages Ravine, and at Laurel Ridge are on the route described for hiking Bear Mountain. Bond shelter is nearby to the south and the Glen Brook shelter is north, over the summit of Mt. Everett.

GETTING THERE

Although most of the hike is in the uplands of the town of Mt. Washington, it begins at the Berkshire School, just off Route 41 in Sheffield. To get to Berkshire School, take Berkshire School Road out of Sheffield at the police station and jog north on Route 41 or, from the north, take Routes 23 and 41 west from Great Barrington. Bear south where 23 continues west, just after South Egremont. The school is 3.5 miles south of the junction.

THE TRAIL

Berkshire School (850 feet in elevation) is most attractive, set into the side of the hills and fronted by rolling, mowed lawns. An education there comes complete with skiing and hiking. Students maintain the Elbow Trail. Rattlesnakes

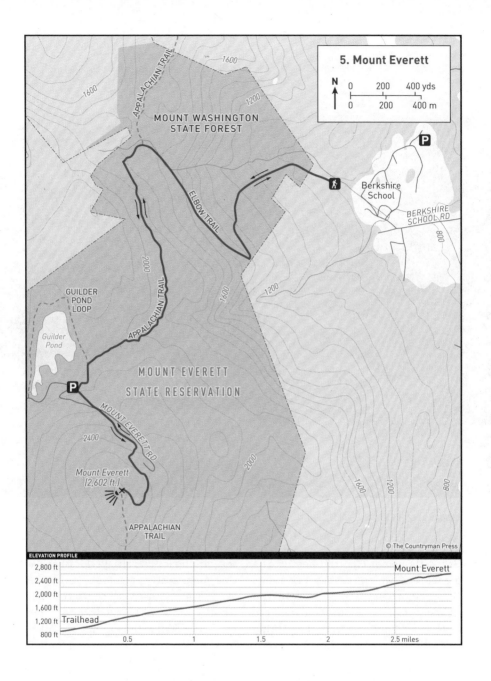

have been seen in the area, so stay on the trails.

To get to the school's visitor parking, bear right at the admissions building, past the tennis court and behind the hockey rink. You may have to ask directions to the trailhead, but you want to walk back towards admissions. Before you get that far, follow the service road by the north end of the main building.

SUNNING NEAR THE MOUNT EVERETT SUMMIT

Go past a home. The trail begins as a gravel road, which reaches a crossing. Go straight past a kiosk, where you should sign in. The Elbow Trail is blazed blue, about 5 minutes from the parking lot. It soon crosses a bridge.

The trail runs 1.2 miles to the Appalachian Trail, through hemlock woods, and gradually increases in steepness. A couple of trails branch off. At the elbow (15 minutes from the house), take a hard right with the trail, which meets the AT .5 mile farther north (40 minutes from the parking lot). As always, look back at this junction so you will recognize it on the way back (there is a sign). Turn left (south) on the AT, blazed white. From the Elbow Trail to the summit: 1.8 miles. In 30 minutes from arriving on the AT, you will reach the road up Mt. Everett at the Guilder Pond picnic area/parking lot (including a privy). A pleasant option takes you around Guilder Pond.

The trail crosses the road and parallels it the rest of the way to the summit. Note that the AT turns left at an

80-foot fire tower (1915-2002) isn't still here and open to the public.

As an alternative, a gravel automobile road (open seasonally) climbs very near the summit from East Street in Mt. Washington (you pass it on the way to Alander). Call 413-528-0330 to find out if the road is open. You could drive into the reservation to picnic at Guilder Pond and walk to the summit from the pond or from the end of the road. It would also be possible to walk north on the AT, to be met by a second car at Berkshire School, or south on the AT to be met at the Race Brook trailhead, having let the car do most of the climbing.

A SERIOUS HIKER CHECKS HIS BEARINGS
Lauren R. Stevens

old tower site (1:25), a site you may want to explore. Over the low shrubbery, including blueberry, scrub oak, and pitch pine, you catch views of Alander Mountain to the west, Mt. Frissell to the south, and, if you move around, other views as well. On a clear day, the Catskills are visible across the Hudson River. The foundations for the old tower make a nice picnic site with vistas, although growth on the summit means that better vistas can be found on the way up and down. Too bad the

6

Jug End

EGREMONT
HIKING DISTANCE: 4 miles
WALKING TIME: 1.5 hours
VERTICAL GAIN: N/A
MAP: Bash Bish

A lovely walk, mixing open fields and deep woods, while exploring the remains of Jug End Resort. The name derives from the German word *jugend* or "youth," perhaps a multilingual pun designed to rally young people to the resort. Or, perhaps a joke or a mistake. An older name for the area is Guilder Hollow, part of a large assemblage of open land in the Massachusetts-Connecticut-New York corner that The Nature Conservancy designates as one of the Last Great Places.

CAMPING

Numerous tenting sites exist in conjunction with the Appalachian Trail in this vicinity: just south of the summit of Bear Mountain, at Sages Ravine, and Laurel Ridge are on the route described for hiking Bear Mountain. Bond shelter is nearby to the south and the Glen Brook shelter is north, over the summit of Mt. Everett.

GETTING THERE

In South Egremont, turn south off Route 23 onto Route 41, and almost immediately turn west onto Mt. Washington Road. In about 1 mile, turn south on Jug End Road, marked by a chocolate-colored state sign. Do not turn in at the private buildings about .5 miles. Proceed to the large parking lot on the right.

THE TRAIL

A number of trails cross Jug End State Reservation and Wildlife Management Area. The Appalachian Trail crosses a short distance farther on Jug End Road, an alternative way of climbing past Mt. Bushnell to Mt. Everett. You are aiming for the Jug End Loop Trail. In case of

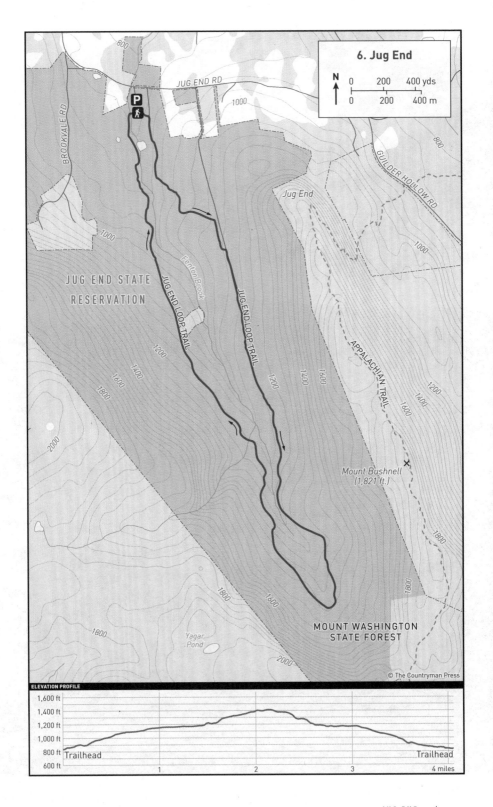

6. Jug End

N
0   200   400 yds
0   200   400 m

JUG END RD

BROOKVALE RD

1000

800

P

Jug End

GUILDER HOLLOW RD

800

1000

JUG END STATE
RESERVATION

Fenton Brook

JUG END LOOP TRAIL

JUG END LOOP TRAIL

APPALACHIAN TRAIL

1200

1400

1600

1200

1400

1600

1400

1200

1800

2000

1600

1800

Mount Bushnell
(1,821 ft.)

1800

1800

Yagar
Pond

MOUNT WASHINGTON
STATE FOREST

1800

1600

2000

© The Countryman Press

ELEVATION PROFILE

1,600 ft				
1,400 ft				
1,200 ft				
1,000 ft				
800 ft	Trailhead			Trailhead
600 ft	1	2	3	4 miles

<blockquote>Lauren R. Stevens</blockquote>

confusion, note that you are heading up on one side of Fenton Brook and back on the other. Before the property was acquired by the state, it was a resort and ski area, which explains the trails on the far hill.

Depart the east corner of the parking lot at an odd foundation and the Nature Conservancy sign on a mowed grass trail that heads uphill; turn right on an old road (17 minutes), following blue blazes. You will notice that the milkweed plants attract butterflies. Cross a field, heading up into the woods; and another field, bearing right, looking across at Mt. Danby. Turn left into hemlock woods off the road, and in 40 minutes cross Fenton Brook at an old cabin site with a fireplace. A blue arrow marks the way, which can be obscure. Follow the jeep road downstream, beside the brook. In about 1 hour, come into an open field again, where trails are mowed. Bear right; go right again at a small bridge. This should return you to the footbridge that leads to the parking lot.

JUGEND FEATURES FIELDS AND WOODED RIDGES

7

York Lake

Stop in at one of the best public swimming areas in the county, which is well-maintained, with clean changing rooms, but no lifeguards. (This popular area is closed when 300 swimmers assemble, so you may be turned away on a summer weekend.) Gasoline engines aren't allowed on the lake, so the water is clean and inviting once it warms up. The Loop Trail explores the periphery.

GETTING THERE

Route 57 drops from Route 23 to New Marlborough. South of New Marlborough, the New Marlborough-South Sandisfield Road passes the Sandisfield State Forest. Don't go by. A modest day-use fee or season pass is required from Memorial Day through Labor Day, and good at all state properties.

THE TRAIL

In 1935, the Civilian Conservation Corps created York Lake (formerly called York Pond) out of swampy wetland. Two hundred men lived in a camp off Route 183, working for a dollar a day to improve the state forest during the Depression. The forest consisted of

A FINE PLACE TO SWIM, BUT NOT THIS DAY

Lauren R. Stevens

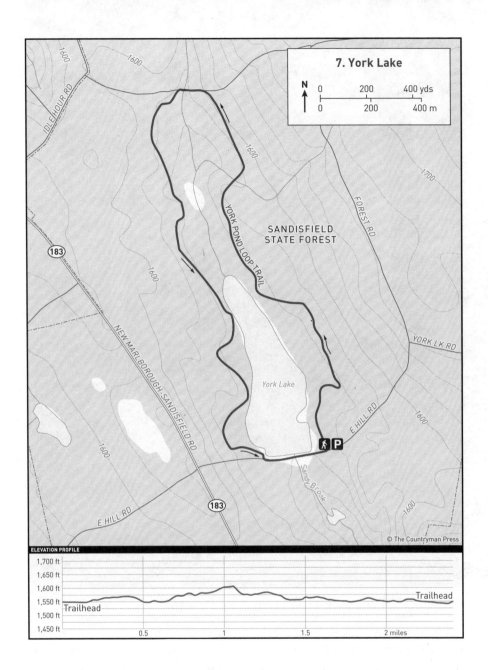

7. York Lake

SANDISFIELD STATE FOREST

York Lake

YORK POND LOOP TRAIL

IDLEHOUR RD

NEW MARLBOROUGH-SANDISFIELD RD

FOREST RD

YORK LK RD

E HILL RD

E HILL RD

Sandy Brook

183

183

© The Countryman Press

ELEVATION PROFILE

1,700 ft					
1,650 ft					
1,600 ft					Trailhead
1,550 ft					
1,500 ft	Trailhead				
1,450 ft	0.5	1	1.5	2 miles	

abandoned farmland and land cut over by the New England Box Company. The CCCs also created the swimming area and cut the trail. They built so many dams in the area that they were called the Sandisfield Beavers. In 1955, Hurricane Diane washed out the dam, which was rebuilt in 1959. A brochure provides this information—and more.

The Pond Loop Trail, which can be

THE OPEN FOREST AND TALL TREES AT YORK LAKE

wet, departs from the picnic area and follows the pond to a gravel road. The trail doubles back on the other, more scenic shore. It is blazed blue. It is possible to pick out remains from the farming days—and from logging, which continues. There are still some large pines and other species near the pond.

Half-mile walks from HQ lead to the former CCC camp and follow a gravel road to the grave of Josh Smith, a local resident. Other lovely walks are available on gravel roads. Just down the road is a memorial to five CCC wardens.

Clam River

SANDISFIELD

HIKING DISTANCE: 1.5 miles

WALKING TIME: 1 hour

VERTICAL GAIN: N/A

MAP: South Sandisfield

This lovely wooded property—with frontage along, you guessed it, the Clam—has become a favorite with its neighbors and, as the Berkshire Natural Resources Council expands the trail system, is likely to attract many more friends. Clam River has long attracted fisher folk. This description focuses on a "lollypop" trail—walking in from the parking lot and completing a loop. The Clam River was dammed above the site as part of flood control in Hartford, Connecticut, as it eventually joins the Farmington River.

GETTING THERE

The trailhead is at The Annex, town offices in Sandisfield, on Route 57. From most of Berkshire, take Route 23 southeast to Route 57 to Sandisfield.

THE TRAIL

Sandisfield town government welcomes hikers to park by the town offices. A kiosk shows the progress of the trail system. The Greenagers, teenagers from Great Barrington, have worked hard constructing trails on property that extends some 550 acres, with 1.5 miles of river frontage.

After a fairly steep descent, the entrance trail meets the loop in 10 minutes. Turn left, following a woods road (which extends to Hammertown Road). Turn sharply right in 5 minutes to work your way down closer to the river. An old wall speaks of farming days. In 20 minutes, pass an ideal riverside lunch spot and soon pass through some large pines. In a half hour, the trail turns right through a stone wall. Follow through a wet area on bog bridging until, at 50 minutes, turn left for the Annex parking lot—another 10 minutes, making for an hour's outing.

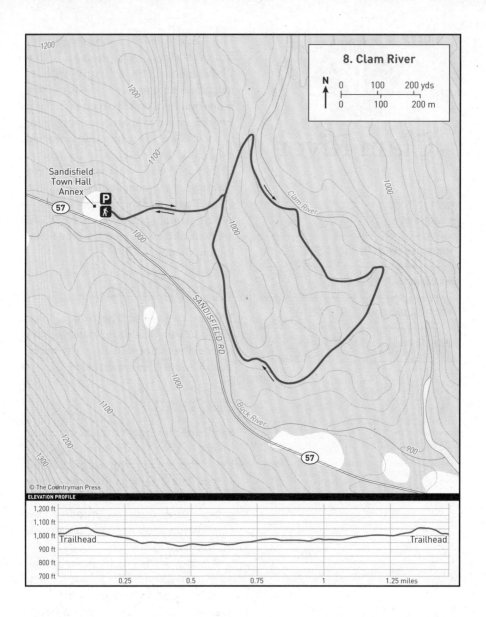

8. Clam River

N
0   100   200 yds
0   100   200 m

1200

1200

1100

1000

1000

Sandisfield
Town Hall
Annex

57

Clam River

1000

1000

SANDISFIELD RD

1000

1000

1100

1200

Buck River

1300

57

900

© The Countryman Press

ELEVATION PROFILE

1,200 ft				
1,100 ft				
1,000 ft Trailhead				Trailhead
900 ft				
800 ft				
700 ft	0.25	0.5	0.75	1	1.25 miles

CLAM RIVER

Lauren R. Stevens

9

Housatonic River Walk

GREAT BARRINGTON

HIKING DISTANCE: Two short sections

WALKING TIME: Including connecting walk through town, .5 hour

VERTICAL GAIN: N/A

MAP: Great Barrington

This project required considerable trash removal and laborious trail construction. As leader Rachel Fletcher says: "I don't think of it as 2,500 feet long, I think of it as 2,300 volunteers long." Since 1988, River Walk has rallied Great Barrington citizens to clean up the section of the Housatonic River that flows through town and to reclaim the banks from generations of industrial waste and neglect. The effort is ongoing.

GETTING THERE

The best starting point is from the Searles Middle School parking lot on Bridge Street in Great Barrington. Heading south on Route 7, Bridge Street is the left turn at a traffic signal in the middle of town.

THE TRAIL

This carefully conceived and laboriously executed project includes the W. E. B. Du Bois Garden, a native species garden at the site of the house where the educator, historian, civil rights activist, and founder of the NAACP was born. The stones are also local samples. The trail, which includes a canoe launch, runs both

GREAT BARRINGTON'S RIVER WALK PANELS TELL THE STORY

Lauren R. Stevens

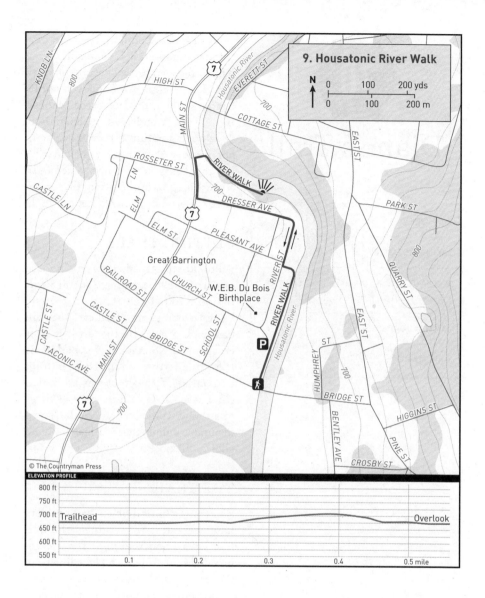

9. Housatonic River Walk

N
| 0 | 100 | 200 yds |
| 0 | 100 | 200 m |

© The Countryman Press

ELEVATION PROFILE

800 ft					
750 ft					
700 ft	Trailhead				Overlook
650 ft					
600 ft					
550 ft					
	0.1	0.2	0.3	0.4	0.5 mile

upstream past the Berkshire Corporation and downstream to Bridge Street, which has a memorial commemorating a battle in King Philip's War. Other aspects of the downstream portion include a nature trail, canoe landing, rain garden, memory bench, and overlook.

That's the river's-edge portion. Upstream is even more gutsy, with many stairs and boardwalks that bring you to the river. Walk up Dresser Avenue and

north on Main Street just beyond Brooks Drugstore. As at the lower entry, kiosks tell the story. Descend the steps to the trail proper and follow downstream for the equivalent of about a block, passing a piece of sculpture through which runoff flows, and a memorial bench. The river stands revealed, its banks stabilized, with native trees and other vegetation planted. Large cottonwood trees stand sentinel.

10

Diane's Trail

MONTEREY

HIKING DISTANCE: 1.5 miles

WALKING TIME: 45 minutes, plus a few minutes from parking to trailhead

VERTICAL GAIN: N/A

MAP: Monterey

Gould Farm, a community-based psychiatric rehabilitation center, has completed more than a century of work thus far. In 1992, an employee's wife, Diane Rausch, died of breast cancer. Along with friends, her husband, Bob, developed a nature trail and bridge in her memory. This nature walk in a wildlife sanctuary is a chance to honor, in a soothing, natural setting, those who have suffered from any affliction.

GETTING THERE

Follow Route 23 to Monterey; turn south on Curtis Road, near the General Store. A sign on Route 23 shows that Gould Farm welcomes trail walkers. The trail begins at a kiosk on the left just after crossing the Konkapot River; parking is 150 yards farther, on the right, in front of a garage. (Konkapot was an Indian chief associated with the area.) Copies of a thoughtfully-written guide, keyed to numbers along the trail, may be available at the kiosk.

THE TRAIL

The trail is blazed blue. Trail builders have worked hard to protect the wetlands with bog bridging. The recommended route follows a fence line from the kiosk to the large wooden footbridge, a particular memorial, over Rawson Brook and then along a property line to gravelly Wellman Road. Turn right on the road, crossing the brook, to the trail entrance (the area is still recovering from the tornado of 1995). The trail follows beside the brook, with lovely views of the water and ridge, back to the kiosk. A spur on the far side of the bridge leads to the confluence of Rawson and Konkapot, where a bench invites contempla-

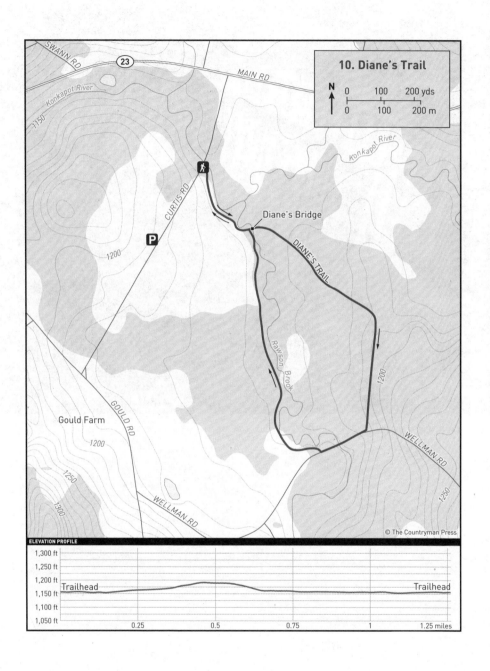

tion. Together with open field, the mix of lowland surrounding a meandering brook and slightly higher land pine forest provides habitat variety.

Lauren R. Stevens

THE MEMORIAL BRIDGE

Benedict Pond

GREAT BARRINGTON

HIKING DISTANCE: 1.7 miles

WALKING TIME: 1 hour

VERTICAL GAIN: N/A

MAP: Great Barrington

This fine swimming area in Beartown State Forest is available for walkers, and includes changing rooms and facilities. The pond is lovely, with dramatic woods and cliffs behind. A walking trail circles the pond; bicyclists may want to do a 3.5-mile road trip around Benedict Pond. A longer hike could include Mt. Wilcox.

CAMPING

Benedict Pond hosts a campground, which requires a modest parking fee. Lifeguards protect the swimming beach in season. At Monument Mountain, on Route 7 north of town, the picnic grove (910 feet) is a lovely, shaded picnic spot—but does not allow camping.

GETTING THERE

This walk can be reached from Great Barrington's Monument Valley Road. Coming south on Route 7, turn left just beyond the high school. Turn left again on Stony Brook Road, which becomes Blue Hill Road. A bicycling expedition from Monument Valley Road is 12 miles. Turn left to Benedict Pond at the chocolate state forest sign to walk a circuit. There is a small parking fee in season.

THE TRAIL

Benedict Pond is a Civilian Conservation Corps project, where Fred Benedict and other local farmers used to cut ice from what was then a much smaller pond. The CCC built the dam in 1934 in what was mostly a red maple swamp. You walk over the dam at the end of the outing. Pick up the self-guided interpretive flyer at the kiosk by the boat launch area. It is keyed to numbered posts

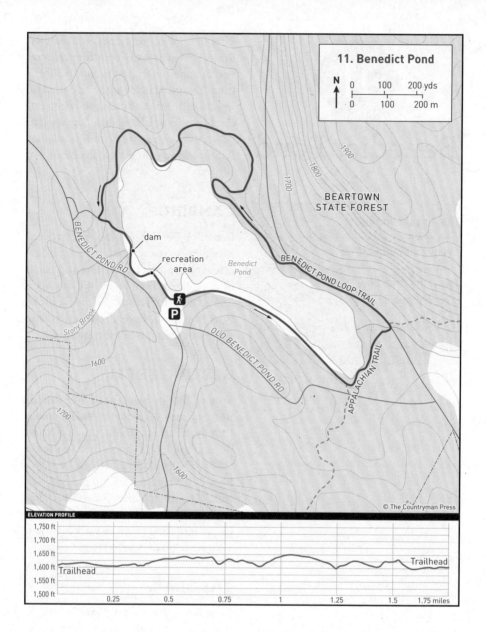

ELEVATION PROFILE

along the blue-blazed trail. While most of the trail is relatively smooth, portions require agility.

The trail passes through azalea and mountain laurel, which is likely to be fragrantly in bloom in June. In 10 minutes, you pick up the Appalachian Trail, which passes through Beartown State Forest, with a shelter south of Mt. Wilcox. The AT does not climb the 2,112-foot Wilcox, which doesn't have much of a view because the lookout tower is closed. It

OPPOSITE: MORNING MIST FLOATS ON BENEDICT POND

Lauren R. Stevens

PART OF THE CHARM: THE LIMIT ON BOATS

is a relatively easy climb (4 miles round trip) from the pond. Beartown is busy in the winter, with visitors on snowmobiles and cross-country skis.

The Loop Trail and AT follow a CCC road and depart it, left, at 20 minutes. By a bench, a box invites people to jot down their thoughts as they contemplate the pond. Other benches are also well placed. Passing beneath oaks and over wet places, you arrive at the dam and retaining wall, some 55 minutes later. In 5 minutes, pass behind the bathhouse to reach the parking lot.

12

Housatonic Flats Reserve

GREAT BARRINGTON
HIKING DISTANCE: .8 mile
WALKING TIME: 25 minutes
VERTICAL GAIN: N/A
MAP: Great Barrington

This 26-acre parcel contains .5 mile of frontage on the Housatonic River. Berkshire Natural Resources Council removed five tons of solid waste from the property. The trail provides peaceful river views, almost right in the middle of the Great Barrington shopping strip.

GETTING THERE

The parking lot is on the west side of Route 7, just north of the WSBS radio station and broadcast tower on the north side of town.

THE TRAIL

The kiosk in the parking lot maps the trail, which, although crossed by power lines, provides maximum exposure to the river, with overlooks and a bench. Go counterclockwise, going straight at the intersection after leaving the kiosk. The mowed trail reaches the river in 5 minutes and continues to provide opportunities for riverine wildlife viewing following the bend in the river. More than halfway to the end of the trail, a bench beckons. Since this is a lollypop trail, you return to the parking lot trail in 20 minutes. Turn right.

THE HOUSATONIC RIVER FROM ITS FLATS

Lauren R. Stevens

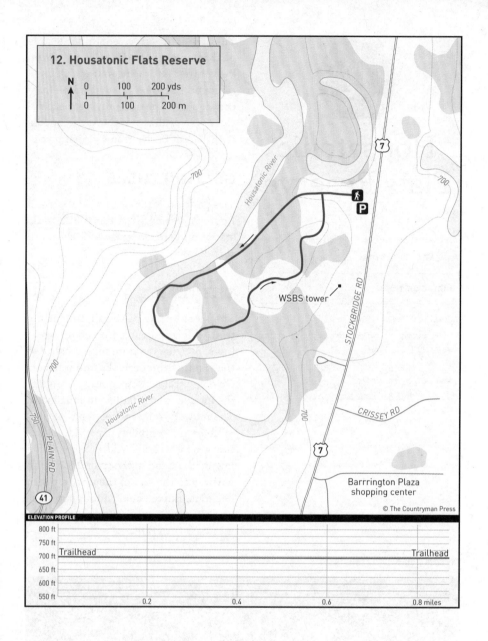

12. Housatonic Flats Reserve

N

| 0 | 100 | 200 yds |
| 0 | 100 | 200 m |

Housatonic River

700

700

7

700

WSBS tower

STOCKBRIDGE RD

700

Housatonic River

CRISSEY RD

700

750

PLAIN RD

41

7

Barrrington Plaza
shopping center

© The Countryman Press

ELEVATION PROFILE

| 800 ft |
| 750 ft |
| 700 ft | Trailhead | | | Trailhead |
| 650 ft |
| 600 ft |
| 550 ft |
| | 0.2 | 0.4 | 0.6 | 0.8 miles |

OPPOSITE: THE FLATS IS A NICE PLACE TO CALL HOME

Lauren R. Stevens

13

Monument Mountain

GREAT BARRINGTON

HIKING DISTANCE: 2.8 miles

WALKING TIME: 1.5 hours

VERTICAL GAIN: 720 feet

MAP: Great Barrington

The Trustees of Reservations maintains this 503-acre reservation (and invites a contribution from hikers). This pile of stones has a largely clear ridge, giving a good view of Beartown State Forest to the east, the Taconic Range to the west, and the valleys in between. If it isn't a tradition at the regional high school below the mountain for seniors to hike to the summit, it should be. This is less of a wilderness hike than others in this guide. From the summit, in addition to the panorama of unspoiled land, you look directly into a former landfill operation and onto the whizzing vehicles of Route 7. As always, it depends where you choose to look.

CAMPING

The nearest campground is at Benedict Pond, Beartown State Forest, east on Route 23 to forest HQ. Follow the signs along Blue Hill Road from there. The parking fee is modest. Lifeguards protect the swimming beach in season. No camping at the lovely picnic spot at Monument Mountain.

GETTING THERE

A familiar sight for motorists on Route 7, Monument Mountain is a pillar of stones located just north of the center of the town of Great Barrington, a few miles south of Stockbridge and slightly south of Monument Mountain Regional High School. Of the several parking lots on the west side of the road, the one at the picnic grounds (with the green TTOR sign) is handiest for this hike.

THE TRAIL

Although not long, this is a steep, rugged climb, and a storied one. In 1850, a publisher arranged an outing on this

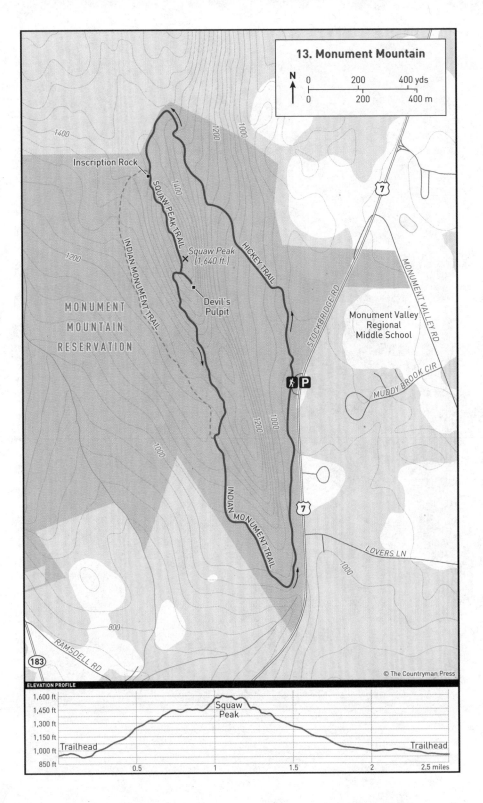

13. Monument Mountain

N

| 0 | 200 | 400 yds |
| 0 | 200 | 400 m |

1400

1200

1000

Inscription Rock

SQUAW PEAK TRAIL

1400

HICKEY TRAIL

INDIAN MONUMENT TRAIL

Squaw Peak
(1,640 ft.)

1200

Devil's
Pulpit

MONUMENT
MOUNTAIN
RESERVATION

1000

1200

1000

INDIAN MONUMENT TRAIL

7

STOCKBRIDGE RD

MONUMENT VALLEY RD

Monument Valley
Regional
Middle School

MUDDY BROOK CIR

P

7

LOVERS LN

1000

800

RAMSDELL RD

183

© The Countryman Press

ELEVATION PROFILE

		Squaw Peak			
1,600 ft					
1,450 ft					
1,300 ft					
1,150 ft					
1,000 ft	Trailhead				Trailhead
850 ft	0.5	1	1.5	2	2.5 miles

mountain for several writers: Herman Melville, Nathaniel Hawthorne, and physician/poet Oliver Wendell Holmes, Sr. The account of the wagon loaded with picnic goods (including champagne), and the liveried servants who accompanied them, may make you wonder how they made it up the trail. You will find out.

The well-trod trail, which is blazed white, leaves from the north corner of the parking lot, near a large map. Follow the yellow dots. It is moderately steep, passing through hemlocks, with scree (rocky rubble at the bottom of a slope) on the left. A trail enters right in 5 minutes. In a quarter hour, faced with a ravine, you swing left. Ignore all other trails, many of which are detours, keeping to the left. The stream on the right flows in lovely cascades in the spring. The trail is badly eroded in places, although the Trustees have labored hard in building stone water bars to try to deflect the freshets.

At 22 minutes, turn left again on the trail to Squaw Peak. Almost immediately, you pass a rock noting the year 1899, when the (then-called) Trustees of Public Reservations acquired the first portion of the property. A former carriage road arrives from the other side of the mountain at that point, which was the way the champagne was hauled to the summit. The trail (blazed red) is quite steep, and requires clambering over quartzite boulders. The lookout left seems to be directly over the school. You will be on the summit ridge in half an hour, but persevere, through the pitch pine, to the peak (1,640 feet) that honors an Indian maid, thought, at least by poet William Cullen Bryant, to have

flung herself to her death. Or worse: she may have hung from a branch for days until a bolt of lightning intervened. Pay attention to your footing on this rough terrain. The rocks themselves, with their lichens, are intriguing. Avoid the area during thunderstorms.

You can see a great deal of the Housatonic Valley and most of the peaks in the area, including Mt. Greylock. One impending rock has the date 1888 carved in it, albeit painted over by recent visitors.

Continue on a short side trail marked by a scenic vista sign (35 minutes) to the close up view of the Devil's Pulpit, a striking pillar of white quartzite. Go back to the Squaw Peak Trail (red) to continue down to the intersection with the old carriage road (called Indian Monument Trail), 47 minutes.

Suddenly you sense something has changed. You hear more birds, not necessarily because they are louder, but because you have rounded a corner of the cobble, leaving the highway traffic noises behind you. Again, keep left as various trails enter this one. The going is much more gradual than on the way up. The hemlocks are larger. Even bigger are the boulders that have tumbled down the steep sides in this romantic spot. In fact, the Mohicans placed a mysterious pile of stones (some "ten cart loads") at the base of the mountain—the source of its name. Treasure hunters removed the stones but the pile has since re-appeared. Pass a short side trail.

Traffic sounds indicate that you are parallel to Route 7 again and approaching the parking lot. In 1:30, plus the time you used to take in the view, you have returned.

OPPOSITE: ABOUT AS CLOSE AS YOU WANT TO GET TO THE DEVIL'S PULPIT
Lauren R. Stevens

14

Tyringham Cobble

TYRINGHAM

HIKING DISTANCE: 2 miles

WALKING TIME: 1.15 hours

VERTICAL GAIN: 450 feet

MAP: Monterey

This Trustees of Reservations property is set in (or above) the idyllic town center of Tyringham. The Tyringham Valley presents one of the most bucolic views in all of Berkshire. The relatively easy climb to a rocky outlook at the summit will make you feel as if you were in another world.

CAMPING

Tyringham remains free of tourist trappings. However, there is a campsite at Upper Goose Pond for Appalachian Trail hikers, just over the line from Tyringham in Lee.

GETTING THERE

To get to Tyringham from the Lee interchange of the Massachusetts Turnpike, at the junction of Route 20, jog briefly right on Route 102 west, then take Tyringham Road due south. Turn right at the town center on Jerusalem Road. Stay right where Church Street enters. Soon you will see a TTOR sign, on the right, just beyond a red barn. Park in the lot. Note the information in the kiosk and follow the trail along the fence.

THE TRAIL

Another lollypop trail, except with a short stick. Follow from the lot through the gate on the mowed path. In 10 minutes, take a left at the T on the blue-blazed trail into the woods. You are making the loop clockwise. The milkweed, as you'll recall, attracts butterflies. You may also observe the bluebird boxes. The trail enters a wooded area, becoming more of a footpath, and passing marvelously eroded sandstone—Rabbit Rock (16 minutes). In 22 minutes,

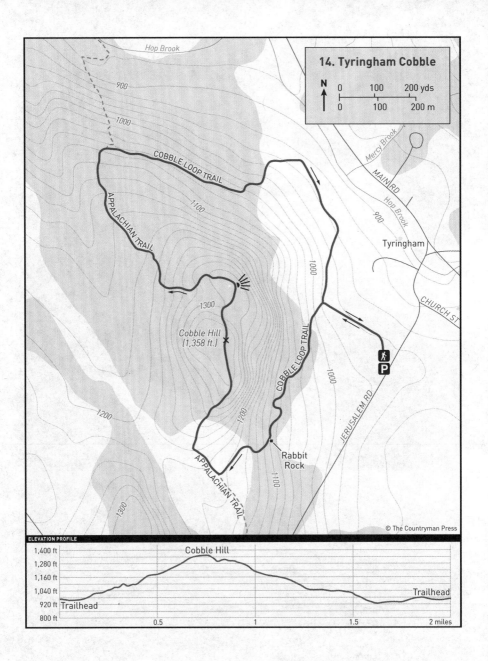

14. Tyringham Cobble

N

| 0 | 100 | 200 yds |
| 0 | 100 | 200 m |

COBBLE LOOP TRAIL

APPALACHIAN TRAIL

1,100

Cobble Hill
(1,358 ft.)

COBBLE LOOP TRAIL

Hop Brook

900

1000

Mercy Brook

MAIN RD

Hop Brook

900

Tyringham

CHURCH ST

1000

1000

JERUSALEM RD

Rabbit
Rock

1200

1300

APPALACHIAN TRAIL

1300

1200

© The Countryman Press

ELEVATION PROFILE

			Cobble Hill			
1,400 ft						
1,280 ft						
1,160 ft						
1,040 ft						
920 ft	Trailhead					Trailhead
800 ft						

0.5   1   1.5   2 miles

join the Appalachian Trail, coming in from the left. Note that you will now follow its white blazes as well as the blue.

Ignore side trails. Begin to climb up rocky ledges and, in 28 minutes, reach the overlook and obvious picnic site. The white church and country town are picturesquely set against the wooded hillsides surrounding Goose Pond. The trail descends, through additional

RABBIT ROCK GUARDS THE TYRINGHAM TRAIL

Lauren R. Stevens

stiles, close to the town's main street. At 43 minutes, turn right to stay on the Cobble Loop Trail, rather than continuing on the AT. Back on a mowed trail, a couple of trails head to town, but stay right on the Loop Trail until, after about an hour, you return to the junction. TTOR owns 206 acres, to which the trail provides an introduction.

Lauren R. Stevens

THE TYRINGHAM VALLEY FROM THE COBBLE

15

Three Trails

STOCKBRIDGE

HIKING DISTANCE: Varies

WALKING TIME: Varies

VERTICAL GAIN: 600 feet to Laura's Tower

MAP: Stockbridge

Strolls in Stockbridge are legion and lovely, not to mention the fact that summer and early fall biking, or even walking, is faster than driving. The Laurel Hill Association publishes a "Hike and Bike Guide," available at the town hall or library, with a useful set of maps. You can also go online. Three trails begin at the Mary Hopkins Goodrich Footbridge at the foot of Park Street. The Mary V. Flynn trail is a restful walk along the Housatonic, with an overlook. Laura's Tower Trail climbs to a metal tower that provides a panorama from Mt. Greylock to the Catskills. The third, Ice Glen Trail, invites you to explore a jumble of rocks, whose crannies are said to hold snow into the summer.

THE GOODRICH FOOTBRIDGE HONORS A FOUNDER

Lauren R. Stevens

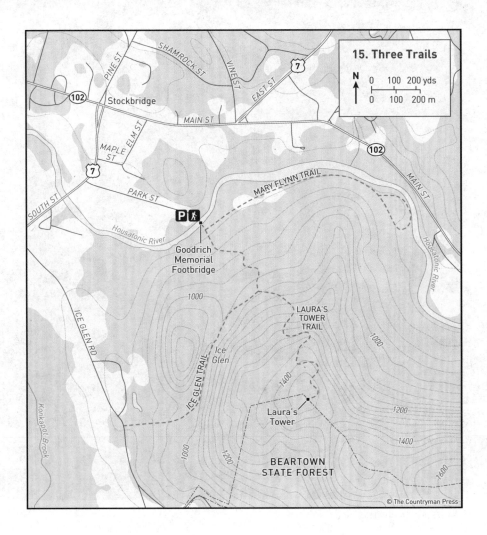

GETTING THERE

Of the several ways to access the trails, the footbridge at the end of Park Street—which juts east of Route 7, two streets south of Stockbridge Center, with room for parking and an explanatory kiosk—seems the most convenient.

THE TRAILS

The Laurel Hill Association, founded in 1853 by Mary Hopkins Goodrich, was the first village improvement society in this country. The trails have the aura of being so well known to local inhabitants that blazing or signage need not be overdone. After crossing the footbridge, proceed over the railroad tracks. After a few hundred yards, bear right where the tower trail swings left. There are other, informal trails in the area. Pass beneath large hemlocks and maples. At the north end of the glen, a boulder honors the donor, David Dudley Field. Whether or not you find snow, you will be greeted by a gush of chilled air from deep in the boulders. In spite of forceful efforts

AN OVERLOOK ON THE FLYNN TRAIL

to create a trail through the jumble of rocks, the going is not easy, although it is less than a mile.

To combine or make a separate trip to Laura's Tower, bear left at the trail intersection. Although steeper, this trail is wider and better marked. A compass rose on the tower labels the sights. The hike is less than 1.5 miles round trip.

The Flynn Trail, easy walking and wheelchair accessible, starts immediately on the left after crossing the foot-bridge. (Do not cross the tracks.) For the most part, the trail follows the bed of the old Berkshire Street Railway line. Starting with 100 feet of boardwalk, the trail crosses several other bridges, including a narrower section. Ferns, euonymus, pine, birch, and cottonwood trees guard the path and the river. The Laurel Hill Association constructed the trail in 2003 to mark its 150th anniversary. About a mile round trip.

16

Olivia's Overlook & Yokum Ridge South

RICHMOND

HIKING DISTANCE: 1.6 miles

WALKING TIME: 1 hour

VERTICAL GAIN: 440 feet

MAP: West Stockbridge

Berkshire Natural Resources Council's Olivia's Outlook has an outstanding view of the Stockbridge Bowl. Olivia Stokes Hatch was the sister of Anson and Isaac Stokes, who donated much of the land across the road to the BNRC. While that view is available from the parking lot, you can combine it with a pleasant hike on Yokum Ridge on a 252-acre parcel, through woods that are largely open (without much underbrush), and a moderate climb to the ridge itself, with additional views.

GETTING THERE

From downtown Lenox, follow Route 183 south for 1.5 miles, just passing Tanglewood's main gate. Where 183 bears left, turn right on the Lenox-Richmond Road (same as to Stevens Glen). Follow up hill for 1.5 miles to parking for Olivia's Overlook, on the left.

THE TRAIL

Yokum Ridge south of Olivia's Outlook has been used for a variety of purposes: from pasture to charcoal cutting and burning for the Richmond Furnace iron production. The woods are now returning to their pre-industrial majesty. The trail begins across the parking lot from the view. Cross a bridge to the kiosk. Go left on the Charcoal Trail (blazed blue) through a hemlock stand and maples. It descends gradually, with occasional side trails. Check for flat, circular areas that might have been used for charcoal kilns.

At .5 hour, cross a small ravine on a stone bridge and begin a fairly steep climb to an overlook, 40 minutes. Turn right for the Walsh Trail. (Or take the Ridge Trail, which is steeper with some tricky footing.) In 20 more minutes, return to the kiosk and parking.

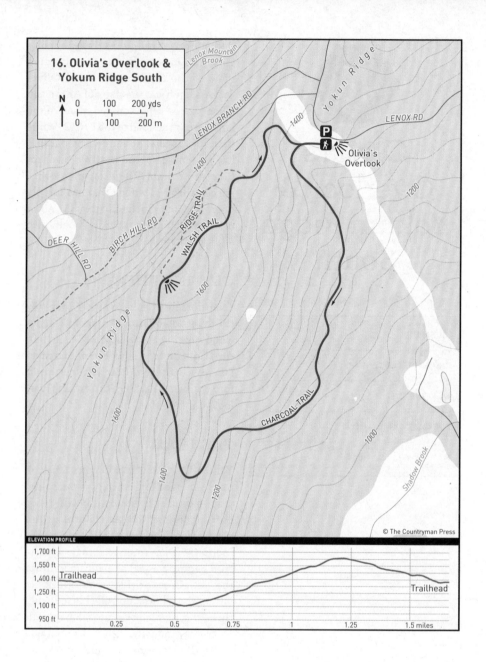

16. Olivia's Overlook & Yokum Ridge South

N
0   100   200 yds
0   100   200 m

Lenox Mountain Brook

Yokun Ridge

LENOX BRANCH RD

1400

LENOX RD

P

Olivia's Overlook

1200

RIDGE TRAIL

WALSH TRAIL

DEER HILL RD

BIRCH HILL RD

1600

Yokun Ridge

1600

CHARCOAL TRAIL

1000

Shadow Brook

1400

1200

© The Countryman Press

ELEVATION PROFILE

1,700 ft
1,550 ft
1,400 ft — Trailhead
1,250 ft
1,100 ft
950 ft

Trailhead

0.25   0.5   0.75   1   1.25   1.5 miles

Lauren R. Stevens

STOCKBRIDGE BOWL FROM OLIVIA'S OVERLOOK

II.

CENTRAL
BERKSHIRES

THE CCC

Civilian Conservation Corps boot prints are all over Berkshire County. The CCCs shaped most of the state-owned land to which this book leads you, on which residents live—the result of the coming together of locally and nationally important episodes in history. One was the carelessness of logging companies that denuded quantities of land in western Massachusetts in order to provide wood for various uses, including furniture making in the central part of the state. Fearful that Massachusetts would run out of forests, the Commonwealth acquired great chunks of abandoned land. Then, as a response to the Great Depression, in 1933 President Franklin D. Roosevelt created the Emergency Conservation Work Act (better known as the CCC), which was designed to find employment for young men and veterans, and to improve the nation's forests and recreational resources. Through 1942, when most of the men enlisted in the armed services, the CCC in Massachusetts employed 100,000 men in 68 camps.

The Commonwealth's Forests and Parks system began in 1898, when North Adams industrialists donated Mt. Greylock to the state. The state, in turn, had to determine how to manage this gift. Until the CCC came along, little was done to improve the forests and parks, or make them accessible to the public. Thus, the Commonwealth's Forests and Parks department welcomed the federal program and turned it toward the large quantities of land, especially in western Massachusetts.

The first step for the CCC was to build their camps, tents initially, but eventually barracks and dining halls. Some buildings are still used as park headquarters. The CCC built roads for access and brought in electricity. The men, who were paid a dollar a day, learned useful skills, such as camp construction, road building, forestry, fire hazard reduction, pest control, wildlife management, and recreational development. More than 75 years later, most of the facilities they built are still in use.

Given the denuded land, the CCCs planted thousands of acres of trees, mostly red spruce, which can be recognized by their straight rows and the regular distance between the evenly aged trees. They practiced timber stand improvement, including thinning, release cutting, and conducting forest type and soil inventories. They tried to eradicate white pine blister rust, gypsy moth, and white pine weevil infestations. They cut brush and created 100-foot-wide firebreaks, dug water holes, and erected fire towers, stringing telephone lines to connect them with sources of help.

The CCCs cut vistas to provide views from their roads. They made miles and miles of trails, often with stone steps, bridges, and water bars as well as wooden ones. They built dams to create swimming holes and stone retaining walls. All this work was accomplished by mostly untrained young men under the skillful leadership of camp superintendents and area craftsmen.

The most obvious CCC contribution for today's hikers is the creation of recreational facilities. The U.S. Forest Service set the style: log cabins, wood guardrails, three-sided lean-tos, picnic pavilions, bathhouses, and other structures, usually made from materials on site. Bascom Lodge, on Mt. Greylock, is a fine example, the stone for its foundation and fireplaces, as well as the wooden walls and beams, native to the mountain. This book explores other parks shaped by the CCCs, including: Bash Bish, Beartown, Monroe, October Mountain, Pittsfield, Savoy, and Windsor.

STEVENS GLEN IS STILL A ROMANTIC SPOT

Lauren R. Stevens

17

Keystone Arch Bridges

CHESTER

HIKING DISTANCE: 3 miles

WALKING TIME: 90 minutes

VERTICAL GAIN: N/A

MAP: Chester

Alexander Birnie built 10 arches between 1839 and 1840, including the first keystone arch railroad bridges in this country, in order to get the Western Railway through the Westfield River Valley and up to the Becket Hills. George Washington Whistler, the painter's father, engineered this feat and then went on to design the Trans-Siberian Railroad. All the stone was laid up dry and still is without mortar. Some bridges have been replaced or avoided by altering the rail alignment. On this walk, you get a look at a double arch bridge, which is still in use; a 65-foot high abandoned bridge; pick and shovel rock cuts and a retaining wall; and a 70-foot high abandoned bridge. As the trail leads onto two bridges, parents and pet-owners should note that there are no fences or guard rails. The CSX line on the far side of the river is still in use. The land belongs to Massachusetts Fisheries and Wildlife, so it is open for hunting.

GETTING THERE

Turn off Route 20 onto the Middlefield Road in the center of Chester. Follow 2.5 miles to parking on the left, which is on the unmarked Herbert Cross Road. Look left to see the double arch bridge. Some trucks belonging to the railroad and off-road vehicles use this road, which soon crosses a tributary on a steel grate bridge. Another parking area is just before the bridge; this is the farthest it is reasonable to drive. Note: Chester has a Railway Station and Museum on Prospect Street.

THE TRAIL

An attractive small cascade flows just above the steel bridge. The route is blazed blue. Follow the road to the sec-

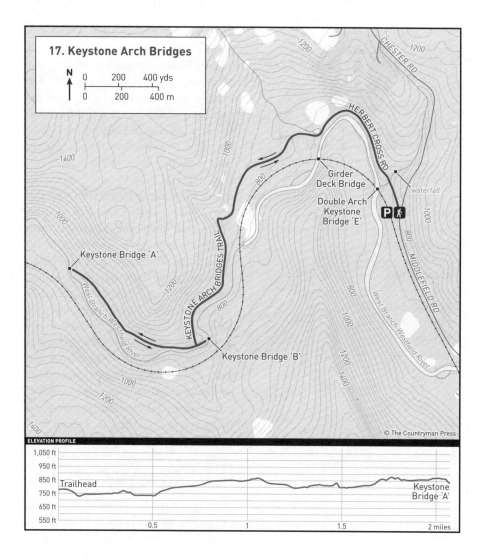

17. Keystone Arch Bridges

N

| 0 | 200 | 400 yds |
| 0 | 200 | 400 m |

1200

CHESTER RD

1200

HERBERT CROSS RD

1200

1000

Girder
Deck Bridge

waterfall

Double Arch
Keystone
Bridge 'E'

1400

P

1000

800

1000

MIDDLEFIELD RD

Keystone Bridge 'A'

KEYSTONE ARCH BRIDGES TRAIL

800

West Branch Westfield River

1200

800

800

West Branch Westfield River

1000

Keystone Bridge 'B'

1200

1400

1000

1200

1000

1400

© The Countryman Press

ELEVATION PROFILE

1,050 ft			
950 ft			
850 ft Trailhead			
750 ft			Keystone
650 ft			Bridge 'A'
550 ft			
	0.5	1	1.5	2 miles

ond right (at a foundation); take another right into the woods on the trail proper. At an intersection of trails, go straight across the brook in spite of an earth berm. You climb and then descend. The woods road that soon enters left is a section of the Old Pontoosuc Turnpike, the stage road to Albany, 100 years older than the railroad. You will be able to pick out other sections of it. Meet the former rail line and turn left to view the 65-foot arch; double back along the right-of-way to see (look down) the stone retaining wall and the cuts. Pass an old signal stand and end on a bridge 70 feet over the river.

18

Basin Pond

LEE	
HIKING DISTANCE: 3 miles	
WALKING TIME: 1 hour, 20 minutes	
VERTICAL GAIN: N/A	
MAP: East Lee	

This lovely parcel tells a story of human's folly. In 1837, East Lee mill owners constructed a dam at the outlet on Basin Pond Brook to stabilize their water supply. Thirteen years later, the dam let go, destroying 25 mills as well as many homes, and killing seven people. The Cromwell-Wright Company built a second dam in the same insecure place in 1965 in order to create a resort community that was to be called Lee Colony on the Lake, a 100-lot leisure home development located near the Massachusetts Turnpike. Three years later, the middle portion of their earthen berm dam collapsed, killing two and causing millions of dollars in damage. Robert Thierot purchased the land out of bankruptcy and donated it to Berkshire Natural Resources Council. With the dam breached, the former lake has returned to wetlands, maintained by beavers rather than engineers. The trails pass artfully through scree (stones that have worked their way down from October Mountain).

GETTING THERE

From Lee, take Route 20 east 4.1 miles to the junction of Route 20 and Becket Road. Turn left on Becket Road and drive north 0.3 miles to a parking area, with sign and kiosk, on the left.

THE TRAIL

You should do a lollypop trail with a side visit to the dam. Master trail builder Peter Jensen laid and executed the trail for BNRC, and traces of his subtle handiwork abound, as in the stone stream crossings. Pass through fine maple and hardwood forest. In 10 minutes, turn right at a junction to which you will return. Pass over additional streams and

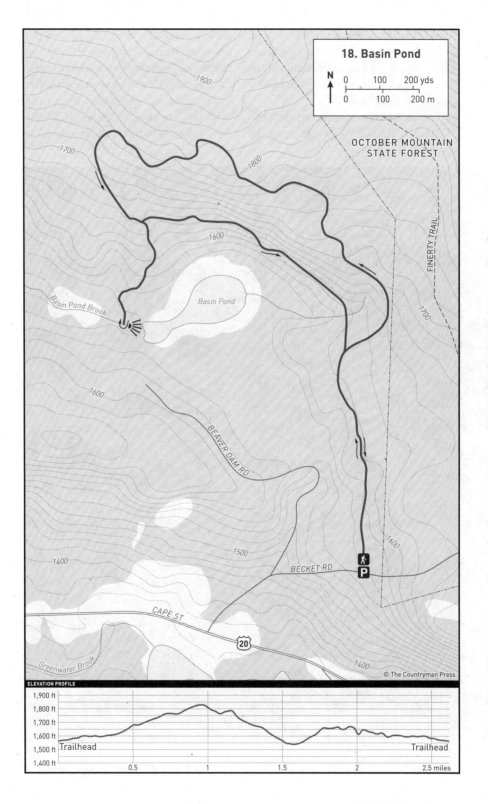

18. Basin Pond

N

| 0 | 100 | 200 yds |
| 0 | 100 | 200 m |

OCTOBER MOUNTAIN
STATE FOREST

FINERTY TRAIL

1900

1700

1800

1600

Basin Pond Brook

Basin Pond

1600

BEAVER DAM RD

1600

1400

1500

BECKET RD

CAPE ST

20

Greenwater Brook

1400

© The Countryman Press

ELEVATION PROFILE

1,900 ft
1,800 ft
1,700 ft
1,600 ft
1,500 ft
1,400 ft

Trailhead

Trailhead

0.5   1   1.5   2   2.5 miles

a boulder field, gaining some elevation. In 20 minutes, come to another junction. Take the side trail to the remains of the dam. The viewing platform provides a good look at the wetlands.

This is a scenic spot, set in the bowl of October Mountain. As wetlands, the spot is home to a diversity of land and water creatures. Return to the loop for further examples of how to thread a trail through significant boulders, including one it nearly passes beneath. In 1:10 minutes, you are back to the original junction. Follow straight to the parking lot.

Lauren R. Stevens

TRAILS SOMETIMES SNEAK AROUND BOULDERS

BASIN POND FROM THE SITE OF THE FORMER DAM

19

Kennedy Park

LENOX

HIKING DISTANCE: varies

WALKING TIME: varies

VERTICAL GAIN: N/A

MAP: West Pittsfield

A history of large estates—as opposed to farmed land, logged land, or developed land—has left some of the county's largest trees in Lenox and Stockbridge, as you can see in Bullard Woods or driving through these fashionable towns. One gorgeous glimpse of this kind of land, that does not consist of recently grown-over farm fields, is Lenox's 502-acre Kennedy Park. The area was the site of the Aspinwall Hotel, built in 1902 to accommodate wealthy tourists who wanted to visit their cottage-dwelling friends. After the hotel burned in 1931, its grounds became the John D. Kennedy Park because he put $12,000 into its development in 1957. The main trail (blazed white) has numerous offshoots. You can design your own route, consulting the map near the entrance or, better, pick up a copy of the trail map at the Arcadian Shop.

GETTING THERE

The original entrance is the gate near the Church-on-the-Hill. You can still use the church's parking lot, except when the church is holding services. Or you can enter across from the state DPW garage on Route 7-A. There is an entrance off West Dugway Road on the way to Pleasant Valley. Perhaps the most convenient entrance is adjacent to the Arcadian Shop, on Routes 7 & 20 south of Pittsfield center, with a 16-car parking lot, picnic area, and handicapped-accessible trail loop.

THE TRAILS

Since there are so many trails (the map lists 31), map-access is important. The T.F. Coakley Trail is the main drag, really a carriage road, running from the Church-on-the-Hill to Reservoir Road.

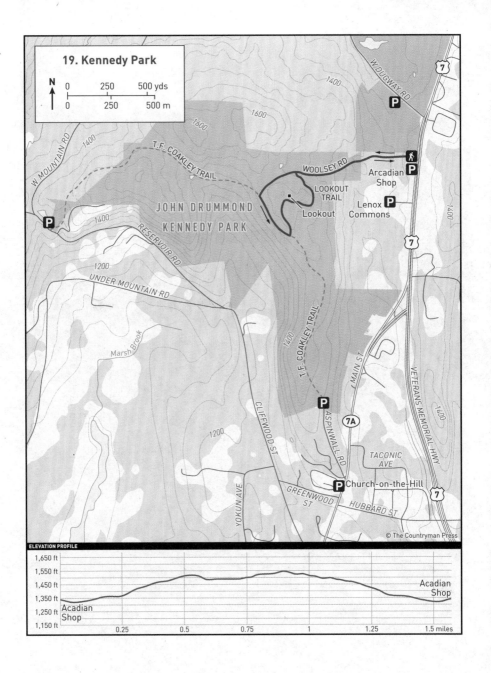

19. Kennedy Park

N

| 0 | 250 | 500 yds |
| 0 | 250 | 500 m |

ELEVATION PROFILE

© The Countryman Press

Bulletin boards with maps are available at the church and at the Arcadian Shop entrance. Most trails are marked with signs at the intersections. Some trails are informal and unmarked. Signs tend to be high on the trees.

To begin, you might like to go from the Arcadian Shop parking to the Lookout—although that lookout shows you more trees than ponds or mountains. Pass through wetlands on a wide trail known as the Woolsey Road. There are too

LENOX IS MAKING AN EFFORT TO REMOVE THE INVASIVE VINES AT KENNEDY PARK

Lauren R. Stevens

many trails to list their crossings here, but some 15 minutes later, you reach the Coakley Trail. Turn left. Pass the Cutoff Trail (left) to turn on the Lookout Trail (20 minutes), also left. That climbs, not surprisingly, to the Lookout (5 minutes), a covered structure. It also continues back down again to the Woolsey Trail; turn right for a return to the parking lot, for a 45-minute stroll beneath large and old Northern Hardwood trees. Note that most of the trails are skiable.

THE KENNEDY PARK LOOKOUT

Pleasant Valley & Lenox Mountain

LENOX

HIKING DISTANCE: 3 miles

WALKING TIME: 2 hours

VERTICAL GAIN: 786 feet

MAP: Pittsfield

The Pleasant Valley Wildlife Sanctuary, one of three Massachusetts Audubon properties in the county, was established in 1929. Seven miles of trails wind through 1,100 acres of Berkshire uplands and beaver swamps. A trailside museum is open from mid-May through October. This is a lovely short hike (for climbing a mountain), and relatively steep, with a rewarding view from the summit of Lenox Mountain. Other strategic lookouts along the trail survey the surroundings. In the spring, trails follow delightful brooks with sparkling waterfalls.

GETTING THERE

Pleasant Valley is off the Lenox-Pittsfield Road (Routes 7 & 20) south of Pittsfield. Turn west on West Dugway Road, at the sanctuary sign, north of the junction with Route 7-A, but south of the junction of Holmes Road. Follow Dugway, a blacktopped road, for a mile until it ends at West Mountain Road. Bear left on this gravel road for .8 mile. The sanctuary has parking on both sides of the road. It is closed on Mondays.

THE TRAIL

Restrooms are available in the barn. Maps and pamphlets are available at the window, where nonmembers of Massachusetts Audubon will be asked to pay a small fee for use of the sanctuary. There are no shelters or camping areas on this hike. Incidentally, no dogs or horses are allowed on this property. No hunting. Cross-country skiing is not allowed. Collecting of plants, of course, is not allowed; nor is it allowed on any public lands or most private lands.

From the Audubon administration

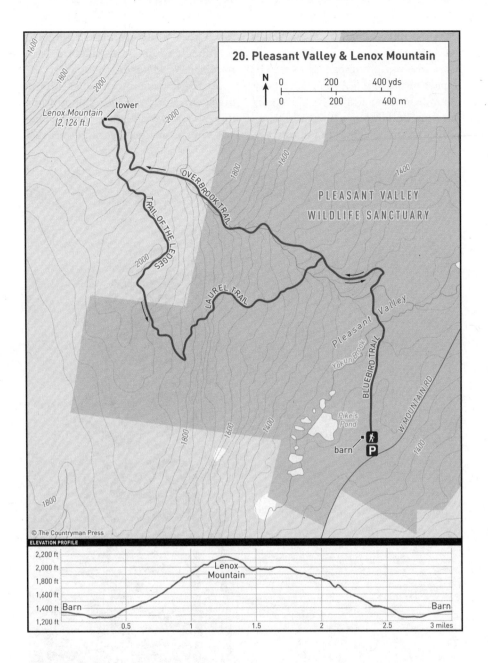

20. Pleasant Valley & Lenox Mountain

Lenox Mountain
(2,126 ft.)

tower

OVERBROOK TRAIL

TRAIL OF THE LEDGES

LAUREL TRAIL

PLEASANT VALLEY
WILDLIFE SANCTUARY

Pleasant Valley

Yokun Brook

BLUEBIRD TRAIL

W. MOUNTAIN RD.

Pike's
Pond

barn

© The Countryman Press

ELEVATION PROFILE

Lenox
Mountain

Barn

Barn

building, follow the main (Bluebird) trail, past the barn on the left and the activity center on the right. From this spot you can see the destination: the tower on the ridge to the west. The Bluebird Trail passes through fields that are beginning to fill in with second growth. Mass Audubon allows the woody stems to replace grass, bushes to replace stems, and gradually trees fill in former farmland. In this area, pines come to shield out undergrowth, and then, finally, hardwoods take over from the pines. That is called "forest succession."

Follow straight ahead as two trails depart to the right. At the sanctuary, all trails heading away from the administration building are blazed blue; all returning to the center are blazed yellow. Cross trails are blazed white. It is difficult to get lost. Bluebird Trail becomes Wood Road.

At the bottom of the slope (5 minutes), cross bridges over Yokun Brook under a stand of tall pines, leave a beaver swamp on the right, and cross a

Lauren R. Stevens

THE FIRE TOWER ON LENOX MOUNTAIN IS MORE OF A COMMUNICATIONS TOWER NOW.

RICHMOND POND FROM LENOX MOUNTAIN

Lauren R. Stevens

second bridge (at 8 minutes), following signs to the Overbrook Trail at various intersections. The trail continues up the brook you just crossed. (You may want to detour on alternate trails to examine the industrious beavers' activities.)

At the 4-way intersection (12 minutes), go straight on the Overbrook Trail (you will return here later). The brook is on the left. As you gain elevation, laurel, which blossoms in June, begins to fill in under hardwood trees. Pass out of the sanctuary land into Lenox watershed lands, but Audubon maintains trails throughout. The trail, climbing fairly steeply over rocks, weaves back and forth across the brook, which runs in the spring with several falls. Large hem-

locks aim to the sky in the ravines and along the ledges. The schist, over which the water runs, contains quartz outcroppings. At 30 minutes, the trail begins to skirt a ledge, left. In 40 minutes, come out on the summit.

The view from the summit looks down onto Richmond Pond, which seems to be very close, despite your elevation of 2,126 feet. The Catskill Mountains rise in the southwest. The Taconic highlands to the northwest are in Pittsfield State Forest. Lake Onota lies to the west-northwest. Looking east, see the highlands of October Mountain State Forest. To the southeast, look down into the extremely Pleasant Valley. The tower adds some 80 feet to the view but, unfortunately, it is no longer open to the public. In fact, it's become more of a communications tower than a fire tower.

The entrance to the Ledges Trail may not be well marked. As you arrive at the summit, it is the opening immediately to your left; take it rather than the jeep road. Remember, returning trails are blazed yellow. There are some sharp turns. In 4 minutes, begin to pass over ledges, descending and climbing along the ridge. At 1:12 from the administration building, come to a trail junction at Fairview, which gives another nice look into the sanctuary's 670 acres. Turn left on the aptly named Laurel Trail, which begins a steep descent, part of which is in an intermittent streambed. The hardwoods now include oak, birch, and beech.

At 1:25, go straight at the intersection with the Ravine Trail. At 1:30, bear right at a familiar 4 corners. You are now back on the trail you began climbing, appropriately known as Overbrook. Although you have been traversing rocky outcroppings, the valley lies atop limestone, buffering the effects of acid rain and affording hospitable conditions for certain ferns and other rare species. Bear right at the Y. At 1:45, cross the first bridge and, at 2 hours, pass the administration building.

The sanctuary map shows numerous strolls and hikes, the one to the tower being the most rigorous. You could spend a full day walking through this beautifully maintained property and enjoying a picnic. Massachusetts Audubon organizes many educational activities, including cross-country skiing and snowshoeing at Canoe Meadows, another Berkshire sanctuary, located a few miles north, off Holmes Road in Pittsfield (see description below).

Old Mill Trail

DALTON/HINSDALE
HIKING DISTANCE: 1.5 miles
WALKING TIME: 70 minutes
VERTICAL GAIN: N/A

Aside from the Appalachian Trail and The Boulders (below), the Old Mill Trail is the first and only public trail in Dalton. (Part is in Hinsdale, as well). Created by the Housatonic Valley Association, it accesses approximately 1.5 miles of scenic and historic riverfront along the East Branch of the Housatonic River. The trail traverses a wild river environment. Along the way, remnants of early mill operations reflect how this industry influenced the development of neighboring communities. When the river is high, segments of the trail may be underwater. The initial portion is suitable for wheelchairs. As a bonus, the trailhead is conveniently adjacent to a store that sells beer and pizza.

GETTING THERE

The Old Mill Trail starts at the trailhead on Old Dalton Road off Route 8 in Hinsdale, on the east side, north of the town center and just south of the Hinsdale/Dalton line.

THE TRAIL

The trail runs primarily on land belonging to Crane & Co., the paper and U.S. currency manufacturers based in Dalton, with an easement from the Massachusetts Department of Fish & Wildlife. It runs from the kiosk in the parking lot on the gravel portion of the trail to a lovely footbridge over the East Branch of the Housatonic River. This trail was expertly laid out and constructed by Peter Jensen. As a sign of history, perhaps, you soon pass an old automobile. Walking through mixed hardwood forest, pass a dam site and then, after 15 minutes, arrive at the end of the gravel section and an opportunity to log in (that is, in a log book; no wifi).

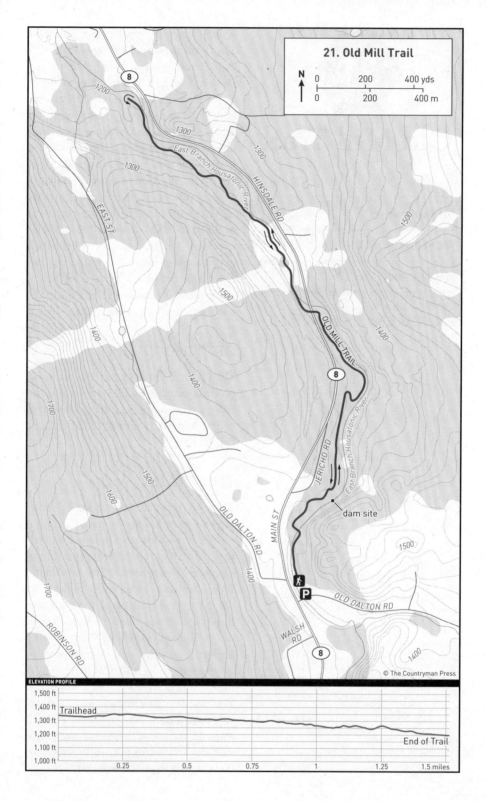

21. Old Mill Trail

N

| 0 | 200 | 400 yds |
| 0 | 200 | 400 m |

1200

1300

East Branch Housatonic River

1300

HINSDALE RD

1300

1500

EAST ST

1300

1500

1400

1400

OLD MILL TRAIL

1400

1700

8

1500

East Branch Housatonic River

1400

JERICHO RD

1600

dam site

1500

OLD DALTON RD

MAIN ST

1500

1700

1400

P

OLD DALTON RD

ROBINSON RD

WALSH RD

1400

8

© The Countryman Press

ELEVATION PROFILE

1,500 ft	
1,400 ft	Trailhead
1,300 ft	
1,200 ft	
1,100 ft	End of Trail
1,000 ft	
	0.25 0.5 0.75 1 1.25 1.5 miles

Lauren R. Stevens

WELCOME TO THE OLD MILL TRAIL

The trail crosses Route 8. Pay attention! By dint of artful rearranging of the existing stone, the trail then follows along the bank of the river, in some places quite close. A bridge crosses what looks to be a former mill run into a deeply forested area. In 35 minutes, the trail ends near an old pipe at a loop. Return the same way.

Berry Pond

PITTSFIELD/HANCOCK

HIKING DISTANCE: 5 miles

WALKING TIME: 2 hours, 10 minutes

VERTICAL GAIN: 1,217 feet

MAPS: West Pittsfield/Hancock

This moderately steep hike passes the common corner of the towns of Pittsfield, Lanesborough, and Hancock—the town in which Berry Pond is actually located. The pond is named for William Berry, a Revolutionary War veteran who owned land in Pittsfield. Near the beginning, Lulu Brook drops in a series of picturesque cascades. At the top, you pass through 65 acres of extraordinary azalea fields, which bloom in early June; by a fine overlook into New York State; and on to Berry Pond (2,060 feet), the highest natural body of water in Massachusetts. (A beaver pond off the Hoosac Range Trail may exceed. The highest, at 3,200 feet, is on Mt. Greylock, dug as water supply for Bascom Lodge.) Pittsfield State Forest, the area you are exploring, entertains a variety of uses common to urban parks, hence efforts to separate motorized from non-motorized trails. The hike described below parallels the automobile road and uses its shoulder briefly.

GETTING THERE

From Park Square, Pittsfield, follow west on West Street, 2.5 miles; turn right on Churchill Street for 1.25 miles; and turn left at the chocolate-colored state forest sign on Cascade Street, from which it is .5 mile to the state forest entrance. There is a small fee for parking, to use the bathing beach at Lulu Pond, or for camping.

From the north, turn right on Bull Hill Road, off Route 7 in Lanesborough, and go .5 mile; jog left and then right on Balance Rock Road, which swings south for 1.3 miles to a Pittsfield State Forest gate. Drive .5 mile to see an extraordinary balanced rock, on a delicate base. The painted rock has been sandblasted to remove fools' names, which—fools

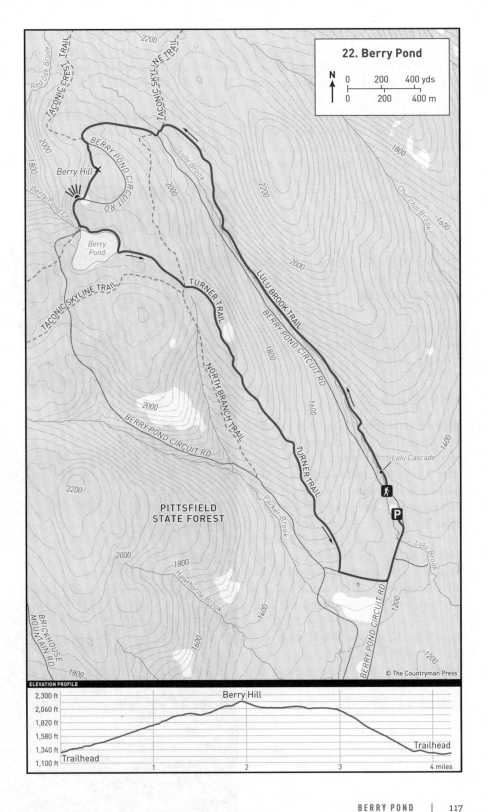

22. Berry Pond

N

| 0 | 200 | 400 yds |
| 0 | 200 | 400 m |

TACONIC CREST TRAIL

Red Oak Brook

TACONIC SKYLINE TRAIL

2200

2000

1800

Berry Pond Ct.

BERRY POND CIRCUIT RD

Berry Hill ✕

Lulu Brook

2000

2200

1800

Churchill Brook

1600

Berry Pond

TACONIC SKYLINE TRAIL

TURNER TRAIL

LULU BROOK TRAIL

BERRY POND CIRCUIT RD

2000

1800

1600

NORTH BRANCH TRAIL

2000

BERRY POND CIRCUIT RD

2200

Lulu Cascade

1400

Parker Brook

TURNER TRAIL

PITTSFIELD
STATE FOREST

2000

1800

Hawthorne Brook

1400

1900

Lulu Brook

1200

BERRY POND CIRCUIT RD

1200

BRICKHOUSE
MOUNTAIN RD

1800

© The Countryman Press

ELEVATION PROFILE

Berry Hill

| 2,300 ft |
| 2,060 ft |
| 1,820 ft |
| 1,580 ft |
| 1,340 ft |
| 1,100 ft |

Trailhead

Trailhead

1   2   3   4 miles

being fools—have reappeared. The rock is what is known as an "erratic," carried in from the north by a glacier and deposited when the ice departed. Many trails lead to the part of the forest where you are headed, but consider Balance Rock a side trip; drive out the road and follow right to either Hancock Road or Dan Casey Drive; turn right, and then left, on Churchill to Cascade; go right at the State Forest sign.

CAMPING

Pittsfield State Forest has two campgrounds. The one at Parker Brook, to the west of the HQ, has 18 sites. The "comfort station," in state parlance, has flush toilets. The one at Berry Pond, your destination, has 13 sites, with pit toilets, meaning privies.

THE TRAIL

Because the blazing and signing of trails at Pittsfield has been erratic, you may wish to stop in at forest HQ to pick up the latest map or inquire about the route. The problem is a bewildering excess of trails, some casually made by four-wheelers. From the state forest entrance, it's a half-mile to the Lulu Pond picnic area, where you park—and where you may want to swim or wade at the end of the hike. Cross the road from the parking lot. Take the Lulu Brook Trail, the first past the gate, or the Honwee Trail, the second by the gate—a woods road. It is blazed yellow, parallel to, and only a few feet above, the Lulu Brook Trail and the Berry Pond Circuit Road. While easier walking, it is a multiuse trail, meaning

that, especially on weekends and holidays, you could experience off-road vehicle traffic. This book describes the Lulu Brook Trail (blazed blue). It is pleasant to look down at the brook itself as you pass through beech, maple, and birch forest, with azaleas prominent on the understory or lower foliage.

BERRY POND WELCOMES CAMPERS

Lauren R. Stevens

While trying to navigate the narrow space between the brook and Honwee, Lulu Brook Trail sometimes follows beside the brook, but occasionally climbs steeply. Furthermore, the footing on the rocks can be tricky. Pass through a stand of pines. At a major intersection (38 minutes) with the Taconic Skyline Trail, really a dirt road, turn left across the brook, and then up Berry Pond Circuit Road. Although the traffic can be heavy on a weekend during azalea season, the shoulders are walkable. At about this point, the three towns come together just south of the road.

At 43 minutes, on a sharp curve to

CAN YOU SMELL THE AZALEAS?

the southeast, the Taconic Crest Trail (blazed white) exits the road, on the right. To the left is your first chance to get on Turner Trail. Or, stay on road. Walk into the overlook at 52 minutes. The mountains before you are the Catskills. Berry Pond, surrounded by tent sites, is 3 minutes ahead.

Follow unmarked trails on the side of the pond (trails may be wet), past an intersection with the Berkshire Hills Ramble (blazed blue). When in doubt, head east. Cross the Skyline Trail (1:05 minutes). As the sign says, you are now on the Turner Trail, which has been blazed blue, but not consistently. At first it passes along a plateau, with an overlook to the left, but eventually begins to descend steeply. Here, a

mountain bike trail, with switchbacks, crisscrosses the relatively direct Turner Trail (no motorized vehicles are allowed). Take your pick. Depending on what you choose, you will come out in approximately 2 hours on the Circuit Road going down or a gravel, connecting road. Turn left on the gravel road through the campground, and left again on Circuit Road after 5 minutes In 4 more minutes, you return to the parking lot, ready for a dip.

Many combinations of trails are possible. The route described here is skiable, as are many of the other trails and unplowed roads. One special trail, the Tranquility Trail, at Pittsfield State Forest west of the HQ building, is wheelchair accessible.

Stevens Glen

RICHMOND
HIKING DISTANCE: 2 miles
WALKING TIME: 45 minutes
VERTICAL GAIN: 320 feet
MAP: Stockbridge

Lenox Mountain Brook drops 100 feet through the rock walls of the Glen—a romantic sight 120 years ago when farmer Romanza Stevens (no known relation to the author!) charged visitors 25 cents to visit his attraction. He built a dance pavilion at the site, which attracted 900 visitors on one evening in 1913. Today it's free to visit due to the generosity of the Pryor family, who donated the land to the Berkshire Natural Resources Council in 1995. It remains a romantic sight/site.

GETTING THERE

Take Route 183 south from the center of Lenox, as though heading to Tanglewood. Turn right up the hill at the fork just beyond and across from Tanglewood's main gate. After passing Olivia's Overlook at the summit, turn left down a road marked Lenox Branch. Approximately .75 miles down the hill, avail yourself of a parking pull-off at the trailhead, on the right. The trail departs through wooden guardrails. A sign says, tersely: "S. Glen." (Which a larger sign spells out.)

A FOOTBRIDGE AT STEVENS GLEN

Lauren R. Stevens

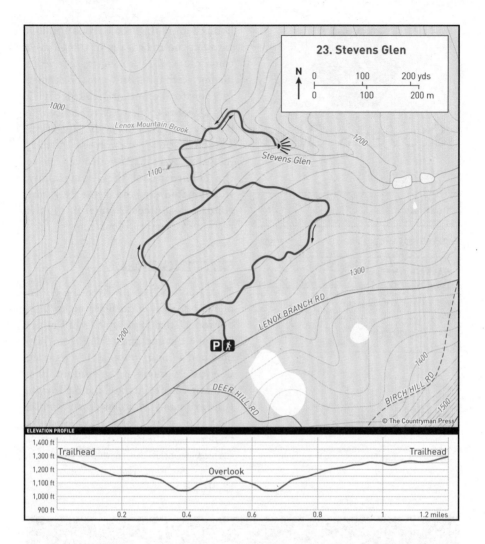

© The Countryman Press

THE TRAIL

A spur from a loop trail leads to a platform that provides the best view. The trails (blazed blue) descend 320 feet from the kiosk to pass through trees planted close together, perhaps by the Civilian Conservation Corps. After crossing some scraggily second growth, you arrive at a combination sign, map dispenser, and donation box (5 minutes). Turn right for a more leisurely, less steep descent; left for a more direct, steeper path. Following left, cross under utility lines and turn left on the spur before the bridge (12 minutes). You will be in a shaded area of large hemlocks. Cross a bridge over a smaller watercourse that parallels Lenox Mountain Brook, then a larger bridge over LMB—which provides a nice view. Steep stone steps lead up to metal steps that take you to viewing platform (18 minutes), with suitable safety warnings. For your return trip, the alternative route loops the opposite direction, with different foliage and wetter terrain.

THE CASCADE FROM THE STEVENS GLEN OVERLOOK

24

Rice Sanctuary

PERU

HIKING DISTANCE: 1.5 miles (includes Rice Road)

WALKING TIME: 75 minutes

VERTICAL GAIN: N/A

MAP: Peru

Dorothy Frances Rice died of tuberculosis in the 1920s, shortly after graduating from Smith College, in Northampton. She loved the site of the family summer home. After her father, architect Orville Rice of New York City, died, her mother, Mary Rice, set up a trust to maintain the 300-acre property, named for her daughter. The family home partly burned and was partly chewed down by voracious porcupines.

People in Peru still talk about two Smith College girls who lived in the visitors' center for one or more summers while studying the plants and animals. In 1974, the trust turned the property over to the New England Forestry Foundation, along with an endowment. In season, a caretaker comes to maintain the trails and the building.

GETTING THERE

Take Route 8 to Hinsdale; turn east on Route 143 to the center of Peru, recognizable because of the church on the left and the road junction. Turn right on South Road for .8 mile, then left at

CHOICES, CHOICES AT THE RICE
Lauren R. Stevens

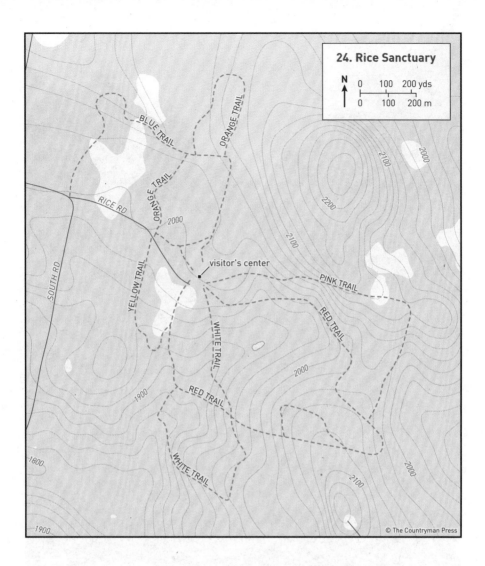

Rice Road. Park at the gate rather than driving in.

THE TRAIL

If you arrive during daylight hours from May 28 to October 12, you will see a sign welcoming you to the Dorothy Frances Rice Wildlife Sanctuary. Local people also ski here in the winter. Walk up the road to the small visitors' center. Nearby, most of the trails come together (their arrows color-coded) at a busy sign. Choose your color and follow in the direction of the arrow, because some of the trees are only blazed—often with colored blocks of wood—on one side. If you go the "wrong" way, you won't see any blazes—though the trails are easy to follow, some sections even mowed. The area is logged occasionally; however, no hunting, trapping, or motorized vehicles are allowed.

The blue trail (at first blue and

Lauren R. Stevens

A MOWED TRAIL THROUGH FIELD AND FOREST

orange) leaves the visitors' center and passes beneath large pine, with occasional glimpses of stonewalls. It could take you on a pond circuit or drop you by the gate. It may be a bit wet. Though as many as 1,500 people a year wander through the sanctuary, you probably won't see any of them. For the most part, the trails pass through old field growth laced with stone walls. The lengths of the walks vary and, of course, it's possible to connect them in different ways as they cross. Plan on an hour or more. Yes, those are bear scratches on the shed. The Peru wilderness is alive with fauna as well as flora.

Canoe Meadows

PITTSFIELD

HIKING DISTANCE: 1.5 miles

WALKING TIME: 40 minutes

VERTICAL GAIN: N/A

MAP: Pittsfield East

This Massachusetts Audubon Sanctuary consists of 262 acres of wetlands bordering the Housatonic River. The property, with its 3 miles of trails, is open from 7 a.m. to dusk, Tuesday through Sunday. The foliage filters the sound of traffic and the sight of nearby homes, so while it's located in a residential area, the property carries you to the open fields of an earlier Pittsfield. In fact, the property once belonged to the Holmes family (Oliver Wendell Senior and Junior) who gave it its name. No restrooms, but privies are available.

GETTING THERE

Drive south on Route 7 from the center of Pittsfield. Turn left onto Holmes Road at the light at the bottom of the hill. Access is from Holmes Road just to the north of its junction with Pomeroy Avenue. (The community gardens on the property are off Williams Street.) The trails are well used.

THE TRAIL

From the kiosk, follow the Maintenance Road through open fields and, in spring, enjoy the fragrance of honeysuckle. In 5 minutes, turn left on the Wolf Pine Trail. You indeed pass beneath wolf pines, those exceptionally large trees that have seeded the rest of the wooded lands. Walk along a berm: a man-made way of getting the trail out of the wetlands. The Owl Trail takes off to the left, but continue on Wolf Pine through skunk cabbage. You might want to follow the Maintenance Road, left (20 minutes) to see the work being done to restore Sackett Brook, but do not enter the Conservation Research Area.

Returning by the Maintenance Road,

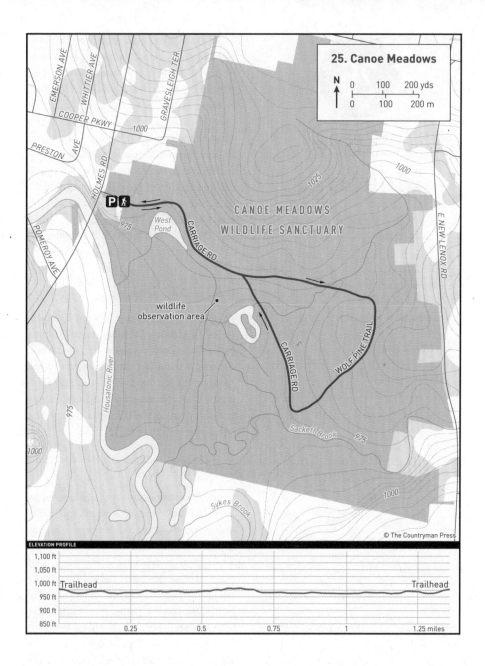

25. Canoe Meadows

N
| 0 | 100 | 200 yds |
| 0 | 100 | 200 m |

CANOE MEADOWS
WILDLIFE SANCTUARY

West Pond

CARRIAGE RD

wildlife observation area

CARRIAGE RD

WOLF PINE TRAIL

Housatonic River

Sackett Brook

Sykes Brook

© The Countryman Press

ELEVATION PROFILE

1,100 ft
1,050 ft
1,000 ft — Trailhead   Trailhead
950 ft
900 ft
850 ft

0.25   0.5   0.75   1   1.25 miles

pass the trail (30 minutes) to a wildlife observation area at the end of a causeway. The building burned in 2015 but may have been rebuilt. The essentially level trails, across meadows and occasional bridges, are skiable as long as wet areas are frozen. There is a self-guided nature tour. A donation is requested from nonmembers.

Lauren R. Stevens

A WOLF PINE IN CAPTIVITY AT CANOE MEADOWS

Lauren R. Stevens

PERHAPS THIS WILDLIFE OBSERVATORY WILL BE REBUILT

26

The Boulders

PITTSFIELD/DALTON/LANESBOROUGH

HIKING DISTANCE: varies

WALKING TIME: varies

VERTICAL RISE: 175 feet to The Boulders themselves

MAP: Pittsfield East

In 1994, Crane & Co., headquarters in Dalton, opened the site of a former family lodge to the public. (The buildings have been removed.) It is a wonderful piece of wooded land surrounded by urban sections of Dalton, Pittsfield, and Lanesborough. Besides the fun of investigating the property, there is a fine view of the surrounding countryside from the eponymous boulders at nearly 1,375 feet. In late 2015, Crane turned the property over to BNRC, which promises to improve the trail system.

GETTING THERE

Although a path leaves directly across from Crane & Co. Government Gate on Route 9, you get more of a feel for the property by parking at either the Gulf Gate or a corner of the Appalachian Trail, both at the Dalton end of Gulf

A TRAIL TO THE BOULDERS FROM GULF ROAD
Lauren R. Stevens

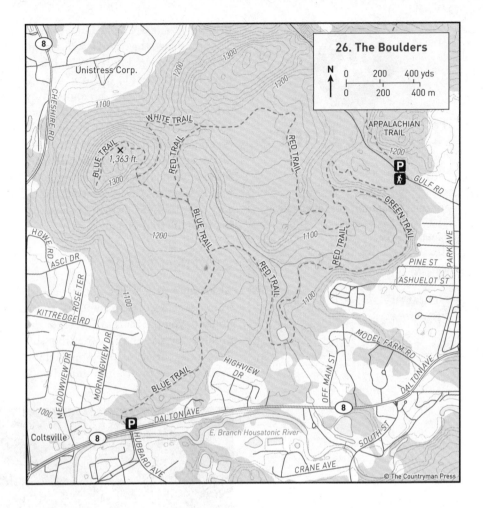

Road. From Route 8, turn east at Arizona Pizza (note: this road is not plowed in the winter). (There is a Gulf Road sign.) From Dalton, take Park Street past the DPW garage. (Warning: watch out for people driving too fast on the narrow, twisty, gravel Gulf Road.)

THE TRAILS

Study the trail map carefully and pick your route. Although there is logic to the trails, with the main trail looping through the property, intersections with side trails can be difficult to pick up, especially if logging disrupts the marking. From either entrance, you will soon make your way to the main woods road, formerly the driveway to the estate. Trails are blazed different colors on blocks of wood, which may help you keep track of the route back. There are signs at some intersections.

As you begin to climb, you hear industrial noises, perhaps from Unistress, and traffic from Routes 8 and 9. An initial look out, shortly before turning south to the summit, is a short scramble

Lauren R. Stevens

TALL MAPLES IN THE BOULDERS

off the road. The road ends at the circle (about 40 minutes from Gulf Road) just before the major lookout, which reveals a surprisingly bucolic view of Pittsfield. People have been unable to resist applying graffiti to the boulders, reminding visitors that they are only a few hundred yards from downtown.

Wahconah Falls

DALTON

HIKING DISTANCE: a few hundred yards

WALKING TIME: a few minutes

VERTICAL GAIN: N/A

MAP: Peru/Windsor

Another of the waterfalls of Berkshire County, Wahconah, like most, is technically a cascade—the water drops several times rather than just once. The lowest and largest drop is 40 feet. The popular site and gorge is located at Wahconah Falls State Park on Route 9 in Dalton.

GETTING THERE

Coming from Dalton center on Route 9 east toward Windsor, turn right at the sign. The parking lot is on the right about 1 mile up the gravel Wahconah Road. No fee, no camping, no lifeguard, but a composting toilet.

THE TRAIL

A sometime party spot, at last visit it had been meticulously cleaned. The public should treat a beautiful resource with respect. Like all state properties and most town and private ones, there are no trash barrels. Visitors are asked to remove what they bring in; some do. On this 53-acre tract, you will find a deep gulf, rocky ledges, large hemlocks, and a scattering of picnic grills. Trails meander through the woods on either side of the brook. The falls dive deeply over ledges below Windsor Reservoir on a tributary of the Housatonic. Deep pools below beckon to cool your feet. However, swimming is not allowed, due to the unsafe conditions.

According to legend, Wahconah was an Indian maid who fell for the handsome Nessacus rather than the older, politically expedient suitor. Of the several versions of the myth, one describes a contest to see which man could leap across the brook above the falls. When Nessacus doesn't make it, Wahconah leaps in after him, and both tumble to their deaths over the falls.

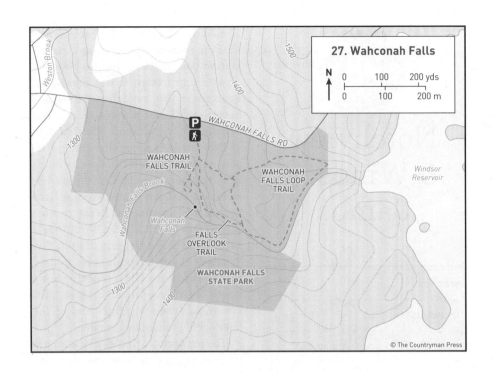

27. Wahconah Falls

WAHCONAH MAY HAUNT HER FALLS

Lauren R. Stevens

Notchview & Windsor Jambs

WINDSOR

HIKING DISTANCE: 5.5 miles

WALKING TIME: 2 hours, 30 minutes

VERTICAL GAIN: 300 feet

MAP: Windsor

The Arthur D. Budd Visitors' Center, near the parking lot, serves as an information booth and provides a place for cross-country skiers to wax and warm. Restrooms are available. There are picnic tables and a water source, but camping is not allowed. The Trustees of Reservations maintains this 3,108-acre reservation, which takes its name from the view from Lt. Col. Budd's former home through a notch eastward into the hills of Cummington. Route 9 passes through the Notch. Budd, a World War II hero, donated the property in 1965. The Trustees charge a nominal fee to non-members for use. The property shows traces of farming the soil of these hills, known as "rock farming," and of the later era of gentlemen's estates.

The property's 25 miles of trails pass through trees that have grown up on former fields, as well as some fields that are cut. Although you only climb 297 feet to the summit of Judge's Hill, the highest land in Windsor, you begin at an elevation of 2,000 feet. This quality of highland plateau, complete with evergreen forests, harsh climate, rocky soil, bogs, and deep stream crevasses, distinguishes Notchview. Wildlife here includes whitetail deer, bobcat, nesting hawks, and occasional bear.

At the time of this writing, the future of the Windsor Jambs as a usable state park is unclear, so it is included here as a side trip from Notchview. The cascade for which the Jambs is named can be reached by automobile, but more dramatically by driving to the Jambs Park and hiking the trail described below.

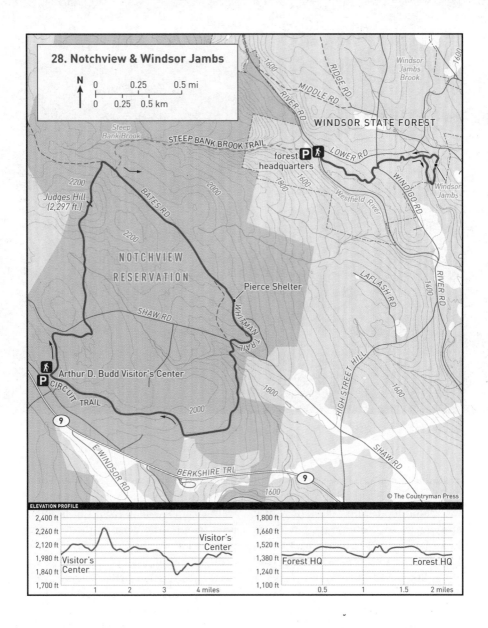

28. Notchview & Windsor Jambs

WINDSOR STATE FOREST

forest headquarters

Judges Hill (2,297 ft.)

NOTCHVIEW RESERVATION

Pierce Shelter

Arthur D. Budd Visitor's Center

STEEP BANK BROOK TRAIL

BATES RD

SHAW RD

CIRCUIT TRAIL

WHITMAN TRAIL

Windsor Jambs

LAFLASH RD

HIGH STREET HILL

SHAW RD

RIVER RD

WINDIGO RD

Westfield River

MIDDLE RD

RIDGE RD

LOWER RD

Windsor Jambs Brook

Steep Bank Brook

E WINDSOR RD

BERKSHIRE TRL

© The Countryman Press

ELEVATION PROFILE

(Left chart) Visitor's Center ... Visitor's Center — elevation axis: 1,700 ft, 1,840 ft, 1,980 ft, 2,120 ft, 2,260 ft, 2,400 ft; distance axis: 1, 2, 3, 4 miles

(Right chart) Forest HQ ... Forest HQ — elevation axis: 1,100 ft, 1,240 ft, 1,380 ft, 1,520 ft, 1,660 ft, 1,800 ft; distance axis: 0.5, 1, 1.5, 2 miles

GETTING THERE

Take Route 9 east from Pittsfield, through Dalton, where 8-A joins, and up the long hill to Windsor. The entrance to Notchview is 1 mile east of the junction where Route 8-A departs north. That road drops south from Route 116 out of Adams, an alternate course for people setting sail for Notchview from North County.

CAMPING

Though it's closed at the time of this writing, in-season camping may be

THE JAMBS ARE A RUGGED SPOT

available for a small fee at Windsor Jambs State Park, which is part of the state forest. The area is just east and north of Notchview, on River Road (signs on Route 116 and Route 9 direct you to the park). A foot trail along Steep Bank Brook connects the Jambs with Notchview, about 3 miles from the Budd Visitors' Center. At the campground, the stream is dammed for swimming, but the area is closed for now.

THE TRAIL

You may choose any combination of well-marked and well-maintained trails at Notchview. Signs at intersections, often including maps, guide your way. For a potential morning's hike of 5.5 miles, walk straight ahead from the parking area, leaving the barn on the left, and turning left on the Circuit Trail. Walk gently up through a wet, spruce area. At 12 minutes, turn left on the Windsor Trail. At first you lose elevation, crossing Shaw Road (gravel) and descending through mixed hardwoods and across a bridge. Begin to climb moderately, through an area marked by large glacial boulders. Note that trails farther removed from the Visitors' Center, and used primarily for skiing, may not be mowed.

After 30 minutes, you achieve the summit, marked by the stone remains of the Judge's "fort," laid up without mortar. Most of the surrounding growth is quite young; the Judge must have had a marvelous view when the land was cleared. Judge James M. Barker was the most prominent member of a social and sporting group known as the Windsor Club, which held weekend hunting and fishing trips on the property. He erected the stone lunch stop, walled around and complete with stone tables and benches, at the turn of the 20th century.

It takes 10 minutes to descend to Bates Road, a gravel surface on which you turn right—or you can choose the Bates Bypass (trail), which is not as easy walking, but off road. Pass between the cellar holes and stone walls of some of the two dozen families who once lived in the area. In one, a rabbit warren has been cleverly burrowed under a concrete slab. Is this the site of the Babbitt Axe Factory? Could these be the Babbitt rabbits? The Steep Bank Brook Trail, which departs left, takes you to Windsor Jambs.

Pick up the Whitman Trail, left, through open fields to General Bates' site. Bates fought Indians in Kansas and Wyoming. His cousin, Herman, was famous for the quality of the butter he produced on this highland farm, becoming known as "Butter Bates." The open fields provide a nice contrast to traveling the woods. The Whitman Trail joins the Bumpus Trail, just before the Pierce Shelter, and turns abruptly right, crossing Shaw Road (1:14) and descending steeply into a gorge. It crosses a bridge over Shaw Brook, then climbs through evergreens. Continue straight at the Y, 9 minutes later. Follow the signs towards the Visitors' Center, coming out on the

Lauren R. Stevens

THE COMFORTABLE VISITORS' CENTER AT NOTCHVIEW

open Sawmill Field, crossing it, and picking up the Circuit Trail back to the parking lot (1:55).

Among the many walking and hiking options is the mile-long, self-guided interpretive trail in the Hume Brook area across Route 9 at Notchview. This trail explains the principles of forest-land management, with an emphasis on forest aesthetics and wildlife. TTOR issues separate maps for hiking and skiing; a large map is posted by the parking lot. Bring a picnic; spend the day.

WINDSOR JAMBS

A visit to Notchview might include a side trip to Windsor Jambs, either by foot on the Sand Bank Trail (3 miles) or, probably better, by automobile. Chocolate-brown state signs will direct you to River Road from both Route 9 and Route 116. If it's open, park in the lot by the HQ. Otherwise, park across the road. When people talk about the Jambs, they mean the state park with its swimming area. Strictly speaking, however, the Jambs is a nearby gorge, the name perhaps derived from the stream's narrowed route through a rock doorway.

You can drive to the scenic gorge on the gravel Lower Road, but you'll miss out on a 3-mile, round-trip stroll through a deep evergreen forest and the sense of accomplishment you'll gain from getting there on your own. Note, however, that the trail is difficult to maintain, beginning in a wet area, climbing fairly steeply, and descending to a stream crossing before the final ascent. Furthermore, while the campground is closed, staff may not be available for maintenance. It is a 3-mile hike, taking about 1.5 hours.

At the beginning of Lower Road, bear

right through the camping area for the Jambs Trail. The trail is wet and requires sure-footedness since it runs beside the Jambs. Wear hiking shoes. The leisurely path (blazed blue), wanders in its own insouciant way through spruce, hemlock, and even some pine and fir. There are bridges, though some are in need of

Lauren R. Stevens

THE JUDGE'S FORT STILL STANDS, ALTHOUGH WITHOUT MORTAR

repair. After 25 minutes, cross Decelles Road. Continue on the other side.

In another 10 minutes, you reach a stream crossing and, on the far side, a junction. For the best effect, follow the trail right to the lower Jambs (40 minutes) then work up along the edge, protected by the fence, to upper Jambs. On the way back, the trail leaves from the parking lot. Jambs Brook has cut deeply into slabs of rock, tumbling over many small falls—a pleasing sight even when, in midsummer, not much water passes through. Note that it may or may not be possible to take a post-hike swim at the public swimming area near where you parked.

29

Shaker Mountain

HANCOCK

HIKING DISTANCE: 6.5 miles

WALKING TIME: 3 hours

VERTICAL GAIN: 1,165 feet

MAP: Pittsfield West

'Tis a gift to be simple
'Tis a gift to be free
'Tis a gift to come down
Where you want to be....
— Shaker Elder
Joseph Brackett, 1848

The first simple gift you will receive from the Shakers, or at least the non-profit corporation that runs their village, is the hospitality of the Visitors' Center. Although you could park at the pullover on Route 20 across from the village and hike in past the Shaker reservoir, why not park in the village lot? There is no charge for hikers and you can stop in to pick up a map. More importantly, before or after the hike, pay your fee and tour Hancock Shaker Village. The first part of the hike is on village property; the rest is in Pittsfield State Forest. This remarkable hike takes you past the un-restored remains of the North Family or industrial grouping of Hancock Shakers. The hike includes the village's water system, mill sites, dams, the foundations of a residence, 150-year-old cart roads, charcoal-burning sites, stonewalls, and hilltop holy sites of both the Hancock village and the New Lebanon, New York, Shaker Village. After that, with any luck at all, you will come down where you want to be, right where you started.

GETTING THERE

From Park Square in Pittsfield, follow Route 20 west for 5 miles. Park in the lot for Hancock Shaker Village, which will be on your left after you cross the Hancock town line and a few hundred yards beyond the village buildings. Most people taking this hike will want to tour Hancock Shaker Village, to learn about the souls who built the industrial

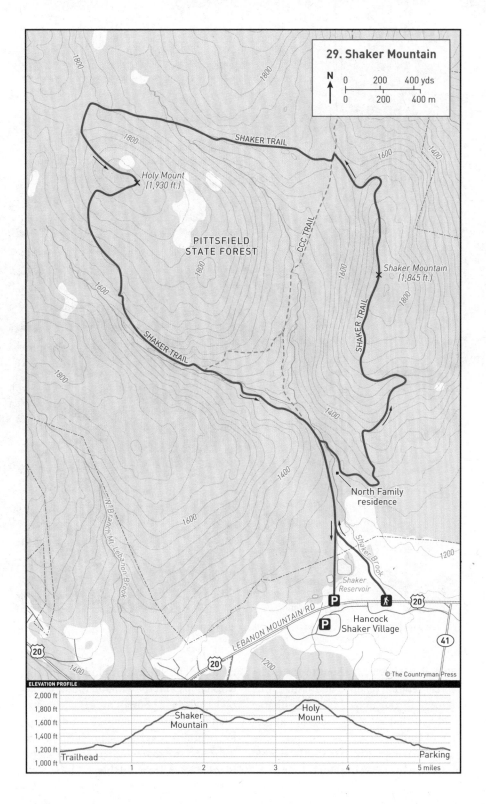

29. Shaker Mountain

N

| 0 | 200 | 400 yds |
| 0 | 200 | 400 m |

1800

1800

1800

SHAKER TRAIL

1600

1400

1800

1600

Holy Mount
(1,930 ft.)

CCC TRAIL

PITTSFIELD
STATE FOREST

1800

1600

Shaker Mountain
(1,845 ft.)

1800

SHAKER TRAIL

1600

SHAKER TRAIL

1400

1400

N. B. Branch Mt. Lebanon Brook

1600

1400

North Family
residence

Shaker Brook

1200

1600

1200

Shaker
Reservoir

P

20

LEBANON MOUNTAIN RD

P

Hancock
Shaker Village

41

20

20

1400

1200

© The Countryman Press

ELEVATION PROFILE

Shaker
Mountain

Holy
Mount

Trailhead

Parking

2,000 ft
1,800 ft
1,600 ft
1,400 ft
1,200 ft
1,000 ft

1   2   3   4   5 miles

THIS DAM MARKED THE BEGINNING OF AN EFFICIENT SHAKER WATER SYSTEM

and holy sites you're about to visit. The Shaker religion reached its zenith in this country in the 1830s. These celibates believed that all work was an expression of God's glory; thus their furniture and craftsmanship are both simple and exquisite. A self-guided tour of 20 restored buildings, including crafts workshops and the famous round barn, takes at least 2 hours. There is a fee. The Visitors' Center, adjacent to the parking lot, contains rest rooms, lunch shop, an information center, and a museum shop. Picnic tables are available.

Berry Pond has 13 sites, with pit toilets (outhouses). However, you cannot drive directly from Shaker Village to the Pittsfield State Forest campgrounds. Return to Pittsfield. From Park Square, follow west on West Street, 2.5 miles; turn right on Churchill Street for 1.25 miles; and left at the chocolate-colored state forest sign on Cascade Street, from which it is .5 miles to the state forest entrance. There is a small fee for parking, to use the bathing beach at Lulu Pond, or for camping.

THE TRAIL

If you park in the Village, you will be asked to sign in—a reasonable request for your own protection. John Manners and his Boy Scouts rediscovered the sites and created the trail, also creating the initial guide. Use the crosswalk to get to the north side of Route 20 and to the fields behind the Meeting House, the most westerly of the village buildings on that side of the highway. Head north to the logging road. The trail proper departs north from a cleared log landing 5 minutes from the highway. Laid out by the Boy Scouts, it is marked by green triangles with white circles (on state forest land accompanied by green blazes). Begin on an unmistakable cart road that soon follows the western side of Shaker Brook. The stone walls may have been laid in 1845. Fifteen minutes from the highway, arrive at the lower dam, the beginning of a sophisticated water system. The pipe filled a reservoir from which it traveled underground to the village where it first powered machinery, then supplied the washrooms, stables, mills, and then the fields to water the cattle. The old bridge above the dam has been replaced. Cross the brook.

As you follow down the eastern side

CAMPING

The closest public camping is at Pittsfield State Forest, with two campgrounds. The one at Parker Brook, to the west of the HQ, has 18 sites. The "comfort station" has flush toilets. The one at of the stream (doubling back), pass an industrial site with a pit for a water wheel, and then the cellar hole for the North Family residence. To imagine its size, compare it to the Brick Dwelling in the village, though this one was made of wood. At 17 minutes into the walk, not counting time spent examining the ruins, turn left up the hill, through second-growth hardwood with some shagbark hickory and hemlock, on what was probably the Shakers' original cart road to their holy site.

At 35 minutes, bear left where a branch of the road continues straight. This was a charcoal-burning site. Cross under power lines that serve airplane beacon lights for the Pittsfield airport. Switch back to cross under the lines again.

At 45 minutes, enter the cleared field that was the Hancock Shakers' holy ground, which they called Mt. Sinai, now referred to as Shaker Mountain. The Shakers did not permit nonbelievers on this site. You are entering consecrated ground. A respectful attitude is appropriate. In 1841 or 1842, all Shaker communities were required to clear the summit of a nearby hill, focusing on a "fountain" (hexagonal fence) surrounding a marble slab, about which they marched, sang, and danced in May and September. A depression in the blackberry bushes beside the trail marks the fountain; you may not notice it. Little else remains at Mt. Sinai; more artifacts are visible at Holy Mount, about a mile as the bird flies across the valley. Shakers called to each other across the chasm.

The trail follows along the ridge and then turns left into the valley. At about 50 minutes, it switches back through a lovely hemlock grove. At 1:03, come out on the CCC Trail (made by Civilian Conservation Corps members). Turn left. If you wish for a 1:30 minute hike, follow straight back to the village. Otherwise, turn right almost immediately. This road follows to the left of a stone wall. At the end of the wall (1:18), bear left down the hill. The trail swings right, between sections of a different stone wall, and across a brook (1:23). The forest in this section has not been lumbered as ruthlessly as the forest in the valley and on Shaker Mountain. Follow up the hill to a junction of walls and trails (1:27), where you turn left and follow a stone wall.

At 1:36, pass an opening in the wall that probably admitted a cart road from the New Lebanon community to its holy ground. At 1:41, arrive at what was a gated entrance, elevation 1,927 feet (higher than Mt. Sinai). Follow the wall, on the inside, left to the feast ground and the foundations of the shelter (1:45). Although the Shakers planted a row of pines around each site, the CCCs planted the pine trees inside in the 1930s. If you head into the woods directly in front of the shelter, you may find the depression in the ground that marks the fountain site. There was once an altar 10 yards west of the fountain.

Downhill from the altar, you'll find a beautiful specimen of the wall-maker's art, probably one day's labor, three feet at the base and tapering to the top, 18 feet long. The brethren must have taken 350 man-days to build the wall around the sacred lot, not including time devoted to the other walls you have seen.

Starting in front of the shelter, head west, bearing right downhill on a trail that reaches an opening in the wall (1:53). Although the path generally follows the wall to the left, it swings out in an arc before rejoining at the corner.

This section of trail, which is not based on an old road and has not experienced much wear, is nevertheless well marked. The corner of the wall encloses a natural amphitheater (2:03), containing a spring. If you did not stop to picnic at either summit, this would be a good spot. Cross the brook below the corner and follow steeply up the hill, along the path, until it comes out on a fire road (2:20). Turn left. The brook is on your right. Pass the first of several wide spots on the road, which were charcoal-burning sites. You may find some pieces of charcoal. Follow the fire road until it turns left, uphill, while the older cart road continues straight to a brook crossing (2:29). From here, follow the green triangles down the branch of the brook to pass by a Shaker marble quarry.

At 2:41, return to the main cart road (bear right) at the site of the high dam, which is largely washed out. It may have been constructed in 1810. Just below, the Shakers built a sawmill that bridged the stream. Logs were loaded at the retaining wall on the far side. The depressions on the near side were mill foundations. This mill, which ran on waterpower—or steam when water wasn't sufficient—was built in the mid-19th century and burned in 1926.

Follow the cart road to Route 20. Total round trip is just about 3 hours, counting only travel time. It would be possible to ski Shaker Mountain, but not Holy Mount. A ski loop, the same as for an abbreviated hike, would return via the lumber road you meet after descending Shaker Mountain.

RAMBLEWILD

LANESBOROUGH

Definitely not a walk in the woods, Ramblewild, located on Brodie Mountain Road in Lanesborough, is a tree-to-tree adventure park. The park, the largest of its kind in North America, is set on 10 acres in the middle of over 1,400 acres of New England forest and mountain landscape. A ravine divides the park, with the sides connected by a 200-foot suspension bridge that hangs 80 feet above the ravine stream. The focal point is a central, wooden, bi-level platform 10 and 15 feet above the ground, from which eight aerial obstacle courses radiate, meandering from tree to tree at various heights through the forest. Each course consists of 15 elements (high wires, zip lines, balancing logs, rope ladders, cargo nets, suspended bridges, etc.) that wander through a hemlock forest. Four of the eight courses cross over the ravine via zip lines that keep you 100 feet above the stream.

The tree-to-tree challenge courses are designed to impact visitors' self-confidence and happiness. Fee charged. Go to www.ramblewild.com.

OPPOSITE: ALONG THE BRADLEY FARM TRAIL
Lauren R. Stevens

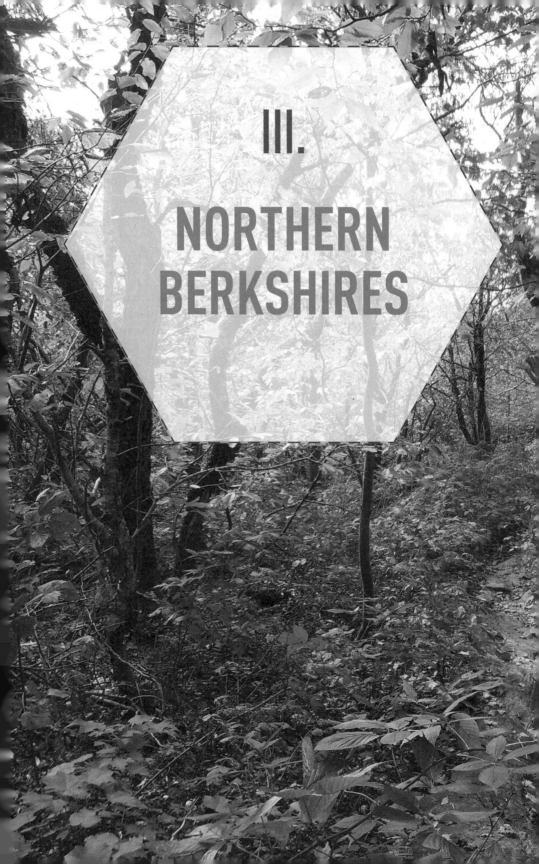

III.

NORTHERN BERKSHIRES

MOUNT GREYLOCK

Although no peak among the Berkshire Hills reaches 4,000 feet above sea level, Mount Greylock comes close, its elevation heightened to the east, north, and west in comparison with the Hoosic and Green River valleys that cut deeply beside it. Those who observe it from the south see it more as a higher rise of a series of hills; those who look from Route 7 across from the high school that bears its name, from the Pine Cobble overlook, from Spruce Hill, or from East Road in Adams get the full effect.

Although the summit of Mount Greylock lies in the town of Adams, the Mount Greylock State Reservation encompasses 12,500 acres of hilly land in the towns of Adams, Cheshire, Lanesborough, New Ashford, North Adams, and Williamstown. But you only have to look up in Adams to understand why the Mother Town, as Adams is called, feels a special regard for the looming mountain. Mount Greylock is a close, intimate friend.

Mount Greylock is the tallest peak in southern New England at 3,491 feet. Well, maybe a couple feet less, as methods of measuring become more precise. It is a massif, surrounded by half a dozen lower eminences, most of which are still higher than anything else in Massachusetts, Connecticut, and Rhode Island: Saddle Ball (3,238), Mt. Fitch (3,110), Mt. Williams (2,951), Mt. Prospect (2,690), Stony Ledge (2,580), and Ragged Mountain (2,451).

Theories compete about how it got its name. Historically it was called Grand Hoosuck, with various spellings: a Mohican Indian name associated with both the river that drains it and the mountain range to the east. Seen from the south, it seemed to have two peaks and was therefore called Saddle Mountain or Saddleback or Saddle Ball, a name that lingers for a lesser peak. You can take the testimony of one Platt, who drove Nathaniel Hawthorne on his visit to a Williams College commencement in 1838. "'That, Sir, is a very high hill. It is known by the name of Graylock,'" Hawthorne recorded, the first time that name appeared in print. He went on: "[Platt] seemed to feel that this was a more poetical epithet than Saddleback, which is the more usual name for it. Graylock, or Saddleback, is quite a respectable mountain; and I suppose the former name has been given it, because it often has a gray cloud, or lock of gray mist, upon his head."

That's one theory. It also happened that an Indian, Chief Greylock, rose to prominence in 1720 for leading fellow Abenaki warriors of the Wabenaki Confederacy against New England settlers. Though no evidence exists that Greylock ever visited Mount Greylock, by the time of Hawthorne's visit, New Englanders were romanticizing the Indians, few of whom remained. The same poetical urge that Hawthorne mentions might have associated the chief with the mountain.

Although Mount Greylock is not as high as some peaks in the Catskills, Adirondacks, White Mountains, or the Green Mountains—all of which you can see from Mount Greylock—it nevertheless dominates Berkshire. At one time the Appalachians, of which Mount Greylock is a part, stood Alpine high, many times their present altitude, but time and weather have eroded them.

A CLOUD LAYER, SIMILAR TO WHAT THOREAU RECORDED, COVERS THE HOOSIC VALLEY

Lauren R. Stevens

In the early 19th century, before the more spectacular, western scenery in this country was accessible, Mount Greylock created much excitement. All the great American writers and naturalists, such as Thoreau, Hawthorne, and Melville, made their pilgrimages to Mount Greylock. The first person to publish an account of his visit to the summit, in 1799, was the president of Yale College, Timothy Dwight, who said "the view was immense and of amazing grandeur . . ." It inspired prose, poetry, painting, and energetic enjoyment of the outdoors.

The summit now has limited development, such as broadcast towers and communications dishes. A 100-foot-high War Memorial Tower, its design clearly influenced by lighthouses along the seashore, 130 miles away, was erected on Mount Greylock in the 1930s to honor the dead of World War I and to call for peace. The state-owned Bascom Lodge, built by the state and Civilian Conservation Corps during the Depression, run by a concessionaire, provides accommodations and good food in season (reservations required). Enthusiastic state interpreters lead walks and conduct programs to explain the natural and human history of the mountain, departing the Visitors Center at the foot of Rockwell Road, the lodge, and the campground.

A 7.8-mile segment of the 2,050-mile-long Appalachian Trail transects the reservation south and north, a ribbon that hangs over most of the peaks. The AT is blazed white. Of the five three-sided shelters on the reservation, two are associated with the AT. Ten side trails to the AT (blazed blue), together with 11 other trails and the AT, make up over 70 miles of hiking total in the Greylock range—routes shorter or longer, steeper or more gentle, fit just about every walker's time and ambition.

On the eastern side, the Thunderbolt Ski Trail, associated with the early days of skiing in this country, is another CCC project. The trail was cut, from August to December 1934, with the aid of 300 pounds of dynamite. The trail—named for a roller coaster ride at Revere Beach, near Boston—originally rolled 1.6 miles from the summit to the Theil farm in Adams. The first United States Eastern Amateur Ski Association (now the US Ski Association) race was held there on February 7, 1935. Richard Durrance of Dartmouth College won in 2 minutes, 48 seconds. Other races attracted international competition and large crowds of spectators, but the east side of the mountain doesn't hold snow well and many scheduled races were cancelled, so when other downhill slopes were developed, with lifts and snowmaking, skiing left the Thunderbolt—until 2008, when the Thunderbolt Ski Runners studied the history, made a movie, reopened the trail for backcountry skiing and boarding, and began to hold an annual race on it.

The CCCs built the ski shelter near the top of the run, now dedicated to Rudolph Konieczny, a member of the 10th Mountain Division ski troops in World War II. Several 10th Mountain skiers were local residents who trained on Greylock. The upper end of the Bellows Pipe hike (below) is on the Thunderbolt.

The War Memorial Tower, closed for repair but expected to reopen in 2017, extends the view from the summit to 70 or 100 miles in clear conditions. It is a tradition for a small group to greet sunrise on the first day of summer from the tower. Innumerable more local views reveal Adams from the east of the summit, the farms of Williamstown from the trail intersection on Mt. Prospect, the peak itself from Ragged, and the lakes and rounded hills of mid-Berkshire from Jones' Nose or Rounds' Rock.

Views on the mountains include tumbling streams. March Cataract flows best when the snows melt. You can see it from Route 7 in front of Mt. Greylock Regional High School. A trail from the campground leads there. The Deer Hill Trail from the campground passes a

A VIEW FROM THE OVERLOOK TRAIL

Lauren R. Stevens

falls on Roaring Brook and through a stand of old growth hemlock. Money Brook Falls, also tucked into the Hopper, can be reached by a short side trail to the Money Brook Trail.

Most of the vegetation on lower Greylock is northern hardwood: beech, birch, maple, with hemlock in the shaded areas. In the southern portions of the reservation, recent second growth fills formerly farmed fields. Here and there on the mountains' steep slopes stand aged trees, in areas too difficult to access for wholesale timber harvesting for railroads or other development. The 1,600 acres of the Hopper, a U-shaped glacial cirque on the west side, contain red spruce stands over 200 years old. The state has designated the Hopper a Natural Area. The federal government, together with the Society of American Foresters, has recognized these spruces as a National Natural Landmark. For protection, the Hopper is a low-impact area, excluding vehicles, campfires, and camping, but available for study and hiking.

Mount Greylock's upper reaches are covered by a boreal type of spruce, balsam fir, and yellow birch forest, probably the only example of such woods in Massachusetts. (See the Dome hike, below. Just over the Vermont border, it also provides a taste of the boreal environment.) The bogs and stunted fir growth near the summits of Greylock and Saddle Ball are similar to the vegetation on the Canadian Shield—the forest of the far north. As a hiker arriving in them, accompanied by the call of white-throated sparrows, you will feel exhilarated. Those in automobiles may be oblivious.

The variety of wildlife matches the diversity of vegetation. Forty state-listed rare or endangered species, animal and vegetable, have been seen on the reservation, as well as birds as unusual as Swainson's thrush and the blackpoll warbler. Viewers come to watch a variety of hawks (and hang gliders) performing their aerobatics by taking advantage of updrafts on the steepest part of the east face. Common wildlife include the whitetail deer, bobcats, snowshoe hares, cottontail rabbits, ruffed grouse, woodcocks, raccoons, red squirrels, chipmunks, foxes, skunks, woodchucks, and porcupines that hang around the shelters to chew unattended hiking boots. As surrounding farm fields grow over, bear, eastern coyote, wild turkey, fisher, and raven have returned to the reservation.

According to Berkshire Natural Resources Council, Berkshire County is blessed with approximately 250,000 acres of land in some form of conservation—approximately 40 percent of its total 600,000 acres. The Mt. Greylock State Reservation stands as the flagship of the state's forest and park system and as the jewel of Berkshire County's public and private holdings.

This book describes walks and hikes at the Visitors' Center, in the summit area and in the campground area. The shorter ones include the Bradley Farm Trail, the Overlook Trail, Campground trails, and Rounds' Rock. It describes longer hikes: Cheshire Harbor Trail, from the southeast; Bellows Pipe Trail from the north; Hopper Trail from the west; Prospect & Money Brooks Trails from the west; and Stony Ledge/Roaring Brook from the southwest. This list is not comprehensive; there are many other trails on the Reservation. Dogs are only allowed on leash at the campground.

Although town bounds with stone markers are maintained on the Reservation, they are of no consequence to

WINTER STALKS ON THE HOOSAC RANGE TRAIL

the hiker. Town names are omitted in the Greylock trail descriptions that follow.

CAMPING

The Sperry Road campground, reached by a trail from a parking lot on Rockwell Road, offers 18 tent sites, 9 group sites, and 3 shelters. The sites, in state parlance, are "primitive" in that they have solar privies but no showers—and no accommodations for vehicles. Water is available from a pump. Tent sites are distributed discreetly in a spruce grove. Shelters are also available at nearby Deer Hill, Wilbur's Clearing on the Money Brook Trail, Bellows Pipe on the ski trail, at Peck's Brook off the Gould Trail, and at the Mark Noepel on the AT

south of Saddle Ball. Dispersed camping is available in the vicinity of the shelters and on the Money Brook Trail near the Hopper trailhead.

GETTING THERE

A popular destination, especially in leaf season, the summit is reached by paved roads from North Adams (Notch Road from Route 2) and from Lanesborough (Rockwell Road from Route 7), which meet a mile from the top, from whence they travel together as Summit Road. A gravel-surfaced road, known as New Ashford or Greylock Road, climbs from the west to Rockwell Road not far below a gravel spur known as Sperry Road, now closed to vehicles.

30

Ashuwillticook Trail

ADAMS CHESHIRE LANESBOROUGH

HIKING DISTANCE: 3.2 miles (the trail currently extends 11 miles)

WALKING TIME: 1 hour, 30 minutes

VERTICAL GAIN: N/A

MAPS: Cheshire

You no longer need to worry about trains along this section of roadbed, although in the mid-19th century the Hoosic River Railroad connected major east-west lines in Pittsfield and North Adams. Now it is a wonderful, water-level route, remade into a popular, paved biking, roller-blading, baby stroller, and walking trail, which joins the Berkshire Mall, on the Pittsfield city line, with the visitors center in downtown Adams. Planning, and even engineering, is underway to extend the route through North Adams and Williamstown. When the Boston & Maine Railroad was about to sell its right-of-way, the Hoosic River Watershed Association intervened, giving then-State Sen. Jane Swift time to arrange for the state to acquire the land. Swift then became acting governor and in short order MassHighway (now Mass-DOT) created the trail. The name comes from the supposed Indian name for this part of the river.

CAMPING

See Mt. Greylock introduction.

GETTING THERE

You can walk any section you like, or the whole thing. The portion along Cheshire Reservoir (a.k.a. Hoosac Lake) is probably the most scenic and the portion through "The Jungle" offers the most wildlife. Here's a bit of each for two cars. Leave auto No. 1 at Cheshire Harbor (turn off Route 8 to the east near the bottom of the hill just south of Berkshire Outfitters, south of Adams center). Parking is just off the road, to keep it out of the way of homeowners. Drive the second car south to Farnam's Crossing, a road running west from Route 8 that crosses the reservoir on a causeway.

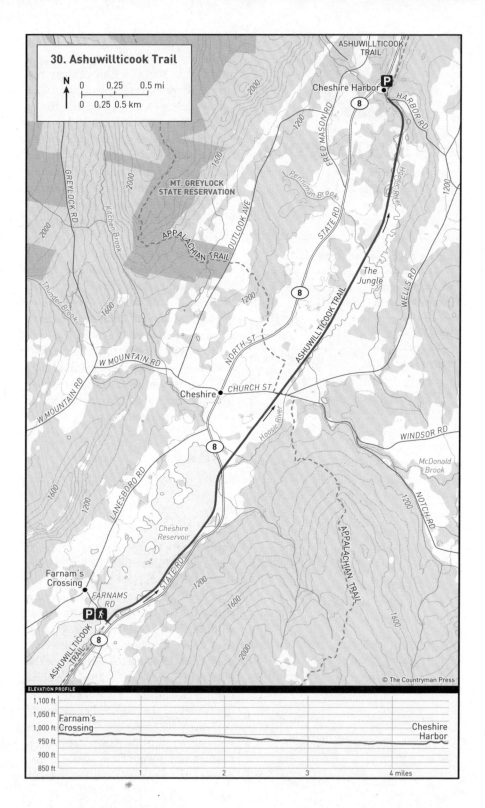

30. Ashuwillticook Trail

N
0   0.25   0.5 mi
0   0.25 0.5 km

ASHUWILLTICOOK
TRAIL

Cheshire Harbor

8

HARBOR RD

FRED MASON RD

2000

1200

1200

Penniman Brook

Hoosic River

STATE RD

WELLS RD

MT. GREYLOCK
STATE RESERVATION

APPALACHIAN TRAIL

OUTLOOK AVE

2000

GREYLOCK RD

Kitchen Brook

1600

Thunder Brook

2000

1200

8

The
Jungle

ASHUWILLTICOOK TRAIL

NORTH ST

W MOUNTAIN RD

W MOUNTAIN RD

W MOUNTAIN RD

CHURCH ST

Cheshire

Hoosic River

WINDSOR RD

McDonald
Brook

8

1600

1200

LANESBORO RD

Cheshire
Reservoir

STATE RD

1200

APPALACHIAN TRAIL

1200

NOTCH RD

1600

Farnam's
Crossing

FARNAMS
RD

P

8

ASHUWILLTICOOK
TRAIL

1600

2000

© The Countryman Press

ELEVATION PROFILE

1,100 ft				
1,050 ft				
1,000 ft				Cheshire
950 ft				Harbor
900 ft				
850 ft				

Farnam's
Crossing

1   2   3   4 miles

THIS DAM ON THE HOOSIC RIVER ON THE ASHUWILLTICOOK TRAIL MAY AGAIN GENERATE POWER

(A universally accessible bathroom is available.)

THE TRAIL

After parking, walk north looking out at the Greylock massif over the water. Just before you reach the Route 8, you will pass the dam that controls the water level. The Hoosic River was dammed in the 19th century to provide a back-up supply for waterpower for a downstream mill. Take care crossing Route 8. (You can control the light with a push button.) Follow the trail behind the restaurant. Cross the bridge over Kitchen Brook. Pass some backyards with barking dogs. Chug-chug across Church Street (and the Appalachian Trail). Soon you are removed from houses and dogs, as South Brook enters from the southeast. Stafford Hill rises northeast and the Greylock massif, northwest.

Natives call this section "The Jungle," since the 10-foot-wide Hoosic writhes through swampland. While you don't need to worry about alligators, nesting snapping turtles can be a problem in late spring. The calcareous (lime-based) wetlands west of the tracks, and marshes and shrub swamps east of the tracks, are fine habitats for a variety of water creatures. Wood duck platforms dot the wetlands, and deer and muskrat tracks follow the stream. You may see snowshoe hare, pheasant, occasional fox, and some wild brown trout that reproduce in the stream, as well as stocked trout. The devices at the ends of culverts are "beaver deceivers," intended to prevent the rodents from damming the pipes. Note that although you are heading north, you are going downstream. Route 8 is close at hand, but not noticeable except for the distant sound of a truck downshifting. You see a gouged hillside of gravel pits to the left.

A brick building belonging to the town of Adams introduces the first road for 3 miles. This is the pumping station for two artesian wells that supply the town of Adams. Around the corner appears a bridge. Welcome to Cheshire Harbor, said to be named because it harbored runaway slaves. It is a lovely spot with an old swimming hole, somewhat silted in. Now the river is on the left, with Route 8 just the far side. Car No. 1 awaits.

Of course the Ashuwillticook is designed for biking, especially family outings, given its flat, paved surface that runs gently downhill. Since the Berkshire Regional Transit Authority buses mount bike racks on the front, you could pedal between the Berkshire Mall to Adams and bus back. The trail is open to cross-country skiing in the winter.

Lauren R. Stevens

BIKING TRAILS ARE OPEN TO OTHER USES

Bradley Farm Trail

GREYLOCK

HIKING DISTANCE: 1.8 miles

WALKING TIME: 1 hour

VERTICAL GAIN: 424 feet

MAP: Cheshire

The Bradley Farm Trail, created by the Student Conservation Association for the Appalachian Mountain Club in 2002, is an interpretive hike, with a brochure available in the Visitors Center. William Bradley was a founder of the town of Lanesborough, acquiring the land around the Visitors Center in 1762. His son, Ephraim, farmed it, as did succeeding generations until about 1822. The land remained agricultural until the early 1900s. Since then it has been returning to forest.

The Bradley Farm stand on Route 7 continues the family name in the area. Ephraim built and endowed the stone schoolhouse that still stands on the road to the Visitors' Center. The family also provided the stone church, St. Luke's Episcopal, on Route 7.

CAMPING

Numerous sites on the mountain; none on this trail.

GETTING THERE

The route to the Visitors Center is well marked from Route 7 in Lanesborough. Turn east onto North Main Street, then right on Greylock Road to Rockwell Road. Note that the Visitors' Center is open year-round, even when the gates to the Reservation are closed, although there are limited hours off-season.

THE TRAIL

The Visitors' Center itself is well worth a stop. This stone, wood, and glass building, built in 1972, sits above a field and commands a view of the Pittsfield lakes and the Taconics. It also provides considerable information about the Mt.

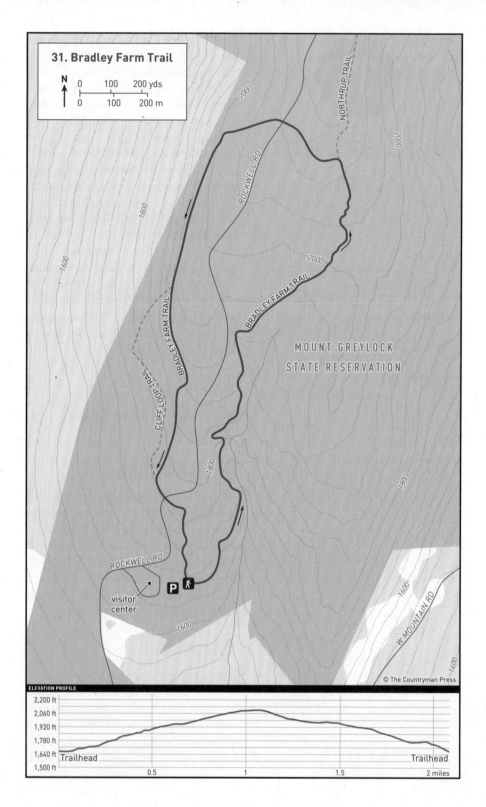

31. Bradley Farm Trail

N

| 0 | 100 | 200 yds |
| 0 | 100 | 200 m |

NORTHRUP TRAIL

2000

ROCKWELL RD

2000

1800

1600

BRADLEY FARM TRAIL

CLIFF LOOP TRAIL

BRADLEY FARM TRAIL

2000

1800

MOUNT GREYLOCK
STATE RESERVATION

1800

ROCKWELL RD

P

visitor
center

1600

1600

W MOUNTAIN RD

1400

© The Countryman Press

ELEVATION PROFILE

| 2,200 ft |
| 2,060 ft |
| 1,920 ft |
| 1,780 ft |
| 1,640 ft | Trailhead | | | Trailhead |
| 1,500 ft |

0.5   1   1.5   2 miles

Greylock State Reservation, including an introductory film. Pick up a self-guided brochure for the Bradley Farm Trail.

The trail begins in an upper corner of the parking lot. Walk through Ephraim's apple orchard, where the remaining trees now provide treats for the animals. In 7 minutes, bear left where the Brook & Berry Trail turns right. The trail rises gently uphill, following a deepening valley, right. Pass over a bog bridge, designed in part to keep your feet dry and in part to protect wetlands. In 25 minutes, the Northrup Trail departs, right, for Rounds Rock. Five minutes later, cross Rockwell Road into cherry, pine, and maple forest.

In 40 minutes, the Lower Cliff Loop Trail takes you on an alternative route—or stay on the Bradley Farm Trail. In either case, in another 10 minutes the Loop Trail returns and you cross Rockwell Road again. Pass through the Continuous Forest Inventory plot, not that you will notice much except that the state measures its holdings. As the guide notes: "Every 5–10 years state foresters visit the plot and record tree species' size, any significant changes and diseases of marker trees." Ten minutes more takes you to the parking lot.

32

Rounds' Rock

GREYLOCK

HIKING DISTANCE: 1.25 miles

WALKING TIME: 55 minutes

VERTICAL GAIN: N/A

MAP: Cheshire

Although you might think this protuberance was named for its shape, Jabez Rounds farmed this area in the early 19th century. He was one of several early farmers who loaned their names to Greylock places. Speaking of protuberances, consider Jones' Nose. Wild blueberry aficionados know of both Jones' Nose and Rounds' Rock. Would you prefer to pick Jones' Nose or berry on Rounds' pate? In season, mostly July, both low bush and high bush produce berries. The Rounds' Rock Trail passes by two fine lookouts, one south and one west, and the remains of a downed airplane. While not strenuous, the treadway is not entirely smooth and easy.

PONTOOSUC LAKE FROM ROUNDS' ROCK

Lauren R. Stevens

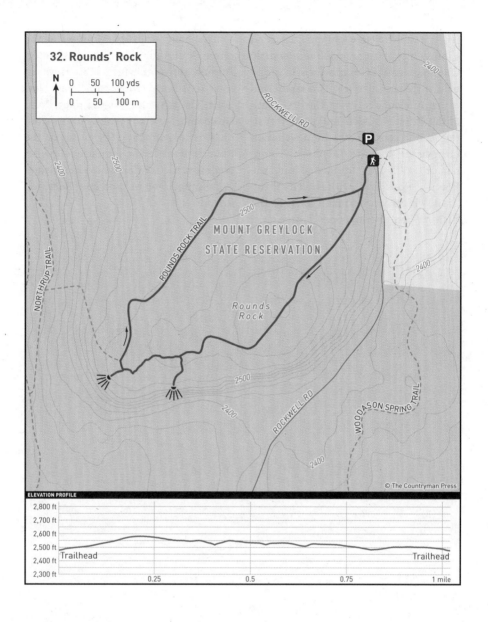

32. Rounds' Rock

N
0   50   100 yds
0   50   100 m

ROCKWELL RD

MOUNT GREYLOCK
STATE RESERVATION

ROUNDS ROCK TRAIL

NORTHRUP TRAIL

Rounds Rock

ROCKWELL RD

WOODASON SPRING TRAIL

2400
2500
2200
2500

© The Countryman Press

ELEVATION PROFILE

2,800 ft
2,700 ft
2,600 ft
2,500 ft
2,400 ft
2,300 ft
Trailhead   Trailhead

0.25   0.5   0.75   1 mile

CAMPING

Numerous sites on the mountain; none on this trail.

GETTING THERE

About 3 miles north of the Visitors' Center on Rockwell Road, you will find a several-car pullover on the right.

THE TRAIL

Signs and crossing markers indicate where to cross the road to pick up the trail. You walk up a wooded hill to what was, until a few years ago, an open field covered with blueberry bushes, but now is growing over. Persist. Continue straight, into deeper woods, passing in 10 minutes by a granite town bound

(N.A. stands for New Ashford). Descend slightly into a wet area defined by rock. Once again pass into an open, stony field with more berries. Two trails lead to magnificent overlooks, the first south to the Pittsfield lakes and state forest; the second southwest to high elevation farm fields and the Taconics. A connector trail, left (15 minutes), joins the Rounds' Rock Trail with the Northrup Trail, which can be taken back to the Visitors Center or to Jones' Nose.

The next stop (17 minutes) is the remains of a plane, which crashed on August 12, 1948, while delivering the *New York Daily Mirror* to Albany, New York. The cross honors the pilot, John Newcomb. For many years, flowers were placed there annually. If you stay on the Rounds' Rock loop and take a left when you meet the trail on which you began (55 minutes), you will end up at Rockwell Road.

Campground Trails

Several trails depart from the campground, including a self-guided nature and cultural walk. Consult the supervisor at the Visitors' Center or the contact station for detailed information on their present state.

CAMPING

You are there.

GETTING THERE

You can only reach the Sperry Road Campground on foot. A 1.3-mile hike brings you in from the parking area on Rockwell Road. You can also reach the campground via the Hopper Trail (2.5 miles), Haley Farm (2.2 miles) or the Stony Ledge (2.1 miles) and Roaring Brook Trails (2 miles).

THE TRAILS

For the most spectacular trail, continue up gravel Sperry Road 1 mile from the contact station to Stony Ledge, for a breathtaking view over the sheer depths of the Hopper to Greylock and Fitch. Though the road rises, this is an easy walk on an open road, suitable even for sneakers. Since the sun strikes on the far ledges, the afternoon is the best time to make the trip. An intriguing alternative from the same perch, however, is watching the sunrise over the highest peak in Massachusetts. The Stony Ledge and Roaring Brook hike ends here. Early on a Friday in the fall, with good weather promised, the President of Williams College calls for the Chapel bells to be rung for Mountain Day, during which students take to the hills. Hundreds assemble here in the afternoon for a cappella singing, cider, and doughnuts.

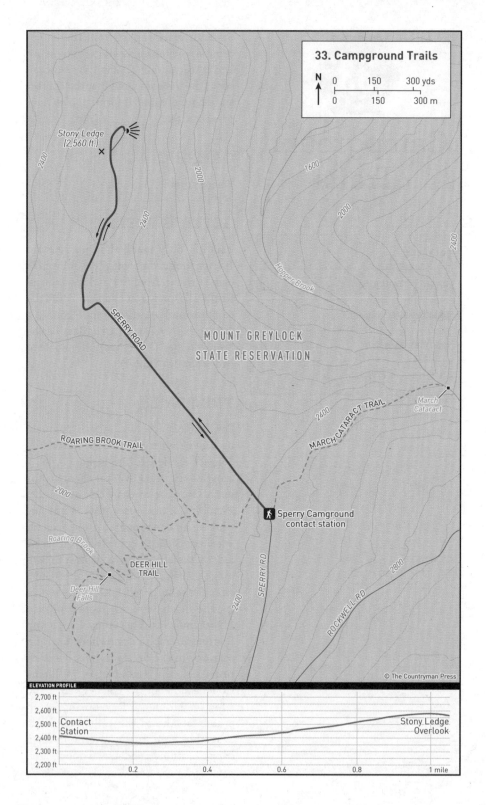

33. Campground Trails

N

| 0 | 150 | 300 yds |
| 0 | 150 | 300 m |

Stony Ledge
(2,560 ft.)

2400

2000

1600

2000

2400

Hooper Brook

MOUNT GREYLOCK
STATE RESERVATION

SPERRY ROAD

MARCH CATARACT TRAIL

March
Cataract

2400

ROARING BROOK TRAIL

2000

Roaring Brook

Sperry Camground
contact station

DEER HILL
TRAIL

Deer Hill
Falls

SPERRY RD

ROCKWELL RD

2800

2400

© The Countryman Press

ELEVATION PROFILE

2,700 ft				
2,600 ft				
2,500 ft	Contact			Stony Ledge
2,400 ft	Station			Overlook
2,300 ft				
2,200 ft				
	0.2	0.4	0.6	0.8	1 mile

Other walks include a good bit of up-and-down, and require stout shoes. A short but rugged trail departs across from the contact station, up a former road and then right, up and along a side hill, then steeply down (less than 1 mile in total) to the foot of March Cataract. Although a good flow of water tumbles down year-round, the walk is especially recommended in high water, when you will be well wetted before you stand on the midstream rocks—if you can—gazing up the gleaming wet stone face. It is dangerous to make this trip in the winter, because the trail can be icy and cuts uncertainly along the side hill, but it's thrilling to hear the water plunging beneath the ice. Note: this trail is less worn than most in the Reservation, and therefore harder to follow.

Departing Sperry Road on the same side as the contact station, but a few hundred feet farther in, the Deer Hill Trail follows Roaring Brook, sharing the Roaring Brook Trail at first, but turning left after 200 yards. Pass Deer Hill Falls (1 mile) and what may be the oldest, untouched stand of trees (hemlock) on the Reservation, and start fairly steeply up, past a lean-to, and come out on the carriage road. Turn left to arrive at Sperry Road and left again to return to the contact station (2.25 miles). If you don't turn on Sperry Road, you will come out on the Hopper Trail above the campground.

34

Overlook Trail

GREYLOCK	
HIKING DISTANCE: 2.5 miles	
WALKING TIME: 70 minutes	
VERTICAL GAIN: -691 feet	
MAPS: Cheshire/Williamstown	

Enjoying a fine dinner at Bascom Lodge at the summit of Mt. Greylock might inspire you to walk off the food with an evening on the Overlook Trail. Resist the urge. The trail is too long and steep, and the footing too uncertain, for evening use. Out-and-backs in either direction on the Appalachian Trail would be better. The Overlook Trail is mostly used to link the Hopper Trail with the AT without going to the summit. However, try the Overlook Trail during the day for fairly rigorous going that passes fine and unique views into the Hopper.

CAMPING

Camping is what this area is about.

GETTING THERE

You could drive or hike to the summit. Or, if hiking on the Hopper Trail, take the signed left turn between the campground and the CCC Pond. Or, if hiking south on the AT, take a right (a crossover, just beyond the junction with the Thunderbolt Trail), then briefly left on Notch Road before turning either way on the Overlook.

THE TRAIL

Depart from the television tower, but turn right instead of following the Hopper Trail. Descent is constant through spruce woods and mixed hardwoods to Notch Road (10 minutes). The trail is blazed blue occasionally. Although this stretch is a former carriage road to the summit, washouts have made some parts difficult going. Cross it into the woods again on what is now more of a trail (rather than old road), continuously losing altitude. Half an hour in, come to

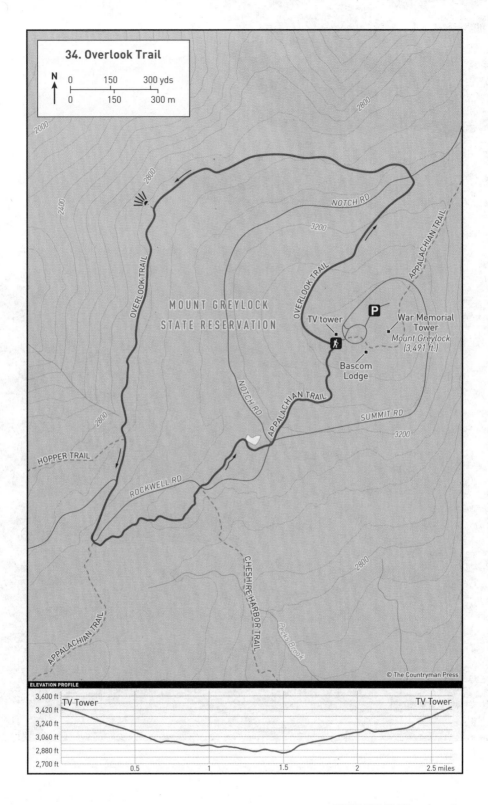

34. Overlook Trail

N

| 0 | 150 | 300 yds |
| 0 | 150 | 300 m |

MOUNT GREYLOCK
STATE RESERVATION

NOTCH RD

OVERLOOK TRAIL

OVERLOOK TRAIL

APPALACHIAN TRAIL

TV tower

P

War Memorial
Tower
*Mount Greylock
(3,491 ft.)*

Bascom
Lodge

NOTCH RD

APPALACHIAN TRAIL

SUMMIT RD

HOPPER TRAIL

ROCKWELL RD

CHESHIRE HARBOR TRAIL

Peck's Brook

APPALACHIAN TRAIL

© The Countryman Press

ELEVATION PROFILE

3,600 ft	TV Tower					TV Tower
3,420 ft						
3,240 ft						
3,060 ft						
2,880 ft						
2,700 ft						
	0.5	1	1.5	2	2.5 miles	

Lauren R. Stevens

LOOKING OUT FROM THE OVERLOOK TRAIL

a fine, 300-degree vista of the Hopper down a short side trail to the right. At the stream crossing just above March Cataract Falls (45 minutes), the trail begins to climb. Don't overlook the overlooks, which are down short, unmarked trails in this vicinity. Shortly, come out on the Hopper Trail (50 minutes), at which you turn left to the AT and climb back up to the TV tower.

BASCOM LODGE OPENING FOR THE NEW SEASON

Stony Ledge & Roaring Brook

Just because you're on Mt. Greylock doesn't mean you always have to hike to the summit. You can call this loop Stony Ledge for the first eminence, with its spectacular view of the Hopper, but you actually hike on the Stony Ledge Trail, which the Civilian Conservation Corps originally cut as one of three downhill ski trails, but has been maintained for hiking. You descend gently along Sperry Road through the campground, and down Roaring Brook Trail. You rise from a deep valley, through the plateau, and streamside down to the valley. Both ascent and descent have steep sections. This hike (or Haley Farm Trail: see Hopper Trail) is the most logical one if your goal is to sit on the edge of the abyss at Stony Ledge. That is sufficient motivation!

CAMPING

You are hiking to a campground—with three-sided shelters—one of the nicest around.

GETTING THERE

Beginning at Field Park in Williamstown, drive south on Route 7, 5.5 miles to Roaring Brook Road, and take a left just before the Mass DOT garage; alternately, coming from the south, after entering Williamstown, turn right immediately beyond the garage. Drive 1 mile up the gravel road until you see the sign indicating the private Mt. Greylock Ski Club, a two-rope-tow holdover from the early days of skiing. Use the parking area large enough for 5 or 6 cars just downstream from the sign; in the unlikely event that this lot is filled, you will have to pull over nearer Route 7.

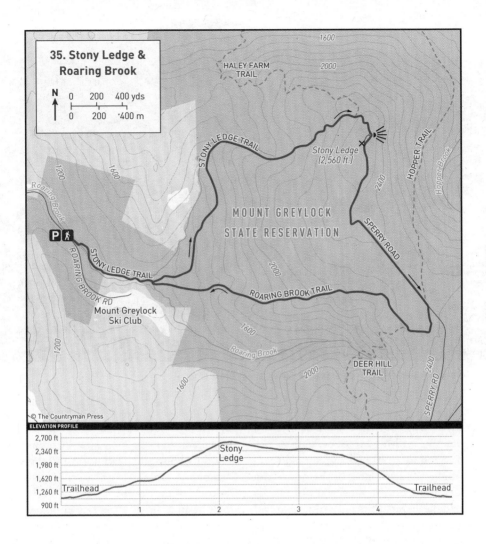

35. Stony Ledge & Roaring Brook

N
| 0 | 200 | 400 yds |
| 0 | 200 | 400 m |

HALEY FARM TRAIL

1600

2000

STONY LEDGE TRAIL

Stony Ledge
(2,560 ft.)

HOPPER TRAIL

Hopper Brook

MOUNT GREYLOCK
STATE RESERVATION

2400

Roaring Brook

1200

1600

P

STONY LEDGE TRAIL

ROARING BROOK RD

Mount Greylock
Ski Club

1200

2000

ROARING BROOK TRAIL

SPERRY ROAD

1600

Roaring Brook

1600

2000

DEER HILL
TRAIL

2400

SPERRY RD

© The Countryman Press

ELEVATION PROFILE

2,700 ft					
2,340 ft			Stony Ledge		
1,980 ft					
1,620 ft					
1,260 ft	Trailhead				Trailhead
900 ft	1	2	3	4	

THE TRAIL

The trailhead is Roaring Brook streamside, across from the ski club sign. Begin on a well-established old woods road, blazed blue for the most part, although some of previous white blazes persist. Cross Roaring Brook on a bridge, beyond the old wagon ford. You climb, passing a trail that rises into the fields, on the left. After 10 minutes, drop down to the brook again to a second bridge. Since the third bridge is out as of this writing, a detour skips the second bridge and climbs the hillside to keep you on the same side of the brook. (This likely will become the permanent route.) At 13 minutes, cross a feeder stream. Just beyond, bear left on Stony Ledge rather than straight on Roaring Brook Trail, on which you will return.

A sign indicates that the wide, grassy trail is an "intermediate ski trail," which refers to downhill skiing. Nordic skiing here is "advanced." Although you can see how the CCC laid it out wide enough to enable some maneuvering, it hasn't been maintained for skiing. Although

Roman Iwasiwka

WILLIAMS COLLEGE STUDENTS CELEBRATE MOUNTAIN DAY ON STONY LEDGE

the area has been cut over, a smattering of large hardwood trees persists.

Soon the trail picks up an old road, which it follows most of the rest of the way. From time to time, you will see the telltale charcoal bits indicating charcoal burning sites. The product was used to smelt iron ore until the late 19th century when the Bessemer process came in. At 30 minutes, the trail begins to bear left and climb sharply, which it continues to do, with a branch of Roaring Brook on the left, to the ridge you soon will see on the right. One of the two branches of the Haley Farm Trail enters at 35 minutes and another at 40 minutes, left.

You arrive at the lean-to after 1:05. Walk straight ahead to the gravel turn-around on Sperry Road. Sit and absorb the summit and ridge across the chasm. The morning is not as good as the evening because of shadows, but on the wall opposite you can see dark stands of red spruce, some nearly 200 years old, probably the oldest stands of spruce in the Commonwealth. You can also see March Cataract to the southeast. However, it won't be prominent when late summer reduces the water flow.

Walk down the road about 1 mile, between azaleas and berry bushes into the camping area. You can easily see why Sperry Road is regarded as the best-laid campground around. Automobile-free camping, the sites are separated from one another for privacy. At 1:10, the Hopper Trail enters the road from the left. You see the Roaring Brook Trail entrance, right (1.5 hours). It is also the Deer Hill Trail at this point, blazed blue. Follow across a bridge, and right along the brook. The Circular Trail leaves left in 5 minutes, but cross the second bridge; just beyond the bridge the Deer Hill Trail leaves left. Stay on the Roaring Brook Trail. Pass through hobblebush, black raspberries, beech, and maple. Descend steadily through hemlock, aware of a brook on each side. The descent becomes steep.

Gradually the two brook branches come closer, as you descend, until you must cross the smaller. You are at the junction with Stony Ledge Trail (2.25 hours). After crossing and attaining some elevation, look down into the scenic, rocky gorge, where you can see the remains of a mill run. Farther down-stream, in the daylilies, is the cellar hole for the mill. At 2:30 minutes, you are back at your starting point.

Skiers should do the loop by climbing Roaring Brook to Sperry Road and returning via Stony Ledge. Hikers go the opposite direction purely for the aesthetic satisfaction of coming out at the end of the climb on Stony Ledge. In season, the hike could be spiced up with a visit to March Cataract or Deer Hill falls. You can link all other Greylock trails to these two, for two-car variations on this hike.

Lauren R. Stevens

IN LATE SPRING, THE GREEN-UP LINE CLIMBS GREYLOCK FROM STONY LEDGE

36

Cheshire Harbor

GREYLOCK

HIKING DISTANCE: 6.6 miles

WALKING TIME: 2 hours, 30 minutes

VERTICAL GAIN: 1,691 feet

MAP: Cheshire

Mt. Greylock feels very close to its east side approaches, although the summit is more of a haul than it appears to be when you stand on the old field at the end of the open section of West Mountain Road. Still, the Cheshire Harbor Trail is the shortest and easiest of the hiking routes to the summit, not only because of its directness, but because it begins at a good elevation, rising from 1,800 to 3,491 feet. It is also the heaviest traveled. Every Columbus Day, hundreds climb this route during the Mt. Greylock Ramble, which is sponsored by the Adams Chamber of Commerce. The trail has been badly eroded, mostly due to off-road vehicles, which have now been banned (except for snowmobiles). Cheshire Harbor is the community in the town of Cheshire where the trail actually starts, about 1 mile southeast of where you begin.

CAMPING

Peck's Brook shelter, a three-sided, Adirondack-type lean-to, is attained by a separate, 1-mile trail that departs from the junction of Rockwell, Notch, and Summit roads. Bascom Lodge, at the summit, has limited accommodations (reservations required) as well as food. Summit buildings are closed from late October until Memorial Day, but some protection may be found at the Thunderbolt Ski Shelter, with fireplace (BYOM— bring your own matches!), located on the AT just below the summit parking lot, to the north of the War Memorial Tower.

GETTING THERE

At the statue of former President McKinley in front of the library in Adams, turn west off Route 8 onto Maple Street. At .4 mile, turn left on West Road; .5 mile

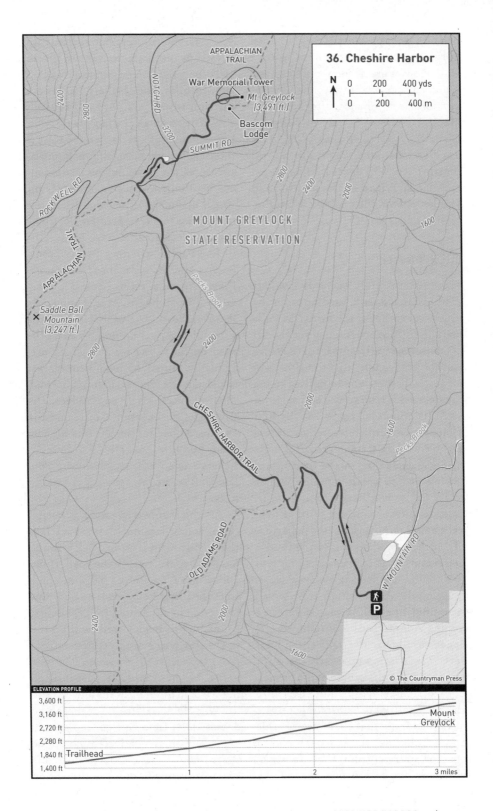

APPALACHIAN
TRAIL

36. Cheshire Harbor

N

| 0 | 200 | 400 yds |
| 0 | 200 | 400 m |

War Memorial Tower

NOTCH RD

*Mt. Greylock
(3,491 ft.)*

Bascom
Lodge

2400

2800

3200

SUMMIT RD

2800

2400

2000

1600

ROCKWELL RD

MOUNT GREYLOCK
STATE RESERVATION

Pecks Brook

APPALACHIAN TRAIL

× Saddle Ball
Mountain
(3,247 ft.)

2800

2400

2000

1600

Pecks Brook

CHESHIRE HARBOR TRAIL

OLD ADAMS ROAD

W MOUNTAIN RD

2400

2000

1600

© The Countryman Press

ELEVATION PROFILE

| 3,600 ft | | | | Mount
Greylock |
3,160 ft				
2,720 ft				
2,280 ft				
1,840 ft	Trailhead			
1,400 ft	1	2	3 miles	

later, go right on West Mountain Road at the sign that says the Mt. Greylock Greenhouses are no longer in business. The road ends at a turnaround, the site of a former farmhouse, after 1.6 miles. Most of the land is part of Greylock Glen, which the town is developing for a recreational area. The trailhead will remain open. Why does McKinley stand in Adams? Friend of the mill-owning Plunketts, McKinley passed a tariff on foreign imports.

THE TRAIL

The un-blazed trail leaves as a woods road (Adams Road), heading from the southwest corner of the field. Old walls mark the site. Almost immediately, the portion of the trail rising from Cheshire Harbor enters left. Riveted drainage pipes and barbed wire hark back to the time when this road served active farms.

At 11 minutes, come to the first switchback and, in 3 more minutes, to the second, where a trail enters left (ignore it). Soon, depending on the condition of the foliage, you see the summit, with its tower rising over Peck's Brook ravine. At 17 minutes, round the third switchback and, 4 minutes later, the departure of Old Adams Road marks the fourth. Old Adams Road follows more or less at this contour to the base of Jones' Nose, crossing the Appalachian Trail, which rises from the south. It was a stage route joining Adams and New Ashford; the Jones' farmhouse (no longer standing) served as a stop. Apparently the place was named for the profile of the farmer.

Bear right, staying on the Cheshire Harbor Trail, and continuing up the moderate grade that characterizes this entire trail. The trail has been blazed blue or orange from time to time, although blazes are not needed. As you rise, the trail erosion diminishes. Scratches on the rocks are not glacial striations, but come from the treads of snowmobiles. The northern hardwoods through which you pass are severely stressed—an effect of atmospheric pollution. Scientists have designated plots in the area to study the decline of high altitude forests in New England. The results are disturbing. You see many dead birch, beech, and maple. The ledges (left) rise to the ridge that connects Greylock with the next peak south, Saddle Ball.

At 54 minutes, cross Peck's Brook. Soon a trail drops right to the Gould Farm. Continue on to Rockwell Road, an hour from the car. At this point, join the AT, following its white blazes to the summit. The next stretch parallels the road but is in the woods—which are, suddenly, boreal, high-elevation forest of balsam firs and bogs, through which the trail meanders on bog bridges. The Civilian Conservation Corps dug the unnamed pond on the left (the highest water body in the state) in a wet spot to serve as a water supply for Bascom Lodge. Beavers are active. You can dig it too.

At the three-way road junction (1:08), follow straight ahead, back into the woods. The trail to Peck's Brook Shelter departs across the road, right. Follow the AT, with the old water pipe from the pump house on the pond; now the lodge has a drilled well. The next sound you hear may well be the wind in the guy wires of the television and radio broadcast tower, which you pass at 1:14. In 3 more minutes, pass through the break in the stone walls and come to the War Memorial itself. For those who do not suffer from vertigo, and assuming it is open, the 92-foot climb up the stairs to the lookout is worthwhile. It is also worthwhile to tour the summit on ground level, especially looking over the eastern side, directly down to the town of Adams—and, considerably closer, Greylock Glen. See if you can count the number of wind turbines visible from the summit.

Remember to start down by the broadcast tower. The road crossings can be confusing. Cross the first, staying on the AT. After the second crossing, the AT continues straight (south) while the Cheshire Harbor Trail bears left. The trip down takes just about the same time as up.

Since the summit is the focus of 70 miles of trails in the Greylock Reservation, numerous variations on this basic, east side climb are possible. If you can get someone to serve as chauffeur, an east-to-west hike across the ridge could begin on the Cheshire Harbor Trail and end on the Hopper Trail. Or, with the aid of a Berkshire Regional Transit Authority bus from North Adams to Cheshire, an east-to-north climb would link the Cheshire Harbor Trail with the Bellows Pipe Trail. (Hopper and Bellows Pipe trails are described below.) A loop, eschewing the summit, begins on Cheshire Harbor Trail, following south on the AT over Saddle Ball and past the Bassett Brook Campsite to Old Adams Road. Follow left (north) 1.5 miles on Old Adams Road until it joins the Cheshire Harbor Trail again (about 15 miles). Cheshire Harbor Trail and Old Adams Road are skiable with deep snow cover, but watch out for the snowmobiles.

37

The Hopper Trail

GREYLOCK

HIKING DISTANCE: 8.8 miles

WALKING TIME: 4 hours

VERTICAL GAIN: 2,390 feet

MAP: Williamstown

This is a classic Greylock hike—from 1,096 feet to 3,491 feet at the summit— on a historic trail through the deeply eroded "grain hopper" that marks the western side of the Greylock massif. Hopper Road didn't originally end at the gate; instead, it passed between the stone walls you walk between and then forded Money Brook, continuing up the far side into the inner Hopper. Almond Harrison laid out the route you follow. He pioneered a farm at the campground site around 1800. President Edward Dorr Griffin dismissed his Williams College students from class on a May day in 1830 to improve this road and extend it to the summit, where they built the first tower. At the time, the summit was covered by trees, so going to the tower was the alternative to shimmying up the stunted fir trees for a better view. The Civilian Conservation Corps later built its camp where Harrison's farm had been; still later, the state developed its campground in the same spot, as the spruces grew into the once-open fields.

CAMPING

Camping is available in the dispersed camping area along the Money Brook Trail, about 12 minutes from the parking lot. The trail leads through the Sperry Road Campgrounds. Accommodations are available by reservation at Bascom Lodge on the Summit.

GETTING THERE

Beginning at Field Park in Williamstown, follow Route 2 east to Water Street, which becomes Green River Road (.5 mile). Turn right. Hopper Road turns left at Mount Hope Park (2.5 miles).

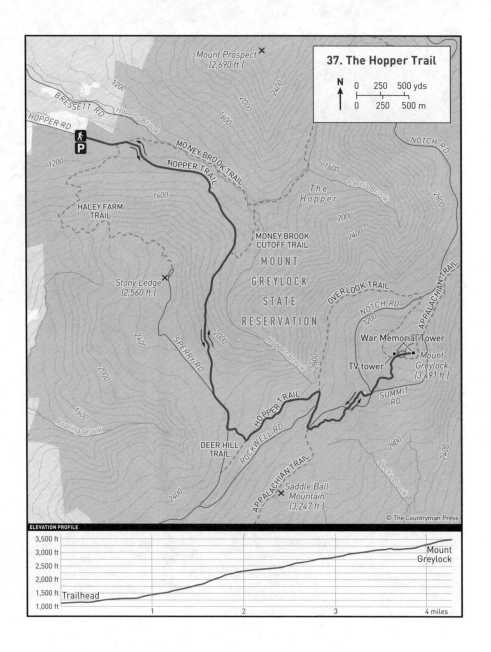

ELEVATION PROFILE

Follow Hopper Road along the brook, past Bassett Road, until it swings left (straight ahead is Potter Road) beyond some open fields. It turns to gravel, ending at a state parking area between a barn and a small farmhouse (2.75 miles).

THE TRAIL

Pass through the farm gates and the state's vehicle gate. No free-running dogs or bicycles allowed. Stroll down the road between the hayfields. Pass Haley

THE CCC DUG THIS POND TO PROVIDE WATER FOR BASCOM LODGE

Farm Trail, right, a good way of making a loop, with the Hopper Trail, to the campgrounds. The Haley Farm Trail goes to Stony Ledge. Leave the colonial road, which continues as the Money Brook Trail, to bear right on the Hopper Trail, blazed blue (8 minutes).

The trail passes by the edge of an upper field and then plunges into the woods. For the next quarter mile or so, bog bridges help to keep your feet dry and to protect wetland. The steady, no-nonsense rise, cut into the side hill, was once the first leg of a Berkshires-to-the-Cape Bridle Trail, which wandered across the commonwealth in the

Brook floating from the floor. Just shy of an hour, reach Sperry Road and the campground. (If you want to make a side trip to Stony Ledge, turn right.) Turn left and, in 5 minutes, turn left again, across from and beyond the contact station, as the Hopper trail (still blazed blue) leaves the road.

This climb has been moved to avoid erosion, so the new route is not well worn. Roots can trip! Turn left on the Deer Hill Trail (1:15), which was once a carriage road. Note this well-marked turn for the return trip. The trail is relatively level and stone-covered, as erosion has removed the thin soil. Where the Overlook Trail exits (1:27), your trail turns and steepens. Large trees are less frequent at higher elevation, giving way to more shrubbery. Nick a corner of Rockwell Road, at a spring, but stick to the woods, which soon turn to spruce. A relatively new section of trail avoids coming out on the road again. From here to the summit, follow the white blazes of the Appalachian Trail. You cross boggy areas on footbridges. At 1:35, pass the pond, no longer used, to serve as water supply for Bascom Lodge. Follow the AT across the road intersection a minute later. Study the road crossings so that you will know what to do on the return trip.

Climb steeply—this section was once known as Misery Mile, although it is hardly a quarter of that (misery or mile)—through fir and spruce, crossing the old water line, for eight minutes until you reach the broadcast tower and two minutes more to the Memorial Tower (1:47).

For the return, the broadcast tower is the landmark for the proper direction to depart the summit on the AT. At 10 minutes, cross the road intersection, still on the AT, even though the "Adams" sign may momentarily confuse you. Pass the

late 19th century. The large birch trees seem to have reached the end of their lives, as beech and maple crowd them out. All trees are under siege, however, whether from insects, disease, acid rain, or climate change. At 34 minutes, the Money Brook Cutoff Trail drops into the valley. Listen for the song of Money

THE HOPPER TRAIL | 183

pond. In six more minutes, you'll reach the next road crossing where, instead of following the AT, you will turn right. Continue on the Deer Hill Trail/Hopper Trail until the Hopper Trail exits, right (35 minutes). After turning right on Sperry Road, look for the Hopper Trail angling off to the right. The return trip takes somewhat less time than the climb, maybe 1.5 hours.

You needn't return the way you came, of course. The most obvious circuit —up the Hopper Trail and down the Money Brook—is lengthy if you include the summit: 11 miles via the AT over Mt. Williams to the Tall Spruces. After you cross Notch Road, take a left toward the shelter that is on the Money Brook Trail. You can save more than a mile by cutting off the AT prior to Mt. Williams and hiking down Notch Road half a mile to the cutoff for the Money Brook Trail. Shorter still would be omitting the summit of Mt. Greylock, which is perfectly acceptable after you've been there a few times. Take the Hopper Trail to the Overlook Trail. Follow Overlook until it meets Notch Road. Take Notch Road 100 yards north to the cutoff to the AT on top of the ridge, and continue as described above (it helps to be looking at a map!).

Lauren R. Stevens

THE FINAL STAGE OF THE HOPPER TRAIL/
AT TO THE SUMMIT: "MISERY MILE"

Prospect & Money Brook Trails

GREYLOCK

HIKING DISTANCE: 7.8 miles

WALKING TIME: 4 hours

VERTICAL GAIN: 1,790 feet

MAP: Williamstown

The climb up Prospect is one of the steepest on the Reservation and the only one with a stretch in which you clamber over rock. You'll enjoy a fine view at an overlook out of the Hopper to the west. Views into the Hopper have been somewhat diminished by tree growth, but remain good when the leaves are down. The real visual treat, however, is the Mt. Prospect Overlook. Where the Appalachian Trail makes an L-turn, the view is down into the farms that crept up the side of the mountain from the Green River—and out beyond to the Taconics. Then, following through where Money Brook makes up in wetlands, you descend to Money Brook Falls, with its 70-foot, multiple drops. Some say Money Brook was named for early 19th-century counterfeiters who supposedly hung out there; others say it was because of the iron pyrite (fool's gold) in the stream. Finally the return, through the heart of the Hopper, has rewards for those who appreciate the age and beauty of old growth.

CAMPING

Camping is available at the dispersed camping site, 12 minutes from the parking lot. The Money Brook Trail, on the return, passes by the Wilbur's Clearing shelter.

GETTING THERE

Beginning at Field Park in Williamstown, follow Route 2 east to Water Street, which becomes Green River Road (.5 miles). Turn right. Hopper Road turns left at Mount Hope Park (2.5 miles). Follow Hopper Road along the brook, past Bassett Road, until it swings left (straight ahead is Potter Road) beyond some open fields. It turns to gravel, end-

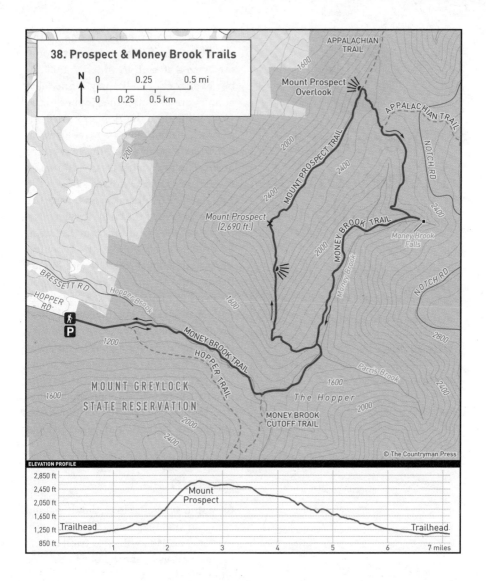

38. Prospect & Money Brook Trails

ELEVATION PROFILE

ing at a state parking area between a barn and a small farmhouse (2.75 miles).

THE TRAIL

The trailhead for Money Brook & Prospect is the same as for the Hopper Trail. Indeed you pass through the same farm gates and state vehicle gate. As before, free-running dogs and bicycles are not allowed. Stroll down the road between the hayfields. Pass Haley Farm Trail, on the right. Stay on the colonial road where the Hopper Trail bears right (8 minutes). The Money Brook Trail is blazed blue. Pass through the dispersed camping by the brook (12 minutes) and enter the Reserved Natural Area, a state designation that reserves the Hopper for walking, skiing, and studying.

The Bob Quay Bridge (look for the small plaque) honors a Williams College '04 student and leader of the Williams Outing Club, who died shortly after graduation. Follow a reroute, left, past foundations for a mill right (30 minutes). Cross another bridge that leaves you at an intersection (32 minutes). Straight ahead is the cutoff trail leading to the Hopper Trail. Turn left, climbing above and then down to the brook—and hop across Bacon Brook, named for the first settler of the Hopper (35 minutes). You are now entering the Inner Hopper, which many regard as sacred space. At 42 minutes, cross a second tributary, Parris Brook, which was the scene of a landslide in 1990. (In the same, particularly wet year, there was also a slide on the east side of the mountain that left what looked like the outline of Chief Greylock's face.) Elkanah Parris was the first settler in the Hopper. The Bacons followed. Almost immediately, wade Money Brook and ascend stone steps.

At 47 minutes, turn left to Prospect, while the Money Brook Trail bears right. There are signs. For the next stretch, you wind through scrubby trees to the base of the rock outcropping, which you soon mount. Although you will certainly not be doing technical climbing, you will be using your hands and watching your footing. Once on the shoulder, you'll see azaleas nearby and, from time to time, views back to Greylock through the foliage if you turn around. You reach a far-viewing lookout on the left at 1:25. There are many views of the Hopper; this one notably looks straight down it to the world beyond. In another 10 minutes, pass by the cairn that is the only sign of the summit of Prospect. There is no view from the trail here. The trail then wanders from side to side along a narrow ridge.

GREYLOCK FROM THE MOUNT PROSPECT OVERLOOK

Lauren R. Stevens

THE PROSPECT FROM THE MOUNT PROSPECT OVERLOOK

In two hours, you reach the Mt. Prospect Overlook, which, like the approach to Race Mountain and Stony Ledge, has special views in Berkshire County and indeed the state. Through-hikers on the Appalachian Trail enjoy this view. Lucky them. Follow the AT right—the sign directs you towards Bascom Lodge. Now the blazes are white. Descend through a dense hemlock forest into the wetlands that make up part of Money Brook. The rest of it drains off the side of Mt. Fitch. Lots of bog bridging.

In two hours, Money Brook Trail departs right from the AT. Again, plenty of signs. The blazes become blue again. The sign notes that you have 3.5 miles to the Haley Farm, where you started. It's mostly downhill! Cross more bog bridging and the Wilbur's Clearing shelter (right). Pass trails coming in from the left and wind down to the side trail to Money Brook Falls, left (2:35). A short, but steep hike takes you to the falls.

Return to the main trail and begin a sharp descent through hemlock. In 10 minutes, cross a tributary and begin a steep climb on steps. Sorry about that. Twenty-five minutes after the falls (really a cascade), come to the intersection with the Prospect Trail. Turn left, wade Money Brook, hop Parris and Bacon brooks, and 50 minutes from the waterfall, arrive at the cutoff trail. Turn right to cross the bridge; then turn left. In 1:05 from the falls, cross the Quay Bridge; and, at 1.5 hours (4 hours total) from the falls, arrive back at the parking lot. Congratulations!

Bellows Pipe Trail

GREYLOCK

HIKING DISTANCE: 9.5 miles

WALKING TIME: 5 hours

VERTICAL GAIN: 2,187 feet

MAP: Cheshire/Williamstown

Though this trail may be too steep for some hikers (see end of description for alternatives), it's hard to think of a better place to be, under certain conditions, than climbing the Bellows Pipe. One set of conditions is a sunny day on light, powdery snow—on skis. Another is a warm morning, as the fog burns off in the valley, perhaps in late May, when the ephemeral flowers are blossoming and all the brooks are running high. The sun bursts yellow through the trees, creating shadows and picking out the dew on the shrubbery. Another may be following Henry David Thoreau's footsteps while reading passages from *A Week on the Concord and Merrimack Rivers*.

CAMPING

You pass a lean-to, a ski shelter, and Bascom Lodge on this hike. The lean-to is a bit more than halfway in time, where the Bellows Pipe Ski Trail meets the Bellows Pipe (hiking) Trail. It faces east. The ski shelter is next to the parking lot at the summit. With a stove in the middle and closed sides, it's meant for day use but is available at night for winter emergencies. Bascom Lodge stands firmly on the summit, a warm and cheery destination in summer and early fall.

GETTING THERE

Turn south on Notch Road, off Route 2 between Harriman and West Airport and the turn that leads to downtown North Adams. The road climbs through a residential area and woods, turning sharply left at Mt. Williams Reservoir. After 2.4 miles from Route 2, turn right on Notch Road and park at the gate to the Mt. Greylock State Reservation; Bellows Pipe Trail is the gravel road that headed straight where you turned right,

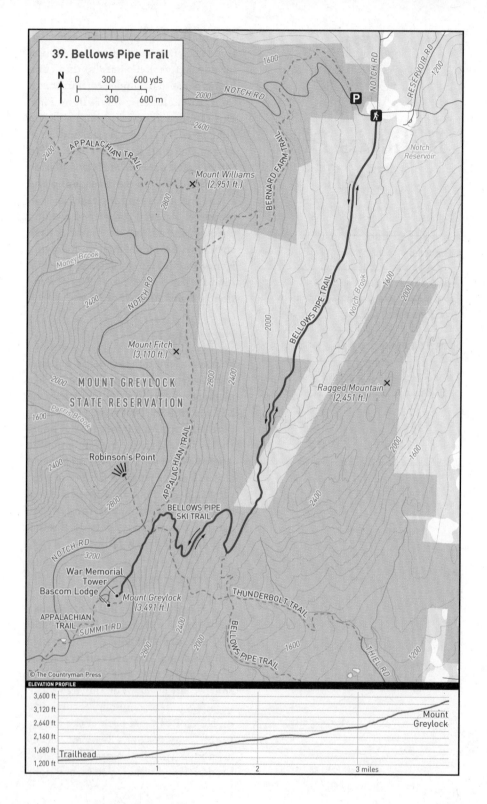

39. Bellows Pipe Trail

N
0   300   600 yds
0   300   600 m

APPALACHIAN TRAIL

NOTCH RD

Mount Williams
(2,951 ft.)

BERNARD FARM TRAIL

NOTCH RD

Notch
Reservoir

Money Brook

NOTCH RD

BELLOWS PIPE TRAIL

Notch Brook

Ragged Mountain
(2,451 ft.)

Mount Fitch
(3,110 ft.)

MOUNT GREYLOCK
STATE RESERVATION

Parris Brook

APPALACHIAN TRAIL

Robinson's Point

BELLOWS PIPE
SKI TRAIL

NOTCH RD

War Memorial
Tower
Bascom Lodge

THUNDERBOLT TRAIL

Mount Greylock
(3,491 ft.)

APPALACHIAN
TRAIL

SUMMIT RD

BELLOWS PIPE TRAIL

THIEL RD

© The Countryman Press

ELEVATION PROFILE

3,600 ft
3,120 ft
2,640 ft
2,160 ft
1,680 ft
1,200 ft

Trailhead

Mount
Greylock

1   2   3 miles

so you must walk down to it. There are a few parking places right at the trailhead. (You can reach the same point via Reservoir Road, also from North Adams, or by Pattison Road, the continuation of Luce Road in Williamstown.)

THE TRAIL

You are starting at 1,304 feet in elevation and climbing to 3,491 feet. In places, particularly on the Bellows Pipe Ski Trail, the going is steep. As you cross the chain meant to keep vehicles off the road, it's clear you're on North Adams watershed property, which protects Notch Reservoir—an impoundment of the brook that cut the valley you are climbing. There are no blazes on city land, which extends almost to the Notch. The large sugar maples beside the gravel road have been there for generations; the pines were planted as a way of having trees beside a reservoir that would not fill the water with leaves. You pass several cellar holes and old walls that may be hidden if the foliage is out.

But you may notice the road was uncommonly well made: edged with stone, built with a crown, ditched on the sides. In steep places, it has been cobbled.

For these and many other man-made features of the route, credit Jeremiah Wilbur (and his descendants), who cut a spacious and productive farm out of the mountain wilderness before the Revolution, built the first road to the summit, grew hay, boiled off enormous quantities of maple syrup, grazed cattle and sheep, killed marauding wolves and bears, built three mills, and raised a dozen children by two wives.

Yours is the route Henry David Thoreau took in 1844, when he heeded Hawthorne's and Emerson's advice to visit Mount Greylock. (Emerson called it "a serious mountain.") At one of these homes, now a cellar hole, Thoreau stopped to converse with a lady who was combing her long tresses. You can read about it in *A Week on the Concord and Merrimack Rivers*. He spent the night in a wooden tower on the summit. When he woke, the clouds had closed in below

THOSE FOLLOWING THOREAU'S FOOTSTEPS PAUSE AT THE BELLOWS PIPE LEAN-TO

him, and he found himself "in a country such as we might see in dreams, with all the delights of paradise."

In 10 minutes, come to a yarding area used for timber cutting, but continue straight on the un-blazed trail. The going gets a bit steeper. Soon, through breaks in the foliage, you can see the ridge of Ragged Mountain, which rises 2,451 feet to the east over Notch Brook Valley. The next landmark, at 31 minutes, is a bridge. This area is called Bellows Pipe, a name that Thoreau used. The name presumably derives from the fact that wind rushes through the notch, just as air rushes through the pipe at the end of a bellows.

Having crossed a dozen or more tributaries, you finally cross the main stem of Notch Brook at 40 minutes and, after a short, very steep eroded section, reach the notch (2,197 feet), which was once cleared as an orchard. At the site of informal camping under spruces at the left, a marked trail follows the wall up to the cliffs on Ragged. Thoreau climbed there to check his bearings before his final bushwhack to the summit. Now that you are on state land, look for blue blazes that lead you to the summit.

Follow a level section, looking down into Adams. At 50 minutes, turn right on the blazed trail. The shelter is on your right, almost immediately. You are now on the Bellows Pipe Ski Trail, cut by the Civilian Conservation Corps in the 1930s, as you will recognize from the series of steep, sharp switchbacks. At 1:02, do not take the unmarked trail straight ahead, which leads to the Thunderbolt. Instead, follow right, on a section that is a real workout if you are on skis. It's also a workout on foot.

The trees are becoming lower and more scraggly on the steep eastern face—more beech and birch, somewhat stunted. After five switchbacks (but who's counting?) and testing ascents, you come out at 1:30 on the white-blazed Appalachian Trail heading south to the summit. In the winter, trees are often ice-covered; if you catch them when the sun hits, the effect is like walking through a lit chandelier. If a breeze is blowing, the branches clink together like cut glass. In a minute, the AT joins the Thunderbolt Trail for the final assault. If you plan to descend this way, be sure to turn around at this point to check the lay of the land, which can be confusing. As the Indians say, "every trail is two trails, one going and one coming." Soon you pass a blue-blazed trail on the right, crossing nearby Notch Road to Robinson's Point. Continue on the steep Thunderbolt to cross Summit Road (1:45). The ski shelter the CCC built at the head of the Thunderbolt is on the right. Skirt the parking lot and arrive at the memorial tower at 2:15.

Remember, if you decide to return by this route, start on the AT north by the parking lot. The AT south takes off by the TV tower only partway around the compass. The Bellows Pipe Ski Trail may be too steep to be a pleasant descent (the knees!), so consider a different way home. To end up where you left your car while adding a mile to the hike, return the way you came on the AT and stay on the AT when the Bellows Pipe Trail veers right. Stay on the AT approximately 2.5 miles to the Bernard Farm Trail, right. Soon after the turn, pass the site of an airplane crash. The Bernard Farm Trail, named for the family that farmed near the Reservation gate, crosses Notch Road and returns you to your car (about 2.3 miles from the AT), for a total return trip of 5 miles. The Bernard Farm Trail is steep in spots, but not as steep as the Bellows Pipe Ski Trail.

Berlin Mountain

This somewhat wet trail wanders over two stream valleys before beginning a satisfyingly direct assault on the summit—a bare rock with a tree fringe. As with other points on the Taconics, the view is nearly 360 degrees, though foliage fringe is beginning to interfere. Still, there are other views as you work back down into the saddle between Berlin and Petersburg mountains. You end up on the remains of a 200-year-old post road with the cellar hole of the toll taker's house and the state line marker.

CAMPING

There are no campgrounds on this route, although camping is permitted along the Taconic Crest Trail in New York. Closest campgrounds are on Mt. Greylock.

GETTING THERE

From Field Park at the Williams Inn in Williamstown, drive south on Routes 7 & 2 for 2.5 miles until they diverge. Follow Route 2 west (right). A half mile up the hill, turn left on Torrey Woods Road. Follow straight at the bottom of the hill onto a gravel road, sometimes called Bee Hill and sometimes Berlin. From the point at which a closed road enters to the right, your route is part of a 1799 post road between Boston and Albany. Bear left at the fork, climbing past a few houses to a small (four-car) parking area on the left. Blue trail blazes head into the woods 150 yards back down the road.

Alternatively, you can continue .5 mile to the old Williams College ski area and leave your car there. The route you will take comes out at the ski area.

Although Hemlock Brook looks pristine, you should carry your own water on this, and all, hikes. At the junction of Routes 7 and 2, Margaret Lindley Park

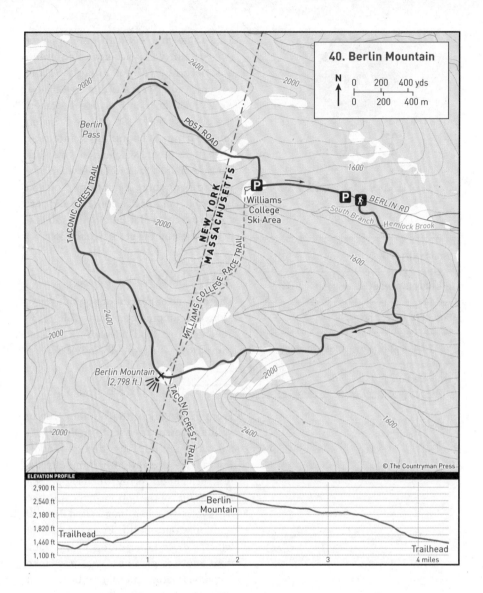

40. Berlin Mountain

N
0   200   400 yds
0   200   400 m

Berlin Pass

POST ROAD

TACONIC CREST TRAIL

NEW YORK
MASSACHUSETTS

WILLIAMS COLLEGE RACE TRAIL

P
Williams
College
Ski Area

P
BERLIN RD
South Branch   Hemlock Brook

1600

2000

2000

2400

2000

Berlin Mountain
(2,798 ft.)

TACONIC CREST TRAIL

2000

2400

1600

© The Countryman Press

ELEVATION PROFILE

2,900 ft				
2,540 ft		Berlin		
2,180 ft		Mountain		
1,820 ft	Trailhead			
1,460 ft				Trailhead
1,100 ft	1	2	3	4 miles

(a town-owned swimming area), provides a pond with water diverted from Hemlock Brook, changing rooms with plumbing, and snack machines, from Memorial Day to Labor Day.

THE TRAIL

From the parking area to the summit is a demanding hike, ascending from 1,400 feet (probably 100 feet lower in the ravines), across two branches of Hemlock Brook, and directly up the side of the ridge to an altitude of 2,798 feet in 2.5 miles. Members of the Williams Outing Club originally laid out the trail in 1933. Clearly they were a no-nonsense group. The remainder of your trip, down into the pass and down the post road, is fairly easygoing. The reward is an unusual 360-degree view. In clear weather, you can see everything from Mt. Greylock to

THE TACONIC RANGE FROM BERLIN MOUNTAIN SKI AREA PARKING

Lauren R. Stevens

the Adirondacks. However, the foliage around the summit is growing up, so you may need to stand on the old anchors of the fire tower. You see some land-use history, as well as sampling old-growth hemlock woods and hardwood forests of more recent vintage. Blueberry picking is good in July and August.

The wind on the summit is apt to be cool, particularly if you decide to take in the sunset, so wear layers. There are wet and steep spots, as well as brook crossings, so wear boots.

Williamstown Rural Lands Foundation has created some trails in the area you may want to explore. While on the '33 Trail, however, be particularly vigilant for the blue blazes at both brook crossings The wet spots begin as you head east to an old woods road for 5 minutes, then turn right to cross the

first branch of Hemlock Brook. Scramble up the far side, jogging right and left as the trail jumps from one logging road to another. This section—a 1980 rerouting to avoid private property—can be hard to follow, since it doesn't seem to be tending in any direction. Soon, however, start up a steep logging road and turn left over the ridge and down to the outing club's former cabin site (26 minutes). Misuse of the old trail and cabin led the landowner to request that the cabin be razed and the trail rerouted. The moral is obvious.

After a sharp right turn, the trail drops down to cross the second branch of Hemlock Brook. Scrambling up the other side, turn right on a broad woods road, following the brook west. Back on this older portion, the trail is easier to follow. Soon it leaves the road (35 minutes) and begins a steep ascent up the side of the valley. The trail levels somewhat in an area of striped maple, hobblebush, and beech. Look back from time to time during the climb for views of Mount Greylock.

At 1:25 a hemlock grove provides a lovely view of the Dome and East Mountain, via an unmarked side trail. The trail rises steeply once again until it joins the upper end of the college's downhill ski trail, just above the site of an airplane crash. Turn uphill (left) for the brief distance to the windswept summit (1:16). The four concrete piers once anchored a fire tower. Someone has pushed them together to create a fire pit. Blueberries and raspberries surround you; this is an excellent picnic site. To the east, the Mount Greylock massif broods over Williamstown. The ski runs you see to the south are cut on the sides of Jiminy Peak. If the weather is clear, you may be able to pick out the Catskills to the southwest and the Adirondacks to the northwest—perhaps even the New York State capitol buildings in Albany. The Green Mountains of Vermont rise to the northeast. You are standing in the township of Berlin in New York State, looking directly down into the valley of the Little Hoosic, which threads through Berlin and Petersburgh. If it is noon, you may hear one bark of the fire siren in Berlin.

The Taconic Crest Trail (TCT) goes off to the south and north. It is marked by diamond-shape white blazes, in most cases superimposed on a blue square. In addition, New York State has its own small, blue disk. You will hardly need these blazes, however, as you follow the deeply rutted jeep trail north—this trail was once the access road to the fire tower. (Detours around large puddles

may be confusing.) After 15 minutes, approach the pass. The former post road rises from Berlin, to the west. You can see the TCT continuing up the slopes of the open ridge to Petersburgh Mountain (sometimes called Mt. Raimer), straight ahead. To the east, the badly eroded post road descends to the start of the hike. You may want to linger in this area to enjoy the view of Williamstown, to pick blueberries, or picnic. The trail bikes and jeeps that come through the intersection can be annoying. However, the state of New York has acquired much of the land along the Taconic Crest in this area and imposed controls on off-road vehicles.

Turn right down the post road for 1 mile. You soon cross near the origin of one branch of Hemlock Brook, high in a mountain spring. Immediately to the right of the trail is a foundation for Alexander Walker's early-19th-century tollgate farmhouse. After about 20 minutes, look left to see the old stone marker at the state line, also left over from post road days. From the college ski area, it is .5 mile down the road to where you began, making for a total of 3 hours of hiking.

An alternative route, shorter but harder on the legs, would be to descend the ski run from the summit to the parking area. Or, if two cars are available, you might consider leaving one at Petersburgh Pass, on Route 2. The distance from Berlin Pass to Petersburgh Pass (1.5 miles) is the same as from Berlin Pass to the parking area. A less strenuous outing, though still a hike, would be to begin at the heights of Petersburgh Pass, climb most of Petersburgh Mountain, and end at the college ski area.

Sheep Hill & Fitch Trails

WILLIAMSTOWN
HIKING DISTANCE: 3.9 miles
WALKING TIME: 1 hour, 40 minutes
VERTICAL GAIN: 600 feet
MAP: Williamstown

The Williamstown Rural Lands Foundation has established its headquarters and education center on the old Rosenburg Farm at Sheep Hill. A kiosk contains information about the property and other Williamstown walking venues. The farm continued small-scale dairying almost to the end of the 20th century and served as a ski area. Visitors will be reminded of the warmth and wisdom that Rosenburg family members extended to Williams College students and faculty, as well as other friends.

CAMPING

Although Boy Scouts had special permission to camp in Flora's Glen, no public camping exists on this route. Closest camping on Mt. Greylock.

GETTING THERE

Williamstown Rural Lands Foundation is located 1 mile south of Field Park, the junction of Routes 7 and 2. Look for a sign and drive right, just south of Fisheries & Wildlife Hemlock Brook access. There is ample parking at the bottom of the drive and in a half-dozen spaces beyond the farmhouse.

THE TRAIL

The proposed loop includes the Rosenburg Ramble on Sheep Hill, the Fitch Trail, the lower RRR Brooks Trail, and a short climb on Bee Hill Road (gravel) back to Rosenburg Ramble. The Rosenburg Ramble, totaling 1.5 miles, begins past the kiosk and barns and tours the perimeter of the property. The lower part of the meadow has wet patches. (The Meadow Walk, also mowed, offers a brief tour of the land just above the

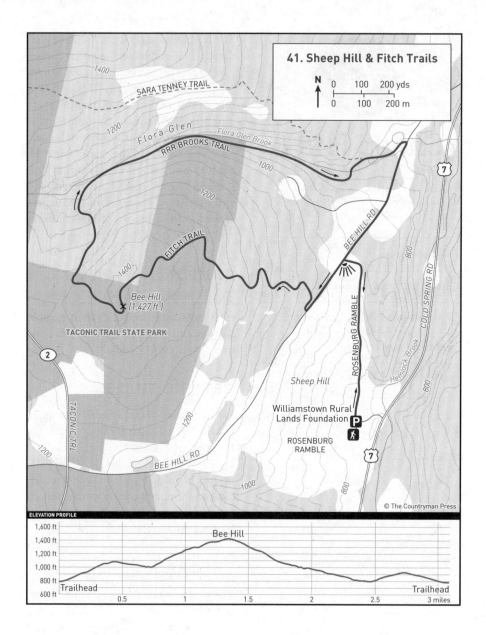

41. Sheep Hill & Fitch Trails

ELEVATION PROFILE

buildings.) Maps are available at the kiosk.

Starting on the Ramble, head cross slope, but generally upwards on the perimeter of the property until you come to the second opening on Bee Hill Road (20 minutes). Take in the views of the old farm and the hills beyond. Turn left and head back down Bee Hill; the Fitch trailhead will soon be on your left (blazed blue). (The Running Pine Trail, with many switchbacks, was cut for skiing.) The Fitch Memorial Woodlands, belonging to Williamstown Rural Lands, contain a variety of ecosystems. Start climbing moderately. The trail

A VENERABLE MAPLE ON THE FITCH TRAIL

FLORA GLEN BROOK

Lauren R. Stevens

has switchbacks and passes signs that interpret the natural scene. Do not turn on Running Pine. Instead, cross a stone wall (33 minutes). A woods road comes in on the right.

Climb into an area of hemlocks, ferns, and very large maples, some over six feet in diameter. A dell near the summit seems to belong to another world. By 45 minutes, you reach the summit (1,427 feet). Turn right just over the summit. The traffic sounds you hear are from Route 2 climbing to Petersburg Pass. You are now skirting an open field that is part of Taconic Trail State Park. In just less than 1 hour, turn right on the RRR Brooks Trail (also blazed blue) in a deep hemlock forest, leading beside Flora Glen Brook. That trail has suffered washouts as it descended into the streambed, so in five minutes, begin a major detour up the side hill. The late Robert R.R. Brooks, a former dean of Williams College, built the trail from his home at its foot.

In 1:15, cross Flora Glen Brook and the entrance to the Sarah Tenney Trail, left and, in 1:20, turn right on Bee Hill Road. Take a left at the first overlook parking, just beyond house number 240 Bee Hill Road (about 5 minutes). Then decide if you want to complete the Rosenburg Ramble loop (right) or head directly back to the kiosk (left), about 7 minutes.

42

Stone Hill

WILLIAMSTOWN

HIKING DISTANCE: 2 miles

WALKING TIME: 1 hour

VERTICAL GAIN: 250 feet

MAP: Williamstown

This leisurely stroll will take you from the Clark parking lot (750 feet) on a meandering path through old-growth, northern hardwood forest, to a stone seat (1,000 feet); then down through open fields, with a striking view of downtown Williamstown and the surrounding hills, and back to the parking lot. Part of the walk is on Clark land, part on Buxton School, and part on town of Williamstown land.

CAMPING

No camping in the vicinity. Closest camping on Mt. Greylock.

GETTING THERE

For Williamstown's favorite walk, drive south on South Street, beginning at Field Park, at the junction of Routes 7 and 2. At .5 mile, turn right into the Clark Art Institute. Pass the buildings to park in one of the lots nearest the main entrance to the museum. Note: the popularity of the Clark may require you to park farther away. There may be more parking available at the Stone Hill Center, up the second drive, from which you can access the same trail system.

THE TRAIL

To find the trailhead, pass through the automatic doors between the new Clark Center and the original museum building. They are open 24/7, as are bathrooms in the wall leading to the entrance, and at the Stone Hill Center. If your walk takes place during the museum's open hours (generally 10 a.m. to 5 p.m.), stop at the desk to pick up a map. Hikers are not charged. Pass through the matching doors and stroll beside the reflecting pools, past the brown

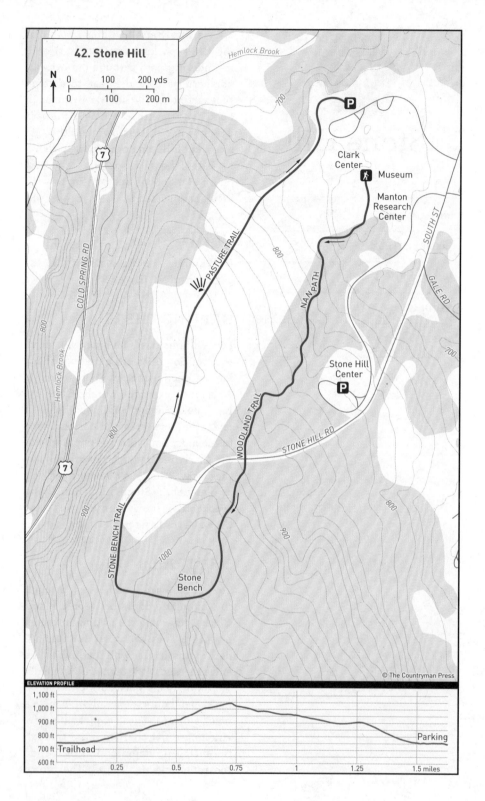

42. Stone Hill

N
0   100   200 yds
0   100   200 m

Hemlock Brook

P

Clark
Center

Museum

Manton
Research
Center

PASTURE TRAIL

NAW PATH

COLD SPRING RD

Hemlock Brook

7

7

WOODLAND TRAIL

STONE BENCH TRAIL

Stone Hill
Center

P

STONE HILL RD

SOUTH ST

GALE RD

Stone
Bench

© The Countryman Press

ELEVATION PROFILE

1,100 ft
1,000 ft
900 ft
800 ft
700 ft
600 ft

Trailhead

Parking

0.25   0.5   0.75   1   1.25   1.5 miles

Manton Research Center on your left. Your immediate destination: the footbridge that is the real trailhead. Copies of the map are available there, as well as inside. Look for two small gravestones that mark the eternal resting place of dogs that belonged to Dr. Vanderpool Adriance, a previous owner of the property. Sterling and Francine Clark purchased his land and built the white marble building for their art collection and, originally, their home. It opened to the public in 1955. The Manton building was built as an addition to the institute in 1973. The trails and footbridge were built in 1985 to help celebrate the Clark Institute's 30th anniversary, and significantly gussied up in 2014 as part of a redo of the Clark grounds that accompanied the construction of the Clark Center.

Take the Nan Path (10 minutes), green on the map, which provides an excellent guide to its features on the back of the map. Marked with clear signs, the trail passes through a variety of birch, beech, and maple stands, as well as hemlock and pine, so that visitors can compare and enjoy as they work gradually uphill.

Go straight to where the Woodland Trail crosses at 22 minutes and then, 2 minutes later, go right on the Pasture Trail and left on the Woodland Trail. (Yes, you could have taken the Wood-

Lauren R. Stevens

LOOKING OUT: THE CLARK AND THE MOUNTAIN BEHIND FROM STONE HILL

LOOKING IN: THE CLARK, WILLIAMSTOWN, AND WILLIAMS COLLEGE FROM STONE HILL

land when it first crossed, but then you would have missed out on station 7 from the guide.) The Pasture Trail crosses on its way to the Stone Hill Center. Continue straight across the remains of the colonial Stone Hill Road (25 minutes), which preceded Route 7 as the main north-south route in North County.

The road has been kept open to provide access to the town's water tank, which is buried under a field. There is a wonderful story about how the town and the Clark got together so that the tank would be buried rather than becoming an eyesore.

You are now leaving Clark trails, the result being that they are less well-marked. Follow up the hill to a somewhat obscure but well-trodden right turn (30 minutes), which leads past the stone seat erected as a memorial to George Moritz Wahl, a professor of German at Williams College who was erroneously suspected of being a German spy during World War I. He was accustomed to climbing to this spot in the evening to watch the sunset—in those days the fields were open. This monument was the town's posthumous apology and tribute.

This is the far point of the hike, but you may want to continue south on the old road and see how the hill got its name. Look through the trees to your left to see the schist outcroppings. After returning, walk through the field across from the seat. Head down, following the open land as it swings right. Although the trail remains clear, it passes through a short stretch of forest, as well as the cleared water tank field. Pass through a gate. Be sure to close all gates behind you, as cows still graze on these fields. Emerge on an open field and, at about 40 minutes from start, face the summit of Stone Hill at the head of a long, sloping field. Set your sights to the right of a clump of trees on the ridge ahead, dipping down and then rising to a view that includes the Clark, Main Street and the college, the Dome in southern Vermont, East Mountain (encompassing Pine Cobble and Eph's Lookout), the Hoosac Valley heading into North Adams, the Hoosac Range beyond the city, and the Greylock Range. A scattering of cut stones represents the site, i.e. Stone Hill. (A small building, an art installation, may be nearby.) The ridge is an ideal picnic site. The view remains in sight as you wander down the field, skirting wet areas.

Proceed across the next field, heading down the hill to the wooden gate. Note: you are now part of the view for museum-goers; perhaps you are being compared to the pastoral subject of an old master. Act accordingly. Staying on the Pasture Trail and its extension, return to the parking lot in about an hour, passing by another viewpoint, which is marked by a bench.

Enlargements of the Williams Outing Club's trail map are featured on the back of the big town maps at the Field Park intersection and at the foot of Spring Street. This town likes trails. Many other strolls in town are yours for the walking. The description of the Snow Hole Trail tells you how to get to a collection of them in Hopkins Forest. Walking guides to the town, available at the Williams Inn or the Chamber Office on Spring Street, show numerous strolls and explain the history of Williamstown. The small house on Field Park was built as part of the town's 250th anniversary in 1953, using the same materials and methods employed in the town's first homes.

43

Mountain Meadow

WILLIAMSTOWN/POWNAL, VERMONT

HIKING DISTANCE: varies

WALKING TIME: varies

VERTICAL GAIN: N/A

MAP: Williamstown

This approximately 85-acre property of The Trustees of Reservations spans Williamstown and Pownal. The grasslands and wetlands are on the Massachusetts end. The upper property, recovering from heavy gravel mining—and from being a teenage party site—is reforesting. The entire property rises from 690 feet in elevation to a summit overlook (1,120 feet). The ruins of an old family resort, Mausert's Camp, provide another overlook on Williamstown. A cellar hole remains from the house Grace Greylock Niles lived in. Niles, a 19th-century naturalist, wrote *Bog-Trotting for Orchids* and a history of the Hoosac Valley, and in later life she became unhinged, terrorizing her few neighbors. The hiker or the cross-country skier enjoys considerable variety from flat, wide trails to steep and twisted ones.

SIGNS DIRECT YOU AT MOUNTAIN MEADOW
Lauren R. Stevens

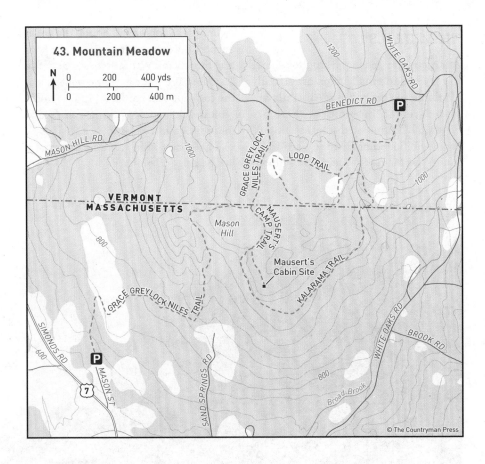

43. Mountain Meadow

N

0   200   400 yds

0   200   400 m

WHITE OAKS RD

BENEDICT RD P

MASON HILL RD

GRACE GREYLOCK NILES TRAIL

LOOP TRAIL

1200

1000

1000

VERMONT
MASSACHUSETTS

Mason
Hill

MAUSERT'S CAMP TRAIL

Mausert's
Cabin Site

KALARAMA TRAIL

800

GRACE GREYLOCK NILES TRAIL

SIMONDS RD

800

P

MASON ST

7

SAND SPRINGS RD

WHITE OAKS RD

BROOK RD

800

Broad Brook

© The Countryman Press

CAMPING

Closest camping on Mt. Greylock.

GETTING THERE

This delightful property can be reached from Route 7, north of Williamstown center, or from Pownal, via White Oaks Road in Williamstown, depending on the landscape you seek. To reach open fields with a side trip to a wooded lookout, follow Route 7 north to Mason Street—the steep, gravel road across from The Chef's Hat. The Trustees of Reservations parking lot is at the end. Ticks—including deer ticks that carry Lyme Disease—have been rife in the fields recently, so tuck your pant legs into your socks and check yourself after walking.

To reach a second growth wooded area that sprouts from former gravel pits, and for a side trip to a higher lookout, take Route 7 north to North Hoosac Road, turning right across from the sign for the town's DPW facilities. Take the second left (north) on White Oaks Road for .5 mile, where the road turns to gravel at the Vermont line. Continue on uphill, bearing left, for a few hundred yards. Go straight on Benedict Road rather than right. The TOR parking lot is soon on the left.

THE TRAILS

A large map at each parking lot shows the trails and small maps are usually available for the taking. All trails are blazed yellow. In addition, there are directional signs at the intersections. From the Benedict Road lot, try walking to the Mausert's Cabin Site (about 25 minutes each way). Though the cabin burned, the chimney remains. The views are mostly of Williamstown and the Taconics. From the extreme west side of the lookout you can see Mt. Greylock. Mountain Meadow is a fine, rolling site for cross-country skiing.

The entire area was once part of a large farm and orchard.

MAUSERT'S CHIMNEY STILL COMMANDS A VIEW

Lauren R. Stevens

Snow Hole

WILLIAMSTOWN/POWNAL, VERMONT

HIKING DISTANCE: 7.6 miles

WALKING TIME: 4 hours, 15 minutes

VERTICAL GAIN: 1,400 feet

MAP: Williamstown

The trip to the Snow Hole is a vigorous outing, climbing from 800 to 2,200 feet. As well as seeing evidence of past land use in Hopkins Forest, you view two spectacular brook valleys and Route 2 as it ascends on the New York side to Petersburgh Pass and the old ski area. Remember that with higher altitudes come colder temperatures, and that the Taconic Ridge can be windy. On the other hand, standing on the top of this piece of the world in snow and ice crystals is unforgettable. Azaleas and blueberries are found here in season. What is equally exciting is that the two states, Williams College, and Williamstown have cooperated to create a public recreation area totaling 3,500 acres.

At the beginning of this hike, the following sites are worth a visit: Buxton Gardens, the re-creation of a 19th-century flower garden; the Barn Museum of farming; and the exhibits in the Rosenburg Center. Hopkins Forest, a 2,500-acre tract bordering New York and Vermont, is an ecology laboratory for Williams College. Please do not wander off the trails, because you might inadvertently disturb experiments. Signs explain some of the work in progress. As alternatives to this route, strolls, hikes, and ski tours beckon in Hopkins Forest. Pocket maps are available at the large map near the barn.

Of course you could reach the Snow Hole by driving up Route 2 to Petersburgh Pass and picking up the Taconic Crest Trail north there, but you wouldn't want to take the easy way, would you?

CAMPING

The Williams Outing Club cabin in Hopkins Forest is available through the club to people associated with Williams Col-

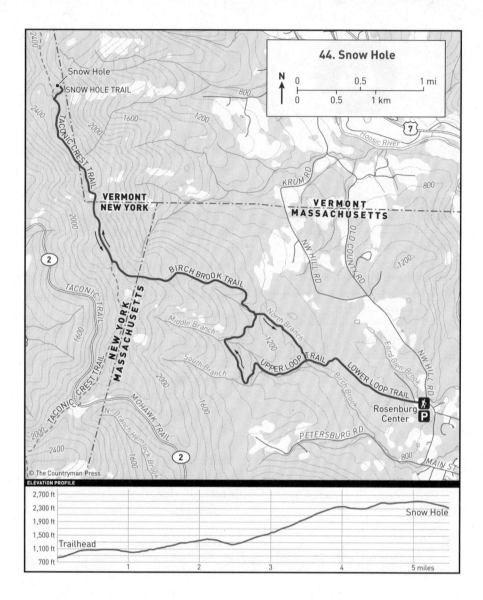

44. Snow Hole

ELEVATION PROFILE

lege. It has a wood stove, running water, and a sleeping loft. Otherwise, closest camping on Mt. Greylock.

GETTING THERE

From Field Park in Williamstown, follow West Main Street down, up, down, up to a right turn on Northwest Hill Road. Pass the end of Bulkley Street and left into a parking lot on the Hopkins Forest drive.

(Do not drive to the carriage house.) You begin and end your trip here.

THE TRAIL

Beginning at the Hopkins Forest lot, walk up the private drive, past the kiosk, and go straight, leaving the barn on your right. The trail climbs and then levels, passing signs that explain the natural and cultural history of the forest. In

AN OVERLOOK OF ROUTE 2 CLIMBING TO PETERSBURGH PASS FROM THE TACONIC CREST TRAIL

Lauren R. Stevens

15 minutes, go left at the intersection, dropping down to the Birch Brook, pass a deep hole known to some as Diana's Bath, cross a bridge (30 minutes) and begin to climb once more—steeply this time. The trail again levels, through hemlocks and an azalea field, and drops to another bridge.

Just beyond (40 minutes), the Birch Brook Trail turns sharply left. Take it. After the broad and carefully constructed Loop Trail, Birch Brook Trail appears indistinguishable in places from a streambed. Nevertheless, follow at a moderate rise for 10 minutes, then follow it right, up the side of a shoulder. This trail soon passes the remains of a stone wall, swings left on top of the rise. Another wall and forest boundary appears on the right. The large maples here were never cut because they were (and are) line trees, marking a property boundary.

At 1:07, the trail crosses a spring, beginning a steep, steady ascent to the ridge on the left. The forest is older, although the birches and maples are showing signs of stress. You think you've been climbing pretty hard, yet if you look sharp to your left, you may see a cellar hole within spitting distance of the trail. People not only farmed these ridges, they lived on them. If you lived up here, you'd think twice about going back to town because you forgot to pick up a spool of thread.

After watching your elevation approach the ridge's for some time and after climbing over phyllite outcrops, at last you attain the Taconic Crest Trail (TCT), blazed with a white diamond on a blue square (1:25). Turn right at the yellow sign. Study this intersection for the return trip. One telltale sign is a "no trespassing" sign just across from the trailhead. Wheeled vehicles are not allowed. You are in New York, .5 mile south of the Vermont border, which juts .5 mile west of Massachusetts. A *New Yorker* cartoon from 1989 showed a real estate broker greeting hikers at the three-state marker, .75 mile to the northeast.

You pass over a wet area on bog bridges and, at 1:52, begin walking through an area Hopkins Forest is cutting to create more varied habitat. Pass three overlooks into New York State. Then at 2:17, the Snow Hole Trail (blazed red) departs on the right. After descending for a few minutes, arrive at a cleft in the ground, created when the side of the hill slid. Although exposed here, the crack continues under the duff through the woods. Though you may not find residual snow at the bottom, you will find curious names and dates carved into the rocks, such as Sullivan, J.M., 1865, or the Troy Motor Club, 1930. When you see a date like C.E. Hyde '94, you can assume that refers to 1894.

The return trip should take less time. Leaving the Snow Hole as you came in, turn left on the TCT (blazed white/

Lauren R. Stevens

THE ENTRANCE TO HOPKINS FOREST, INCLUDING THE FARM SCULPTURE

blue). Turn left on Birch Brook about 3 hours out; then, in 40 more minutes, left this time on the Upper Loop Trail. Pass, but do not take, trails coming in from the left. At a major trail intersection, 4 hours out, turn left. Continue on this well-made woods road, which the Civilian Conservation Corps constructed when the U.S. Forestry Service ran an experimental forest here. Looking down to your left, you will soon see Ford Glen in the chasm it has cut for itself. Pass, without entering, a weather station that gathers important information for experiments in the forest. Pass a sugar shack and the Outing Club cabin, and return to your starting point.

45

Pine Cobble

WILLIAMSTOWN	
HIKING DISTANCE: 3.2 miles	
WALKING TIME: 2 hours	
VERTICAL GAIN: 1,000 feet	
MAP: Williamstown	

Every Berkshire town should have its own mountain overlook—and most do. Pine Cobble, the southernmost thrust of the Green Mountains, is Williamstown's. From here, you get a fine, panoramic view of the Hoosic River valley, including the Williams College campus, Williamstown, the airport, and North Adams. The Greylock massif and the Taconics serve as backdrop. Pine Cobble might be seen as its own peak or as an overlook on East Mountain, which rises to the north. "Cobble" refers to the exposed outcropping of quartzite bedrock, which you clamber onto to get the view. The trail itself is well marked, starts gently upward, dips, then climbs fairly steeply part way up and again, just before the crest.

CAMPING

The Seth Warner shelter, a three-sided, Adirondack-style lean-to, is north on the Appalachian Trail. The local chapter of the Green Mountain Club keeps it well maintained, with firewood and a clean privy. A tent camping area is nearby. Although Broad Brook serves the city of North Adams for drinking water, it is still safer to carry your own. There is a tent site on the AT south. Sand Springs Pool (slightly farther west on Bridges Road than White Oaks Road) is a private swimming spa open to the public for a fee.

GETTING THERE

From Field Park in Williamstown, drive north on Route 7, over the Hoosic River at the bottom of the hill, and go right at the first turn, North Hoosac Road. Follow that past Cole Avenue. Turn left on Pine Cobble Road to a parking lot (on the left), designed primarily for hikers. The

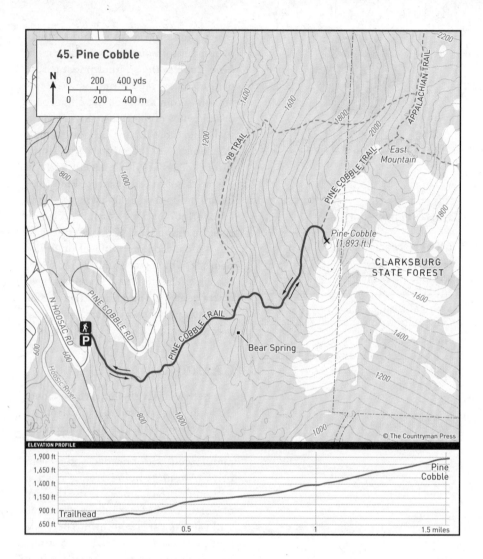

45. Pine Cobble

N
0   200   400 yds
0   200   400 m

98 TRAIL

PINE COBBLE TRAIL

APPALACHIAN TRAIL

East
Mountain

Pine Cobble
(1,893 ft.)

CLARKSBURG
STATE FOREST

N HOOSAC RD

PINE COBBLE RD

PINE COBBLE TRAIL

P

Bear Spring

Hoosic River

© The Countryman Press

ELEVATION PROFILE

1,900 ft
1,650 ft
1,400 ft
1,150 ft
900 ft   Trailhead
650 ft

Pine
Cobble

0.5   1   1.5 miles

trail begins across the road from the lot. It is marked with an informative sign.

THE TRAIL

Pine Cobble is one of the most popular climbs in Williamstown, including weekly sunrise hikes by the Williams Outing Club. Through-hikers on the Long Trail use it as a destination, since there is no direct access to the southern end in Vermont. After climbing the bank across from the parking lot, follow the blue blazes parallel to the road and into the wood. After 10 minutes, start down on a re-route designed to move the trail farther from the backyards of houses in the Pine Cobble development. A water dish provides for "the thirsty dogs of Pine Cobble." Stone steps (20 minutes) help you up a short, steep section. Pass a trail sign where an older version of the trail once entered. At 33 minutes, a side trail leads to Bear Springs (the only spring on the side of Pine Cobble), which attracts animals.

EAST MOUNTAIN FROM PINE COBBLE

A few minutes later, the '98 Trail departs on the left. Cut in 1998, the trail provides a way to reach the Appalachian Trail north of Pine Cobble without summiting to the Overlook. Your trail is now steeply skirting a slide area, eroded by generations of Williams College students. The trail shows some gravel and sand, evidence that the hill was the shore of a glacial lake 10,000 years ago. Pass a sign that indicates Willliamstown Rural Lands Foundation's ownership of the property—and implicitly, the role the land trust played in maintaining trail access after housing development began.

Having crested the shoulder, bear left by a trail entering right and some property signs. Given the poor soil conditions, the second growth birch and oak are thin and small. The trail gradually increases in angle until you

THE PINE COBBLE SUMMIT

pass a large boulder on the left, a resting point for many a weary hiker. At 50 minutes, pass Three Trunk Tree, formed when the original tree died, leaving its offshoots. In an hour from the start, you reach the ridge; turn right for a three-minute scramble to the overlook. Due to fragile conditions, be careful to stay on the trail.

You are looking at Mt. Williams Reservoir and Mountain—one of the Greylock peaks. You overlook Williamstown and, to the east, North Adams, in the valley. The Hoosacs rise farther east and the Taconics west. You are standing on the southern extremity of the Green Mountains. Behind you, in that dark valley of Sherman Brook, rises the AT.

You may decide to return the way you came, meaning back along the ridge and left down the steep slope, past Three Trunk Tree and so forth, for a fine two-hour hike with exceptional views. There are of course alternatives. One would be to continue along the ridge to the high point of East Mountain. The vegetation opens up at a burn area, now covered with blueberries. Blazes are painted on stone; some cairns mark the trail, some are artistic expressions of trail hikers. The highest pile of loose stone is Eph's Lookout (2,254 feet), named for the college's benefactor, Ephraim Williams, a soldier of the king who probably never stood where you do. The Hoosac Valley links the communities of Williamstown and Pownal below you. The dwarfed pitch pine you see among the rocks are at their northern extent. The AT enters right almost immediately, with several handsome signs: Williamstown, 2.1 miles; Route 2, 2.7 miles south; Vermont line, 1.3 miles north. The Seth Warner Camp is ahead. You could then double back to the Pine Cobble Trail, follow the AT south, coming out in North Adams, or follow to the Long Trail, and then return by the Broad Brook Trail (a full day's outing), or follow a few hundred yards farther north and turn left on the '98 Trail, about .5 mile from Pine Cobble. Remember that you passed the other end part way up Pine Cobble. The '98 Trail is 1.5 miles long.

46

The Dome

POWNAL, VERMONT

HIKING DISTANCE: 5.2 miles

WALKING TIME: 3 hours

VERTICAL GAIN: 1,750 feet

MAP: Pownal

There are several reasons not to recommend the Dome Trail. It is not in Berkshire County. Four-wheelers (quads) traffic it, causing considerable erosion. Trees have grown up, diminishing the view from the summit. Yet, at 2,748 feet, it's a favorite hike of the few who know it, especially in cool weather when its rocky crest reflects the sun, and in the winter when its highest vegetation is spectacularly snow-or-ice-covered. Its bald stone summit is unusual. Like Mount Greylock, the Dome allows you to climb out of a second-growth, mixed hardwood forest into a distinctly different environment, with spruce and fir bogs of the kind found on northern Canada's Laurentian plateau. Although the mountain lies in Vermont, it is distinctly a part of the northern Berkshire skyline. Check the view from Stone Hill, for example. Since the trail dead ends, you must come back down the way you went up.

CAMPING

Sand Springs Pool (left at the junction of Sands Springs and White Oaks roads) is a private spa open to the public for a fee. No shelters on this trail. Closest camping on Mt. Greylock.

GETTING THERE

Although located in Vermont, the Dome is accessible by road only from Williamstown. From Field Park, drive north on Route 7 across the Hoosic River. Take the first right onto North Hoosac Road and the second left onto White Oaks Road. Follow White Oaks about 4 miles from Field Park. At the Vermont line, the road turns to gravel; immediately on your right is a parking lot that serves the Broad Brook Trail. You can park here or drive another quarter mile to the Dome

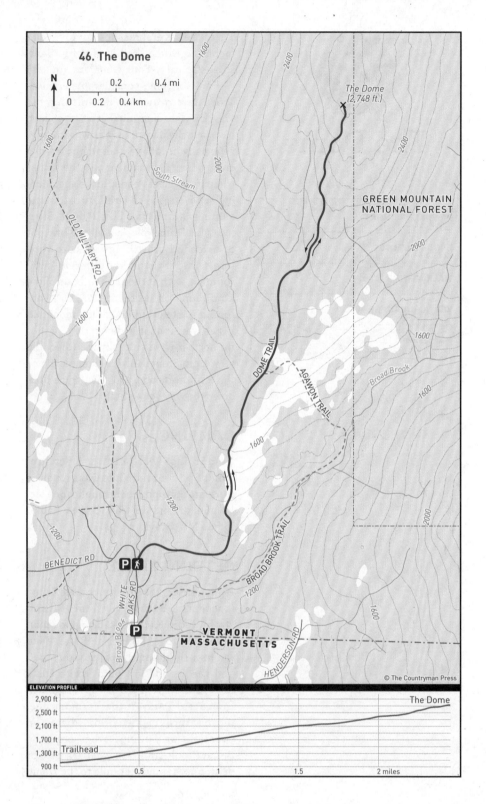

46. The Dome

N
0   0.2   0.4 mi
0   0.2   0.4 km

The Dome
(2,748 ft.)

GREEN MOUNTAIN
NATIONAL FOREST

South Stream

OLD MILITARY RD.

DOME TRAIL

AGAWON TRAIL

Broad Brook

BROAD BROOK TRAIL

BENEDICT RD

WHITE OAKS RD

Broad Brook

HENDERSON RD.

VERMONT
MASSACHUSETTS

© The Countryman Press

ELEVATION PROFILE

2,900 ft
2,500 ft
2,100 ft   The Dome
1,700 ft
1,300 ft
900 ft   Trailhead
              0.5   1   1.5   2 miles

Lauren R. Stevens

THE DOME'S DOME

LOOKING SOUTH TOWARD GREYLOCK FROM THE DOME

trailhead, on the right. Dome trailhead parking assumed. The trail is unusual in that water is available for almost the entire route. Still, it is better to carry your own.

THE TRAIL

From the parking lot at about 1,000 feet, it is a steady, demanding climb. The Dome Trail leaves its trailhead (you can't count on signs) past a cable intended to keep out motorized vehicles, and beside a branch of Broad Brook. If you miss the trailhead, you will soon come to a division of White Oaks Road:

a Colonial military road continuing straight, passing through wild country.

Back on the trail, vehicles drive into former fields, now growing over, that have served as a logging yard and occasionally as a party site. The Williams Outing Club once blazed the trail white; more recently, it has been blazed red. The trail is broad and blazes clear. One stone of a cemetery stands on a knoll to the right: "Polly 1830," it reads. (Perhaps a farm animal?) Continue on the old lumber road, bearing right, out of the second field into the woods.

The road begins a moderate climb along the shoulder of the Broad Brook valley, passing through a gap in a stone wall and continuing up at a steady rate until the first terrace, about 5 minutes later. The lumber road (at 15 minutes), closed by a boulder, goes straight; follow the trail left. The hike becomes more strenuous, with occasional detours around the most seriously eroded sections. Erosion, particularly from motorized vehicles, is severe in this section.

The Agawon Trail (35 minutes) drops off to the right, and heads down to join the Broad Brook Trail. Just beyond is Meeting House Rock, a large boulder more or less halfway to the summit. Just beyond that point, the trail emerges on the second terrace, an open area where azaleas bloom with haunting fragrance in late spring. The trail rises more gently, swinging westerly. In some places the quartzite ledges are covered with gravel and even white sand left over from the time when the sides of the Dome, like all northern Berkshire ridges, were the shores of a glacial lake that inundated the valley to a height of 1,300 feet or more. The deposits left by the glaciers formed the shoulders and plateaus so evident on the Dome, creating a situation typical of Berkshire climbs: the steepest part is at the beginning (you've done it), followed by a leveling or series of plateaus, and ending with a steep but short scramble to the summit.

Surprise: at about 50 minutes, you'll find the remains of an old Chevy truck strewn before you. Presumably someone drove it up the logging road that enters from the left, where it died. Turn right on this road, past intimidating signs that aim to control hunting, not hiking on the trail. Bear left where the logging road continues straight, up a short steep section to the third terrace. Few motorized vehicles get beyond this point.

Now begins a pattern of emerging on successively wetter terraces and bearing right up the slope after attaining each one. There is a short ascent to the fourth terrace. Angle right; there is also a short ascent to the fifth terrace. The trail begins to follow a brook—or to be a brook. Turn right to ascend to the sixth terrace. Right again to the seventh. Cross the brook. Then back across it, right, to the eighth and last terrace. Have you kept count? Turn right through a spruce and fir forest to the rocky ridge.

Follow the ridge to the false summit (1:20): no view because of vegetation. Still following the blazes, push through the fir down into a bog, similar in ecology to what you might find hundreds of miles north. Scramble up the quartzite outcroppings to the ridge that leads to the real summit. The blazes are now painted on the rocks, augmented by a few cairns. You will know you've reached the summit because there won't be any more up (1:25). Furthermore, you get the first real views: west to the tops of the Taconics and southeast to the Hairpin Turn and the Hoosacs. The view of Greylock is pretty well obscured by spruce now, although an ice storm may improve visibility one of these winters.

When descending, while still on the summit ridge, note the blazes and bear left where it appears the trail continues straight. In addition, remember to turn left at the Chevy on the way down. The trip back to the parking lot will take about 1:20, for a 3-hour round trip.

Either coming or going, an alternative route would be to use the Agawon Trail between the Dome and Broad Brook trails. This option is steep and requires a stream crossing, which can be troublesome at high water. Almost the entire Dome Trail is skiable, except for the two summits.

The Cascades

NORTH ADAMS

HIKING DISTANCE: 1 mile

WALKING TIME: 50 minutes

VERTICAL GAIN: N/A

MAP: Williamstown

North Adams' lesser known treasure is the Cascades, which drop 45 feet at the site, and over 1,000 feet as Notch Brook from the Notch between Mt. Greylock and Ragged Mountain. The Cascades are well worth a short hike. Besides, this book promised to introduce you to all the major waterfalls/cascades in the county. These were created as the harder rock eroded more slowly than the marble downstream. Close to downtown and located in the midst of a residential neighborhood, they are a pleasant surprise on a hot summer day.

CAMPING

The AT north of Massachusetts Avenue and Mt. Greylock offers camping.

THE CASCADES, NEARLY DOWNTOWN IN NORTH ADAMS
Lauren R. Stevens

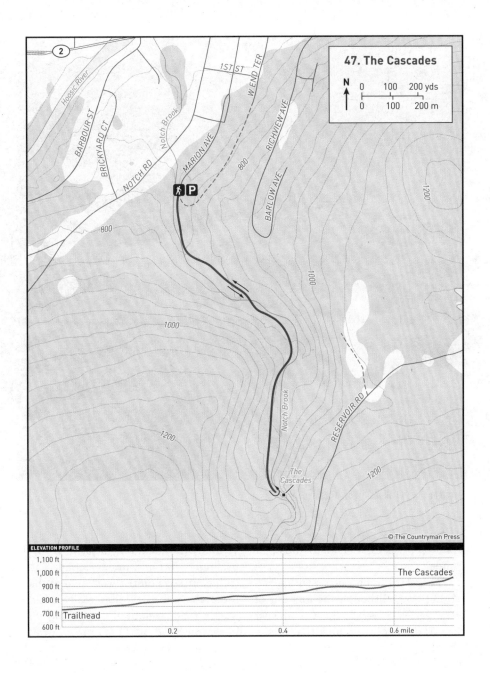

GETTING THERE

Drive west from North Adams to turn left at the *YMCA*. The trail departs from the parking area, crosses a bridge, and follows sidewalks.

THE TRAIL

The trail follows along Notch Brook, first on the east side and then, over a bridge installed by the Berkshire Nat-

NOTCH BROOK CONTINUES BELOW THE CASCADES

ural Resources Council on the west, for .5 mile.

The water tumbles down with a satisfying roar. Although the amount of water varies, generally there is a heavy flow. The folds in the rock that create the falls are worth seeing in themselves. The large hemlocks in the over-story keep the temperature down; the area, virtually in the middle of town, is surprisingly wild and undeveloped. The trail continues on the west side of the brook above the Cascades, really an old woods road, eventually emerging on Reservoir Road. Parts are grown over, however, and may be private property. The Cascades present a fine picnic and cooling off spot.

Hoosac Range Trail

NORTH ADAMS

HIKING DISTANCE: 6 miles

WALKING TIME: 4 hours

VERTICAL GAIN: 700 feet

MAP: North Adams

This is one of the best-laid and constructed trails in Berkshire County. It is a pleasure to walk on Peter Jensen's handiwork, which is brought to you by the Berkshire Natural Resources Council. Furthermore, it takes you to a brief section of the Busby Trail that deposits you on the rocky summit of Spruce Hill for a superb view of the Hoosac Valley and the southern Green Mountains—and of North Adams. Spruce Hill is North Adams' backyard mountain. A shorter, 1.5-mile route to Sunset Rock also provides excellent views to the west. The Hoosac Range Trail is a segment of the Mahican–Mohawk Trail, which currently runs from the Connecticut River to North Adams, with a few breaks.

CAMPING

South Pond, off Strykers Road from Route 2 in Florida, provides tent sites and cabin camping.

GETTING THERE

Leave the center of North Adams heading east on Route 2, up and up (this trail leaves most of the climbing to the automobile), around the Hairpin Turn and the Western Summit for 4.5 miles. Shortly after swinging left at the Western Summit, you'll see the parking lot on the right. The lot is plowed in the winter; snow-shoers take note.

THE TRAIL

The trail (blazed white—with red stripes for winter viewing) rises gently from the kiosk through northern hardwood forest dominated by maples. You'll soon understand that the trail finds its way in harmony with the topography, rather than fighting it. More subtly, the treadway has

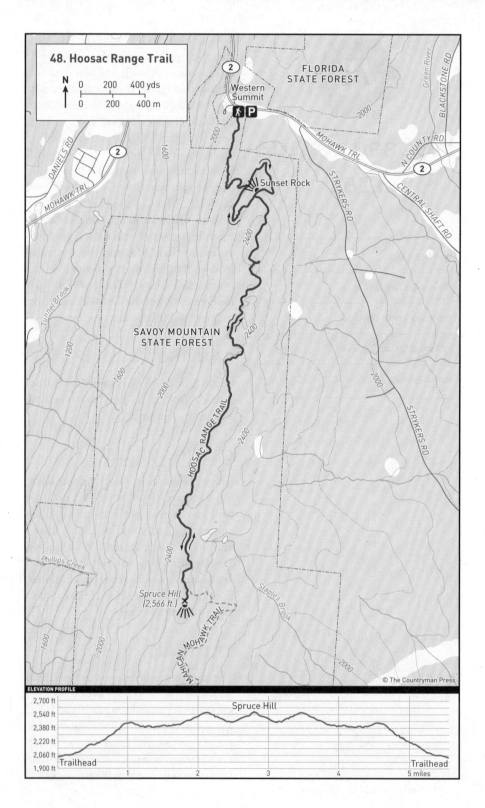

48. Hoosac Range Trail

N

0   200   400 yds
0   200   400 m

FLORIDA
STATE FOREST

Western
Summit

Sunset Rock

MOHAWK TRL

STRYKERS RD

N COUNTY RD

CENTRAL SHAFT RD

Green River

BLACKSTONE RD

DANIELS RD

MOHAWK TRL

Tunnel Brook

SAVOY MOUNTAIN
STATE FOREST

HOOSAC RANGE TRAIL

Phillips Creek

Spruce Hill
(2,566 ft.)

MAHICAN–MOHAWK TRAIL

Staples Brook

STRYKERS RD

© The Countryman Press

ELEVATION PROFILE

2,700 ft			Spruce Hill		
2,540 ft					
2,380 ft					
2,220 ft					
2,060 ft					
1,900 ft	Trailhead				Trailhead

1   2   3   4   5 miles

been improved by small touches, such as ground rock in a wet spot or movements of a stone to improve the footing. You can still hear the traffic on Route 2, which will pick up but then fade. In 10 minutes, take the left at the intersection in order to climb to Sunset Rock for a view of downtown North Adams (15 minutes).

At the next junction, turn left up the hill (if doing the shorter loop, go straight; otherwise save that trail for later). The sedimentary (layered) rock is becoming more of a feature of the trail. Again, the trail doesn't find its way directly, but wiggles with the landscape.

Nor does it climb along the ridge; rather it tends to go to the side the highest land.

At 37 minutes, a sign by a bridge indicates that you've reached the midpoint of the trail (1.4 miles). Twelve minutes later, a side trail on the left leads to a fine vista of the truncated summit of the Hoosacs. Just an hour from the start, pass the remains of the shack and a television broadcast tower. The demise of Adelphia Cable Company provided an opportunity for Berkshire Natural Resources Council to begin purchasing the parcels that make up the Hoosac Range Reserve, thereby creating a cor-

Lauren R. Stevens

THE HOOSAC RANGE TRAIL PASSES ROCK FORMATIONS

NORTH ADAMS IN THE VALLEY AND GREYLOCK BEYOND FROM THE SUMMIT OF SPRUCE

ridor for the trail. Construction began in 2010.

Soon you pass under a wire cut. To the left, on an unmarked trail, is a beaver pond that may be the highest natural body of water on the Commonwealth. A sign that says "Spruce Hill 0.2 miles" signals the end of the Spruce Hill Trail. From this point, follow the Busby Trail (blazed blue) to the summit. There are several open, rocky places in the way, but push through to the actual summit (about 1.5 hours). If you don't feel very winded, remember that the automobile did most of the climbing and that a trail that conforms to topography is easier to follow.

Come out on the outcroppings. This summit rises to 2,566 feet, the highest point on the Hoosac plateau (with the exception of the top of the tower on Borden Mountain). The view down into the Hoosac Valley and up to the Greylock massif rewards your final burst of effort. The view south, over the Hoosac plateau, is no slouch, either. During the fall migration, these cliffs provide an excellent vantage point from which to watch kettles of hawks cavort in the warm air rising from the valley.

Return the way you came, except take a left at the intersection to follow the other branch. Or you could go down the other side of Spruce Hill on the Busby and/or Blackburnian Trails (also part of the Mahican–Mohawk Trail). You would want to have spotted a car near North Pond.

Tannery Falls

SAVOY

HIKING DISTANCE: 3 miles

WALKING TIME: 1 hour, 30 minutes

VERTICAL GAIN: N/A; -200 feet at the falls

MAP: Plainfield/Rowe

In this book's campaign to bring you to every major waterfall (really cascade) in Berkshire County, *voila*, here is spectacular Tannery Falls, notable not because of its volume of water, but because two, and sometimes three, graceful strands come together. Biting insects favor this wet, boggy area, so take precautions. For a stroll on gravel roads, sneakers are adequate.

CAMPING

Camping is available at South Pond, which you pass while driving. In addition to tent platforms, there are three cabins that can be reserved. Swimming and boating are available at North Pond.

GETTING THERE

You can drive directly to Tannery Falls, either up Black Brook Road from Route 2 at the eastern foot of the Trail, or via the gravel Adams or Tannery Roads. However, on the principle that the value of an experience improves if it is earned, follow Route 2 east from North Adams, around the Hairpin Turn, past the Western Summit, and take a right on Strykers Road; go right again on Central Shaft Road, which you follow past North Pond. The road turns to gravel and swings left, becoming, unbeknownst to you, Burnett Road. Park in the snowmobile parking lot to your left just before Burnett meets New State Road. (There are few road signs in Savoy.)

THE TRAIL

Walk right on New State across the bridge over Gulf Brook and turn left on gravel Tannery Road. Simply stay on that road, mostly downhill, for 1.5 miles

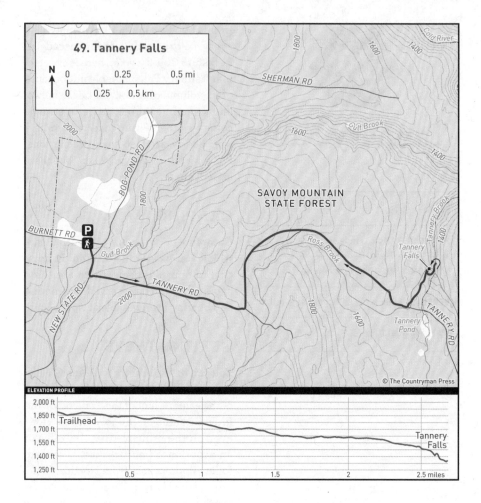

49. Tannery Falls

N
0   0.25   0.5 mi
0   0.25   0.5 km

SHERMAN RD

Cold River
1800   1600   1400

BOG POND RD

2000

1800

Gulf Brook

1600

1400

SAVOY MOUNTAIN
STATE FOREST

BURNETT RD   P

Ross Brook

Tannery Brook

Tannery
Falls

1400

NEW STATE RD

Gulf Brook

TANNERY RD

2000

1800

1600

Tannery
Pond

TANNERY RD

© The Countryman Press

ELEVATION PROFILE

2,000 ft					
1,850 ft	Trailhead				
1,700 ft					
1,550 ft					Tannery Falls
1,400 ft					
1,250 ft	0.5	1	1.5	2	2.5 miles

(about 40 minutes). New State Road, incidentally, was not a MassDOT project. Instead, it was named for a fundamentalist community that lived there in the 19th century.

You probably won't see a sign for Tannery Falls, but you will see a parking lot on the left. You have gone past it when Tannery Pond appears on your right. Follow the blue blazes from the parking lot as you work your way down Ross Brook, under wonderful hemlocks. The first falls and chasms in the folded rock are a prologue. Follow at the top of the long, delicate falls, some 80 feet over a slab of rock. As you work your way to

its foot, you will discover another brook and falls entering, in season, to the south, and to the right, Parker Brook—the one the Civilian Conservation Corps dammed to make Tannery Pond. After the brooks unite, they become Tannery Brook, joining Cold River. Be sure to allow plenty of time to observe the rock, the water, and the trees. Read a book or have a picnic here, at least.

Many of the trails in the area are designed for snowmobiling, kept up either by the state or a club, Adams Sno-Drifters. They are not all blazed. One unmarked trail to the south leads to a balanced rock.

HIDDEN BUT DELIGHTFUL TANNERY FALLS

Dunbar Brook

SMONROE

HIKING DISTANCE: 4.2 miles

WALKING TIME: 2 hour, 20 minutes

VERTICAL GAIN: 700 feet

MAP: Rowe

Saving what may be the best for last: a truly scenic walk along the Dunbar Brook Trail, beside the tumbling waters of the clear, mountain stream, through glades of enormous hemlock, which look as though the underbrush were swept every day. Like Alander Mountain and the Hopper on Mt. Greylock, the Commonwealth has declared the Dunbar Valley a special Backcountry Area. This walk takes you through and near ancient and undisturbed stands of trees, some of which are more than 250 years old. Some are large, but conditions, more than age, determine size. Note: if the bridge has not been replaced, you will have to wade the brook.

Do not confuse the Spruce Hill hike in Florida with this one, Spruce Mountain in Monroe. Several other spruce hills and mountains exist in the area, for obvious botanical reasons.

CAMPING

You will pass a well-maintained lean-to (three-sided) shelter—kept up by the state and power company—as well as numerous fireplaces and informal camping areas. Up the hillside, there are two more shelters on another trail. A word of caution, though: the shelters are within a mile of a road and show evidence of being sites for parties. Ideally, shelters should be located a bit off the trail. Using these is a little like sleeping in the hall.

GETTING THERE

Go east on Route 2 in North Adams, 6.7 miles up and into Florida on what is known locally as The Trail (the Mohawk Trail); take the next left on Whitcomb Hill Road after Whitcomb Summit; then the next right. Head down on a steep

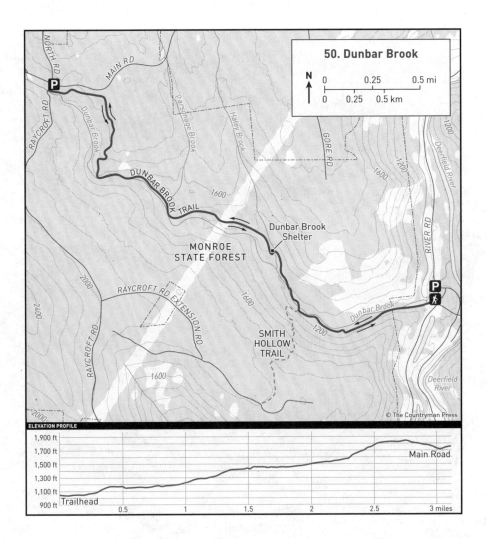

ELEVATION PROFILE

| | Trailhead | | | | | | Main Road |

road to a T at River Road (2.5 miles). The river is the Deerfield. Go left at the T, continuing through the village of Hoosac Tunnel. Soon you pass the Bear Swamp Visitors' Center, on the right, where you might wish to stop. Bear Swamp is a pumped-storage electricity generation station. The parking area you want to find for the Dunbar Brook hike is on the left, .75 mile beyond the Visitors' Center, 4.8 miles from the Mohawk Trail.

THE TRAIL

The Dunbar trailhead is located across River Road from the picnic area maintained by TransCanada, which owns hydroelectric facilities on the Deerfield, and the Massachusetts Department of Conservation and Recreation. Start up to the power line, by the kiosk at the southwest corner of the lot. Do not take the trail, which is gated, down

Lauren R. Stevens

to the dam. Above the dam, your trail detaches itself from the jeep road and drops towards the brook, which it follows under spreading hemlock. Look for the blue blazes. Solomon's seal, trilliums, and other spring ephemerals flower in profusion. In late May, it's impossible to avoid stepping on their beautiful blossoms. After 12 minutes, the trail turns left at a bench and fireplace, following close to the river for 3 minutes until you come to the bridge site. Tropical Storm Irene washed out the bridge. As of this writing, no date has been set to replace it, so you may have to ford.

Once across the brook, turn left. In 25 minutes, cross Haley Brook on a bridge, with a three-sided shelter on the other side. The trail, however, bears right, following an old carting road. You are in a heavily forested area, moving away from the brook. In 35 minutes, pass through a wire cut, and five minutes later, returning toward Dunbar Brook, you cross Parsonage Brook on a bridge. You are skirting some 150 acres, the largest tract of old growth forest in the state. The Student Conservation Association did the most recent work on this trail.

Turn away from Dunbar again, advancing up the slope by some large boulders and under magnificent hemlock, whose needles cushion your every step, until you again meet a woods road that takes you to paved Tilda Road (1:10 minutes). You could have started at this point and hiked the trail the other direction. If you want a good view of the brook and a picnic spot, turn left to the wooden bridge, where a kiosk shows the trails. The best picnicking might be

DUNBAR: AN AUTHENTIC MOUNTAIN BROOK

THE DUNBAR BROOK TRAIL BRUSHES A BOULDER

streamside, rather than in the parking lot, which tends to be cluttered. If you look on the north side of the brook, you will see the foundations of an old mill.

You have options for returning to your starting point. The first, of course, is the way you came, for a four-mile-plus round trip. For an 8-mile round trip alternative, cross the bridge and hike up South Road (gravel) to Raycroft Extension, left and down to the south side of the brook at the former bridge crossing. This is a route that distance runners like to jog. A detour would take you to Raycroft Lookout—another CCC project, with a stunning view of the Deerfield Valley.

Long Distance Hikes

50 Hikes in the Berkshire Hills is designed for day-trippers, and only tangentially describes the county's long-distance trails. Those are covered in specific guides noted in the bibliography. Nor does this book cover more than a fraction of the trails in the county. Many more hikes in northern Berkshire are described in the Williams College Outing Club's _North Berkshire Outdoor Guide._

The Appalachian Trail

In the 1920s, Benton McKaye and others used available state-owned land located between convenient small town inns and lodges to plan the Berkshire section of the 2,050-mile footpath from Springer Mountain in Georgia to Mt. Katahdin in Maine. It is intended to be a passive, recreational trail. No vehicles are allowed.

The more than 90 miles of the AT in Berkshire enter in South County at Sages Ravine and wander through Mt. Everett State Reservation, East Mountain State Forest, Beartown State Forest, October Mountain State Forest, Mt. Greylock State Reservation, and Clarksburg State Forest, and exit the county into Green Mountain National Forest. In recent years, the National Park Service has moved sections in between state forests off roads and onto protected lands, departing from the original concept of connecting towns. Several hikes in this book follow parts of the AT, which is blazed with white rectangles; side trails blazed blue.

The goal, as yet unrealized, is to place shelters within a day's hike of

Lauren R. Stevens

BOG BRIDGING ON THE HOPPER TRAIL

each other over the entire length of the trail. Bascom Lodge, on Mt. Greylock, is a storied rendezvous for through-hikers. Great Barrington and North Adams have been designated as Appalachian Trail Communities, officially going the extra mile, so to speak, to welcome through-hikers. See: _Appalachian Trail Guide—Massachusetts-Connecticut._

Long Trail

The 262-mile Long Trail, spanning the length of Vermont between Massachusetts and the Canadian border, begins on the AT at the Vermont line. Hikers must enter or depart from Pine Cobble in Williamstown or the AT from North Adams, since there is no direct road access to the south end. The Long Trail and the AT are the same from the Vermont line north to near Rutland, Vermont. See the Green Mountain Club's *Long Trail Guide*.

The Mahican–Mohawk Trail

Following up on a 1990 feasibility study conducted by Williams College students, the Appalachian Mountain Club, Deerfield River Watershed Association, Friends of Mohawk Trail State Forest, and Hoosic River Watershed Association began the process of laying out a 100-mile re-creation of Indian trails connecting the Connecticut and Hudson rivers by following the Deerfield and Hoosic rivers. Recently, the Massachusetts Department of Conservation and Recreation has played a key leadership role, along with the Student Conservation Association, Berkshire Natural Resources Council, and the Manice Center. The trail has been extended west through Franklin County, and now links campgrounds at Mohawk Trail State Forest and North Pond in Savoy Mountain State Forest. Its marker is a green maple leaf on a yellow disk (while the trail is blazed white). The Hoosac Range Trail (number 48 above) is a segment.

Since this is an ongoing project, more up-to-date information is available at Massachusetts Greenways and Trails: www.mass.gov/dcr.

The Taconic Crest Trail

The Taconic Hiking Club, founded in 1932 in Troy, New York, sponsors various kinds of outings. In 1948, its members began to develop the Crest Trail: 29 miles from Berry Pond in Pittsfield State Forest to Route 346 in North Petersburg, New York. The Snow Hole hike (number 44) follows it in part. The trail runs generally north and south along a ridge through three states. White, diamond-shape markers on blue squares mark the Taconic Crest Trail; side trails are marked by blue. Frequent overlooks east and west distinguish the trail. As well as Pittsfield State Forest, the TCT runs through New York Department of Environmental Conservation property, Williams College's Hopkins Forest, and other private land. Every other year, the club sponsors a one-day, end-to-end hike, beginning with breakfast before dawn at Berry Pond and continuing past dusk. See: *Guide to the Taconic Crest Trail*.

The Taconic Trail System

The entire Taconic system includes the Taconic Crest Trail, the Taconic Skyline Trail, and the South Taconic Trail. The 23-mile-long Skyline Trail runs from Richmond to Williamstown, including the 7-mile section south of Berry Pond maintained by the Taconic Hiking Club. It follows along the Brodie Mountain extension to the Taconics. About half is in Pittsfield State Forest and half on private land. The blazes are painted white, round or square in shape. The trail is used primarily by off-road vehicles.

The South Taconic Trail extends 15.7 miles, mostly in New York State's Taconic State Park and Mt. Washington State Forest in Massachusetts. It runs parallel to the AT, to the west, and is maintained by volunteers from the New York chapter of the AMC, the Mid-Hudson chapter of the Adirondack Mountain Club, the New York–New Jersey Appalachian Trail Conference (NYNJTC), and the Sierra Club. The crest it follows provides almost continuous, open, and extensive views east and west, including Alander and Bash Bish (see the description of hike number 4). Numerous side trails and camping areas provide circuit routes. See: *Guide to the Taconic Trail System.*

Williams Outing Club Trails

Founded by Albert Hopkins as the Alpine Club in 1863, the Williams Outing Club is the oldest mountain-climbing organization in the United States, preceding both the White Mountain and Appalachian Mountain Clubs. Students maintain some 75 miles of trails in northern Berkshire, southern Vermont, and eastern New York. The organization's trail guide, *The North Berkshire Outdoor Guide*, details trips on some 60 trails in the Williamstown area.

Berkshire Culture

All folks, certainly all families, will want to augment hiking with some of that famous Berkshire culture. After all, glorifying God's grandeur by gracefully combining Art and Nature was the goal of Stockbridge's Laurel Hill Association—America's oldest village improvement society, founded in 1853. By the mid-19th century, communities had moved beyond a strictly practical look at the landscape, such as hills and lakes getting in the way of the plough, to seeing its inherent beauty. Although the cultural awareness of the area's founders led to well laid-out town centers and well-proportioned architecture, it took writers, painters, and musicians to absorb the Berkshire's beauty and to teach the local populace a fuller appreciation of it. The county's artistic abundance grew out of proportion to the size of the area. In the latter half of the 19th century, as the well-heeled sought to escape the hectic and hot nature of their city lives, they came to Berkshire by the droves, bringing more culture with them. During the Gilded Age, the taut, lean architecture became considerably more indulgent and major museums were founded.

Of the intelligentsia who developed around Stockbridge and Lenox in the early 19th century, no single family was more dynamic than the convivial and civic-minded Sedgwicks of Stockbridge. Novelist Catharine Sedgwick shares honors with poet William Cullen Bryant as Berkshire's—and America's—first native-born published writers in their fields. The Sedgwick house and family still grace Stockbridge—and film—today.

Other writers, such as Herman Melville and Nathaniel Hawthorne, cross-fertilized their fiction in Berkshire in the 1850s, along with the popular Oliver Wendell Holmes, the doctor/poet who returned to his roots by summering in Pittsfield. Henry David Thoreau beheld a transcendental sunrise on the summit of Mount Greylock. Edith Wharton moved here, recreating the kind of opulent European lifestyle that she skewered in her fiction. Williams College became a scientific and literary center. The list of famous artistic residents is lengthy and impressive.

When the Berkshires became the "inland Newport" during the late 19th-century Gilded Age, culture rode into Berkshire along with big money. The area benefits from much inherited culture. Many of the family estates have become cultural centers, such as Tanglewood for music and the Mount for literature. As a reminder that beauty need not be ornate or expensive, the Shaker Village at Hancock is also a Berkshire cultural legacy of remarkable value and vitality.

Furthermore, Berkshire families have been patrons both of the arts and the landscape. For example, the Crane family of the Crane Paper Company of Dalton founded the Berkshire Museum, Francine and Sterling Clark created the Art Institute in Williamstown, and the Tappan family gave Tanglewood to the Boston Symphony Orchestra.

Many artists drawn to the Berkshires

lived here seasonally, like Wharton; others, like Norman Rockwell, stayed year-round. Thousands more have come just to perform or exhibit. Berkshire has left its mark on each. When asked what the Berkshires and Tanglewood mean to him, Seiji Ozawa, former music director of the Boston Symphony Orchestra, replied: "Tanglewood has an absolutely special connotation for me. It was the first place I ever saw in America, since I came to Tanglewood as a student in 1960 at the invitation of Charles Munch. For me and the orchestra, Tanglewood represents an opportunity to appreciate both the beauty of the Berkshires and of the music we make here."

Art combines with nature, from the fine woodwork in colonist John Ashley's study at Ashley Falls, to the nation's four founding documents in Williams College's Chapin Library; from dioramas and an aquarium at the Berkshire Museum in Pittsfield, to beautiful flowers and shrubs at the Berkshire Botanical Garden in Stockbridge. In performance halls, museums, libraries, theaters, nightclubs, and historic homes, Berkshire is rich in art and its accompanying pleasures. The following material is adapted from the eighth edition of *The Berkshire Book*, The Countryman Press, 2006.

ARCHITECTURE

Those who enjoy roaming through New England in search of handsome buildings will find Berkshire County a delight, displaying styles from colonial times to the present. Few counties anywhere can claim this much architectural variety.

Berkshire is justly famous for the scores of mansions built during the opulent Gilded Age. "Historic Homes" below describes several of the best surviving examples of these great "cottages." Yet the saga of the sumptuous cottages isn't half the Berkshire building history.

Humbler examples include one-room schoolhouses or steeple churches, icons of America's simpler past. Still performing as designed in some Berkshire towns, adapted to alternative uses in others, these white-clapboard structures are often handsome and always charming. Some of the best can be found in Alford, Lenox, Lee, New Ashford, Washington, and Williamstown. A beautiful c.1800 stone church is located in Lanesborough.

Many Berkshire villages seem like architectural set pieces, with artfully coordinated building styles and locations. The villages of Alford, New Marlborough, Stockbridge, and Williamstown have this look. Neon and plastic commercial clutter is conspicuously absent. Feelings of space and grace predominate. Yet each town also suggests the heart of a community where religion (churches), education (schoolhouses), government (town hall), domestic life (private homes), and the honor due the dead (cemeteries) all naturally fit together. People who live in cities or suburbs will find the centralization of Berkshire villages intriguing, as well as architecturally beautiful. New Marlborough bears all of this out with its archetypal village green surrounded in part by the colonial-style Old Inn on the Green (1760), a fine Federal-style house (1824), and a Greek Revival-style Congregational Church (1839).

Farms have long formed the Berkshire landscape. Almost any country road leads past splendid examples of old farmhouses with numerous outbuildings. Some of the barns precede the homes. Good rides for farm viewing include Routes 57 (New Marlborough); 41 (south from South Egremont or north from West Stockbridge); and 7 (north from Lanesborough). Dramatic Tudor-style barns from the Gilded Age are still in use at High Lawn Farm (on Summer St. off Route 7, Lee), but the most famous barn in Berkshire is the round stone barn at Hancock Shaker Village, described under "Museums" below.

South County towns have many impressive buildings, among them several notable industrial sites. Rising above them all is the Fox Paper Company's Rising Paper Mill (c.1875; Route 183 in Housatonic), with its handsome mansard slate roof. A similar mansard slate roof style is pushed to artful extremes on campus buildings at Bard College at Simon's Rock (on Alford Road, Great Barrington).

The village of Lee boasts the tallest wood-framed steeple in the county atop its Congregational Church. In South Lee, Merrill Tavern (Route 102), a Federal-period building, which still functions as an inn, is exquisitely maintained by the Society for the Preservation of New England Antiquities.

Architecturally lovely and filled with antiques shops, Sheffield appropriately prided itself on having preserved the oldest covered bridge in Massachusetts (1837) until it burned in 1994. The Massachusetts Department of Transportation erected a duplicate. Otis, a Berkshire hill town, is graced with St. Paul's Church (1829), a fine example of the Gothic Revival style.

Stockbridge dazzles. Architect Stanford White's turn-of-the-century work appears in impressive diversity here: a casino (now the Berkshire Theatre Festival; Route 102 and Yale Hill Road); a mansion (Naumkeag; on Prospect Hill Road); a former railroad station on Route 7 south of the village; and a church (St. Paul's Episcopal; center of town). Two other noteworthy Stockbridge churches are the red brick Congregational Church (Main Street, next to Town Hall) and the chapel at the Marian Fathers Seminary (on Eden Hill, off Prospect Hill Road). Whereas the interior of the Congregational Church has a powerful, simple beauty, the beauty of the Marian fathers' chapel comes from its finely crafted stone, woodwork, painting, and fabrics—much of it produced by transplanted European artists. A description of the Mission House, a colonial "Historic Home," follows later.

Three outlying sites in Stockbridge are worth a drive. The district originally called Curtisville—now known as Interlaken (Route 183, north of Route 102)—boasts several strikingly pretty 18th- and 19th-century homes and a remarkable former tavern-inn, as well as Citizens Hall, with its Victorian era, Second Empire–style exterior details. Another building of note in rural Stockbridge is at Tanglewood's Lions' Gate (Hawthorne Street, off Route 183), where the replica of Nathaniel Hawthorne's "Little Red House" overlooks Stockbridge Bowl and the distant mountains. The estate known as Linwood has opened to the public as the site of the Norman Rockwell Museum, a Robert A. M. Stern–designed New England town hall. Charles E. Butler's unpolished marble cottage, Linwood (1859), remains the architectural highlight of this delightful Berkshire hilltop.

Finally, in South County, a ride out on the Tyringham Road (off Route 102, south of Lee) and then upland on Jerusalem Road will lead to "Jerusalem"—the remnants of a Shaker settlement dating from 1792. Five buildings remain, none open. Jerusalem Road begins in tiny Tyringham Village. Along the Tyringham Valley Road is the Gingerbread House, a thatched-roof English cottage built by sculptor Henry Kitson in the late 1800s and known currently as Santarella.

Central County abounds with notable architecture. In Dalton, a ride along Main Street (Route 9) provides views of the Crane Paper Mills (the Old Stone Mill, dating to 1844, is open as a museum in season) and several Crane family estates. In addition to other fine papers, Crane manufactures U.S. currency paper in these venerable mills. In 1816, company founder Zenas Crane built a dignified Federal-style house, which still stands. In Dalton proper, there are also three 19th-century Richardsonian Romanesque churches on Main Street.

In the hill town of Hinsdale on Route 8, visitors will find some architectural surprises—vestiges of more prosperous, populous times when various mills were alive and well in the Berkshire highlands. The oldest (1798) Federal-style church in Berkshire is here. A Greek-Revival town hall was built in 1848. The public library is in the high Gothic style, designed in 1868 by architect Leopold Eidlitz, who did St. George's Church in New York City and the New York State Capitol in Albany.

Aside from Williams College's Thompson Memorial Chapel (1903–04), the only stone early-Gothic-Revival church in the county is St. Luke's Chapel (1836), in Lanesborough (on Route 7). Like many other buildings cited here, St. Luke's is on the National Register of Historic Buildings.

Impressive architectural set pieces can be found in stately Lenox, especially in the historic center of the village, including: the Lenox Academy (Federal style, 1803), the photogenic Church-on-the-Hill (1805), and the Lenox Library (1815; see "Libraries" below). All three buildings are on Main Street (Route 7A). The Curtis Hotel, dominating the center of town, has been restored and converted to an apartment complex. From the Gilded Age to recent times, the Curtis was one of Berkshire's most fashionable addresses for travelers. Not far from Lenox village, on Route 20 heading toward Lee, is Cranwell, once a Jesuit-run school, now a resort, golf club, and condominium complex.

Pittsfield's architectural record is distinguished, though problematic. Preservation and restoration nowadays receive good attention, as a walk around Park Square reveals. Several new buildings integrate well with the ornate elegance of the old Venetian Gothic Athenaeum, the two churches, the bank buildings, and the courthouse—all dating from the 19th century.

The former *Berkshire Eagle* newspaper building (on Eagle Street, off North Street) is a fine example of the Art Deco style, set on a triangle like a miniature of Chicago's Flatiron Building. Another important business structure in Pittsfield is the General Electric Plastics House, a handsome and curious experimental display house in the Plastics Division's world headquarters complex. The address? "Plastics Avenue," of course (between Merrill Road and Dalton Avenue).

North County provides stark contrasts in architecture and what the buildings reveal about social history. The communities of Adams and North Adams owe their expansion to past industrial times. However, revitalization proceeds, the most spectacular being the conversion of the idle Sprague Electric plant (formerly textile mills) into a mammoth museum of contemporary art (visual and performing): MASS MoCA. Although urban renewal hit the downtowns unkindly, Adams and North Adams have recently beautified their main streets. In North Adams, Western Heritage Gateway State Park celebrates a 19th-century architectural and engineering wonder, the Hoosac Tunnel. (See "Museums" below.) The spires of North Adams's many churches are a pretty sight when one is descending into the city from the east on Route 2. In Adams, suffragettes will want to pass the Susan B. Anthony Birthplace (1814; a private home near the corner of East Road and East Street) and the Quaker Meeting House (1782; near the end of Friends Street), another National Register of Historic Places building. Most spectacular is St. Stanislaus Kostka Church (1902; 25 Hoosac Street). The interior is a hymn to Polish culture in this country.

Williamstown contains homes from colonial to contemporary, a college that has been adding buildings almost since the country began, quaint shops, and two masterfully designed art museums (the Clark Art Institute and the Williams College Museum of Art, both described under "Museums"). It's worth touring the campus to see West College (1790), Griffin Hall (1828), the oldest (1838) extant college observatory in the United States, and the 1802 President's House. Visitors can consult a large map in front of the main administration building, Hopkins Hall, or refer to brochure maps available at the information booth. The much-photographed First Congregational Church (1869) has a replica of an colonial one in Old Lyme, Connecticut, superimposed. The Milne Public Library faces the 1753 House, built with authentic methods and materials for the town's bicentennial on Field Park.

CINEMA

Images Cinema
413-458-5612
www.imagescinema.org
50 Spring Street, PO Box 283, Williamstown, MA 01267

Eclectic, exciting films—independent first-run flicks, as well as the best from camp to classic—are the order of the evening in the only year-round, single-screen, independent movie house in the county. Its survival as North County's most dynamic movie house is a wonder. In 1989, when it was threatened with closure, the late actor and former resident Christopher Reeve pulled together support to keep the theater open. In 1998, it became a nonprofit organization under the leadership of energetic managers and support from the community. Today, Images lives on in refurbished modernity. Memberships, printed or e-mailed schedules, and special programs.

Little Cinema
413-443-7171
www.berkshiremuseum.org
At the Berkshire Museum
39 South Street (Route 7), Pittsfield, MA 01201

This is a great little film program in Berkshire, featuring state-of-the-art projection and sound. Films are shown in the summer, with special showings during the year. Fine independent and foreign films, shown downstairs in the Berkshire Museum auditorium.

Other cinema . . .

South County

Bard College at Simon's Rock (413-644-4400 www.simons-rock.edu; 84 Alford Road, Simon's Rock, Great Barrington, MA 01230). Occasional classics and fun films, open to the public.

Triplex Cinema (413-528-8885 info; 413-528-8886 office; fax 413-528-8889; www.thetriplex.com; 70 Railroad Street, Great Barrington, MA 01230; Mail: PO Box 508, South Egremont, MA 01258). An art venue, as well as cinema, with surround sound.

Central County

The Beacon Cinema (413-358-4780; 57 North Street, Pittsfield, MA 01201) bills itself as an independent triplex.

Regal Berkshire Mall 10 (413-499-3106; Berkshire Mall, 123 Old State Road, Lanesborough, MA 01237; off Route 8). Dolby stereo, action, adventure, drama, comedy, popcorn.

North County

North Adams Movieplex 8 (413-663-6300; www.northadamsmovieplex.com, 80R Main Street, North Adams, MA 01247). North County's multiplex, with eight screens.

DANCE

Albany Berkshire Ballet

413-445-5382; 800-476-6964
www.berkshireballet.org
Mail: 116 Fenn Street, Pittsfield,
MA 01201

The Albany Berkshire Ballet includes a school and professional performances in numerous sites in New York State, Berkshire County, and the Northeast. Highlights of past seasons include lavish productions of *Cinderella* and *Giselle*. Fall and winter concerts are capped with the traditional *Nutcracker*, staged at Berkshire Community College and throughout New England in November and December.

Jacob's Pillow Dance Festival

413-243-9919
www.jacobspillow.org
358 George Carter Road, Becket,
MA 01223
Off Route 20, 8 miles east of Lee

Founded in 1933, Jacob's Pillow is America's first and oldest summer dance festival. The Pillow keeps step with the times, presenting the best in classical, modern, postmodern, jazz, and ethnic dance. It offers a Who's Who of contemporary dance, with past performers including: Merce Cunningham, Dame Margot Fonteyn, Peter Martins, Alicia Markova, Twyla Tharp, Alexander Gudunov, Martha Graham, Paul Taylor, Alvin Ailey, Phildanceco, the Pilobolus troupe, Jane Comfort and Co., and many others.

High on a hillside in Becket is the farm that famed dancer Ted Shawn bought after successfully touring with his wife, Ruth St. Denis, and the Denishawn troupe in the 1920s. Here, Shawn worked to establish dance as a legitimate profession for men, founding a world-class dance-performance center and a school for dance. The school continues to flourish along with the festival, honoring its founder's heartfelt philosophy that the best dancers in the world make the most inspirational dance instructors. In addition to performing here, some of the Pillow's visiting dance luminaries stay on to teach master classes in the compound's rustic studios.

A visit is more memorable for those who drive to the Pillow early to stroll among those studios where works are in progress, and dancers in development. Through a window, lithe figures create choreography. Down at the Pillow's rustic outdoor theater, "Inside/Out," all forms—from experimental to ballet—are rehearsed and performed for free. After savoring that dance hors d'oeuvre, strollers might wish to sup at the Pillow. There are several lovely options: the Pillow Café, feasting under a brightly colored tent; or the picnic area, possibly glimpsing a dancer who will be performing later in the Ted Shawn Theatre. The Pillow's Studio/Theatre adds a separate 10-week schedule of new and emerging offbeat companies, complementing the Ted Shawn Theatre's exciting dance schedule.

Olga Dunn Dance Company, Inc.

413-528-9674
olgadunndance.org
46 Castle St., Great Barrington,
MA 01230

Since its founding in 1977, the Olga Dunn Dance Company has enjoyed such success that it spawned the Junior Company and the Olga Dunn Dance Ensemble. Performing a free mix of exuberant and witty jazz, modern, and ballet, frequently with live musicians, the company has also toured area schools, exposing children to the creativity of dance and the excitement of movement. Annual performances at its own studio, at the Berkshire Museum, and at other theaters in the tri-state area are highlights of the dance year. As Marge Champion—famed dancer and Berkshire resident—put it: "The Olga Dunn Dance Company has become the radiating center of our experience in appreciating and participating in the art of the dance."

Other dance . . .

With Jacob's Pillow bringing the world's best dancers to the Berkshires, it's not surprising that quality dance troupes would spring up throughout the county.

In **South County**, Great Barrington leads the dance. Many of the most innovative performances take place at the Daniel Arts Center at Bard College at Simon's Rock, located on Alford Road (413-644-4400. The center has been offering student/faculty dance programs in December and May that feature original music and choreography by members of the school's dance program. Laurie McLeod is an award-winning dancer, choreographer, and filmmaker who, with her company, Victory Girl Productions (413-298-3006; PO Box 141, Stockbridge, MA 01262), presents innovative works at such places as Jacob's Pillow's and MASS MoCA. Modern dancer and choreographer Dawn Lane is the program director and choreographer for the Community Access to the Arts (414-528-5485; 40 Railroad Street, Great Barrington, MA 01230). CATA is a nonprofit organization that brings visual performing arts experiences to the disabled community. There is also a flourishing country and contra dance network in the Berkshires. Check newspapers and bulletin boards for listings.

In **Central County**, Susan Dibble (413-637-1199; www.shakespeare.org) is resident choreographer for Shakespeare & Co. She also leads Dibbledance, presenting one or two weekends of dance at Shakespeare & Co.

In **North County**, the Berkshire Dance Theater (413-743-4645; 21 Maple St., Adams, MA 01220) provides instruction and performances for aspiring dancers. The dance program at the

Massachusetts College of Liberal Arts appears to be taking shape. The Fine and Performing Arts number is 413-662-5255. The Williams College Dance Department (413-597-2425), located in the '62 Center for the Theatre and Dance, sponsors an ongoing, energetic series with student and faculty choreography, and visiting notables. Chen & Dancers, a Chinese company, has been the artists-in-residence; the Chuck Davis African Dance Collective has also been seen and heard in Williamstown. Kusika and Zambezi is the college's African dance company, which accompanies itself with drumming. Other companies burst on the scene. MASS MoCA (massmoca.org; 413-662-2111; 1040 MASS MoCA Way, North Adams, MA 01247) presents numerous dance companies.

HISTORIC HOMES

Arrowhead
413-442-1793
www.mobydick.org
780 Holmes Road, Pittsfield, MA 01201
About 1.5 miles east of Route 7

In 1850, seeking to escape what he later called "the Babylonish brick-kiln of New York," Herman Melville gave in to his yearning "to feel the grass" and moved with his family to the Berkshires. By the time he arrived, Melville had already published two tales of his South Sea adventures, *Typee* and *Omoo*, earning a reputation as a man "who had lived among cannibals." Longing to be known as a great writer and fresh from a new "close acquaintance" with the "divine" writings of Shakespeare, here he took off on the grand literary whale hunt that was to become *Moby Dick*.

Arrowhead is home to the Berkshire Historical Society, which offers excellent guided tours of the house. The second-floor study is where Melville wrote his great novel, looking northward at the Mount Greylock range, its rolling form reminiscent of a giant whale. He dedicated his next novel, *Pierre*, to "Greylock's most excellent majesty." Here you'll find the implements of the writer's trade and duplicates of many important books in his library.

The other thoroughly "Melville" room is the dining room, dominated by a grand stone hearth. His brother inscribed the mantle with the opening of Melville's story, *I and My Chimney*. The house contains 19th-century period furnishings, fine arts, and textiles with Berkshire origins, several pieces of which belonged to Melville. The Ammi Phillips folk-art portraits are of particular interest. Outside, the piazza is the site of another story. The grounds include an extensive herb garden and a vintage cutting garden. Arrowhead also makes for a lovely picnic spot.

The barn behind the house is the site of cultural programs such as literary readings and historical talks. A video about Berkshire literary figures and artists takes 20 minutes. Those hungry for more Melville can visit "The Melville Room" at the Berkshire Athenaeum on Wendell Avenue, also in Pittsfield. (See the Berkshire Athenaeum entry under "Libraries" below.)

Ashintully Gardens
413-298-3239
www.thetrustees.org
Sodem Road, Tyringham, MA 01264
Follow signs from Main Road toward West Otis

Ashintully is Gaelic for "Brow of the Hill" and, indeed, the grassy terraces, fountains, statuary, and ponds descend gracefully from the pillars that remain of the "marble palace," a mansion completed in 1912. A property of The Trustees for Reservations, a state-wide group that has done well by Berkshire County.

Colonel Ashley House

413-298-3239
www.thetrustees.org
Mail: PO Box 792, Stockbridge 01262
Cooper Hill Road, Ashley Falls, MA
01222, off Route 7A

In his military role as a colonel and as a political radical, John Ashley was destined to become as prominent a citizen as Berkshire would produce in the Revolution. He began his Berkshire life as a surveyor, trudging through the woods and swamps of Sheffield and mapping the wilderness with compass and chain.

Ashley loved what he saw. By 1735, he had built a handsome home on the west bank of the Housatonic River, now the oldest extant house in Berkshire County. Framed of well-seasoned oak with chestnut rafters, it was the finest house in Sheffield. Woodworkers from across the colony came to carve paneling and to fashion the gracefully curved staircase. The craftsmanship of Ashley's study, with its broad fireplace and sunburst cupboard, inspires confidence. It was here that Ashley met with a group of his neighbors in early 1773 to draft "The Sheffield Declaration," stating to the world that all people were "equal, free and independent." They asserted their independence from Britain some three years before Thomas Jefferson and associates did so in Philadelphia. One of his slaves, Mumbet, overhearing the conversations, thought she should be free too, and approached lawyer Theodore Sedgwick, who won her case.

The house was rescued, moved a quarter mile, restored, and turned over to The Trustees of Reservations. TTOR has seen to it that the Ashley House, listed on the National Register, lives on to tell the history of the Ashley Family. An herb garden flourishes outside, while colonial furnishings, redware, and the original wood paneling survive inside. A visit can complement viewing the extraordinary flowers at Bartholomew's Cobble or antiques hunting in the Sheffield–Ashley Falls area.

The Sheffield Declaration, 1773

Resolved that Mankind in a State of Nature are equal, free and independent of each Other, and have a right to the undisturbed Enjoyment of their lives, their Liberty and Property.

Resolved that it is a well known and undoubted privilege of the British Constitution that every Subject hath . . . a Right to the free and uncontrolled injoyment and Improvement of his estate or property. . . .

Resolved that the late acts of the parlement of Great Breton expres porpos of Rating and regulating the colecting a Revenew in the Colonies: are unconstitutional as thereby the Just earning of our labours and Industry without Any Regard to our own consent are by mere power ravished from us. . . .

The Bidwell House

413-528-6888
www.bidwellhousemuseum.org
PO Box 537, 100 Art School Road,
Monterey, MA 01245
2.5 miles from town center, turn left on Art School

Located at the end of the traveled section of Art School Road, Bidwell is one of Berkshire's oldest homes, dating to 1750 and listed on the National Register. Because the center of town moved on, Bidwell is now surrounded by 196 acres of pristine Monterey woodland, looking much as it might have back in the 18th century. Two designers from New York discovered the abandoned former home of the Reverend Adonijah Bidwell in the 1960s, brought it back to fine condition, and left instructions in their wills that it continue as a museum.

An active slate of lectures, workshps, and hikes (in the fall, along historical Royal Hemlock Road) takes place.

The William Cullen Bryant Homestead
413-532-1631
www.thetrustees.org
207 Bryant Road, Cummington,
MA 01026
Off Route 9, on Route 112 in
Cummington

William Cullen Bryant was born in 1794 in a small gambrel-roofed cabin of roughhewn lumber, two miles from the frontier village of Cummington, on a farm of 465 acres. He stayed at Williams College only eight months, shortly thereafter taking up the law. From 1816 on, Cullen, as he was called, practiced law in Great Barrington, where he wrote about 30 well-respected poems on such local themes as Monument Mountain's Indian legend, the Green River, and native waterfowl. With the influence of Catherine Sedgwick's brothers, Bryant became coeditor of the *New York Review* and *Athenaeum Magazine*, editor at the *New York Evening Post* (one of America's oldest and most influential newspapers), and ultimately America's first popular and widely respected native-born poet.

Bryant returned to and added substantially to his Cummington homestead; today it has 23 rooms. Visitors should read the poems first to capture the tour's fine points. Well managed by The Trustees of Reservations; National Historic Landmark; interpretive trail.

Chesterwood
413-298-3579
www.chesterwood.org
Mail: PO Box 827, Stockbridge,
MA 01262
4 Williamsville Road, Stockbridge,
MA 01262
Off Route 183, Glendale

At age 25, Daniel Chester French was commissioned by his hometown of Concord, Massachusetts, to create his first public monument, *The Minute Man*. Its lifelike pose and exquisite sense of surface modeling won the artist national acclaim, and the statue became an American icon.

Years and scores of sculptures later, French sought a permanent country home to augment his studio in New York City. In 1896, he and his wife, Mary, were shown the old Warner Farm and Boys School in the Glendale section of Stockbridge. After taking in the magnificent vista southward, toward Monument Mountain, French pronounced it "the best dry view" he had ever seen and promptly arranged to buy the property. Thereafter, he and Mary spent half of the year in New York City, half at Chesterwood. Glendale "is heaven," he said. "New York is—well, New York."

In Glendale, he built a grand residence, studio, and garden complex, which are an enduring and eloquent tableau of his artistry. Here he created his masterpiece: the *Abraham Lincoln* statue that sits in the Lincoln Memorial in Washington, DC. "What I wanted to convey," said French, "was the mental and physical strength of the great President." Visitors are invited to handle sculpting tools in his studio. Highlights include his marble *Andromeda*, a surprisingly erotic work, and the "railway" to move his works-in-progress out into the daylight.

French designed magnificent gardens, maintained today after his fashion by the property's managers, the National Trust for Historic Preservation. The grounds host special exhibits during the season.

Samuel Harrison House

413-445-5414

samuelharrison.org

82 Third Street, Pittsfield, MA 01201

The Samuel Harrison House is newly open to the public. It was the home of the Rev. Samuel Harrison, chaplain to the Massachusetts 54th Regiment, the first all-black infantry to fight in the Civil War, and pastor of the Second Congregational Church in Pittsfield. He was active in the American abolitionist movement.

His former homestead has become the Harrison House Museum, an archive and research center on African-American history in New England. It is a site along the Upper Housatonic Valley National Heritage Area's African-American Heritage Trail.

The Merwin House

413-298-4703

www.spnea.org

14 Main Street, PO Box 72,

Stockbridge, MA 01262

Center of town

"Tranquility," a bit of 19th-century Berkshire refinement stopped in time, is the former home of Mrs. Vipont Merwin. Built around 1825, this charming brick mansion is filled with mostly Victorian antiques; furnishings and collectibles reflect global travel and domestic dignity. Merwin House is maintained as a property of the Society for the Preservation of New England Antiquities. For Stockbridge strollers, evening views through the multi-paned front windows provide an inviting glimpse of an elegant world gone by.

The Mission House

413-298-3239

www.thetrustees.org

19 Main Street, Stockbridge, MA 01262

Corner Main & Sergeant Streets

In 1735, an earnest minister from Yale College came to the Berkshire wilderness to preach to the Mahican Indians. John Sergeant learned the Indian language in which he preached two sermons every Sunday. In the springtime, he went out with the Indians to tap the maples, writing the first account in English of this sugar production method. He talked with the Indians in the back of his simple log cabin. Under Sergeant's leadership, the Stockbridge Mission flourished.

To please his wife, Abigail, the Reverend Sergeant built what is now called Mission House, high on Prospect Hill. The tall and ornate Connecticut doorway, with beautiful panels, was carved in Westfield, Massachusetts, and dragged by oxen 50 miles over rugged terrain to Stockbridge. This front door and the front rooms were Abigail's domain; in the back, a separate entry and long corridor allowed the Indians access to Sergeant's study.

When he died in 1749, the days of the Stockbridge Mission were numbered, too, although eminent theologian Jonathan Edwards succeeded him. By 1785, the Indians had been displaced from Stockbridge, driven out for the most part by land speculators.

In 1927, Mabel Choate—the art collector and philanthropist who was heir to Naumkeag—acquired the Mission House. She moved it to its present Main Street location, near the site of John Sergeant's first log cabin. Boston landscape architect Fletcher Steele, who had designed the gardens at Naumkeag, planted an orderly, symmetrical 18th-century herb, flower, and fruit garden beside the restored and relocated Mission House. Today apple and quince trees; herbs such as lamb's ear, rue, and southern wood fern; bright flowers; a grape arbor; and a "salet garden," filled with garden greens, greet visitors.

The Trustees of Reservations maintains Mission House, which is a National Historic Landmark. Tours of the house capture the 18th century's furnishings, kitchen implements, and the feeling of humble domesticity that gathered around the dominant central hearth. An adjoining museum focuses on Native Americans.

The Mount

(413) 551-5111
www.edithwharton.org
2 Plunkett Street, Box 974,
Lenox, MA 01240
Near southern junction of Routes 7 & 7A

It is amazing what a difference a few million dollars make. With federal money and match, the building has been repaired. Even more spectacular is the restoration of the grounds.

In February 1901, writer and heiress Edith Wharton arrived at the Curtis Hotel in Lenox for a week in the country. She had summered in the area for the preceding two years and now, having found the "watering place trivialities of Newport" all but intolerable, sought a new site on which to realize the design principles incorporated in her book, *The Decoration of Houses*. The Georgian Revival house she built was modeled on Christopher Wren's Belton House in Lincolnshire, England. At first Wharton retained as architect her associate, Ogden Codman. When his design fees grew exorbitant, she called on Francis L.V. Hoppin to complete the job.

Wharton supervised creation of the gardens, orchards, and buildings while finishing her novel *Disintegration,* writing as always in bed and tossing the pages on the floor for the staff to assemble. The Mount, elegant throughout, boasts marble floors and fireplaces and originally required 12 resident servants. Besides the 14 horses in their stables, the Whartons owned one of the earliest motorcars, a convenience that thrilled the visiting Henry James. In the fall of 1904, James and Wharton motored through Berkshire's autumnal splendor daily, enjoying social afternoons and evenings with visiting sophisticates.

"The Mount was to give me country cares and joys," she wrote, "long happy rides, and drives through the wooded lanes of that loveliest region, the companionship of a few dear friends, and the freedom from trivial obligations which was necessary if I was to go on with my writing. The Mount was my first real home . . . and its blessed influence still lives in me."

Happily, its blessed influence lives on for the public as its physical and spiritual restoration continue. The National Trust for Historic Preservation bought the Mount to save it from commercial exploitation; the Edith Wharton Restoration, Inc., manages the house.

Naumkeag

In-season (June 1–Oct.13): 413-298-8138; Off-season (Oct.14–May 30): 413-298-3239 x3013
www.thetrustees.org
5 Prospect Hill Road, Box 792,
Stockbridge, MA 01262

During the Gilded Age of the late 19th century, men and women of power played out their fantasies in Berkshire, dotting the hillsides with dream houses. A most livable example is the mansion of illustrious lawyer Joseph Choate, the summer "cottage" that the Choate family came to call *Naumkeag* (a Native American name for Salem, where Choate was born). Here, Choate found both a retreat from New York City life as well as an enclave of great legal minds in Supreme Court justices Field, Brewer, and Brown—all Stockbridge contemporaries.

Choate bought the property from David Dudley Field in 1884 and began construction. By the autumn of 1886, the 44-room, shingled, gabled, and dormered Norman-style house was complete, with architectural design by McKim, Mead & White and imaginative gardens by the landscaping pioneer Nathaniel Barrett.

The house eventually came into the hands of Choate's daughter, Mable, who maintained it while adding extensively to the gardens under the direction of landscape architect Fletcher Steele. The Fountain Steps, framed by birches; the Afternoon Garden, an outdoor room; farther southward, the Chinese Pagoda and Linden Walk; uphill, the brick-walled Chinese Garden, mosses and stone Buddhas gathered with carved lions and dogs, all shaded by ginkos; to the north, the topiary of the Evergreen Garden and the fragrance and color of the Rose Garden—all reflect decades of inspired and distinctive garden design.

Now held by The Trustees of Reservations, Naumkeag still includes its gardens, furnishings, and an extraordinary porcelain collection, much of it from the Far East. The tours are excellent.

Searles Castle
413-528-9800
389 Main Street, Great Barrington, MA 01230

When Mark Hopkins, a founder and treasurer of the Central Pacific Railroad, died, his widow, Mary, consoled herself with the creation of a grand home in Great Barrington. Stanford White designed this 40-room castle, which was constructed between 1882 and 1887 using locally cut blue dolomite stone. Upon its completion, Mary Hopkins married her interior decorator, Edward Searles, a man 20 years her junior. Searles had spared no expense on the castle's interior. Many of the major rooms feature massive carved wood or marble fireplaces, each unique. More than 100 of the world's best artisans and craftsmen were brought on site to work with oak carvings, marble statues, atriums, columns, and pillars. The bills totaled $2.5 million.

The castle now serves as the home of the John Dewey Academy, a residential therapeutic prep school. In 1982, Searles Castle was added to the National Register of Historic Places. Usually closed to the public, the building and grounds are visible to pedestrians walking along Main Street. Several times a year—for an Antiquarian Book Fair, for the Stockbridge Chamber Concerts, and for other special events—Searles Castle is open to the public and well worth a visit.

Ventfort Hall
413-637-3206
www.gilde
104 Walker Street, PO Box 2424, Lenox, MA 01240

This Berkshire cottage's Elizabethan Revival style was already out-of-date when George and Sarah Morgan built their summer home in 1893, but it's fun to imagine the life lived within. For those who need more visual stimulus, Ventfort served as the set for the orphanage in the 1999 movie *The Cider*

House Rules. Unlike the other cottages open for our inspection, Ventfort aims to be a museum of the Gilded Age.

Sarah, sister of J. Pierpont Morgan, kept her last name by marrying a cousin. Their Boston architects Rotch & Tilden designed four other homes nearby in Lenox—all different from this one. Placed on the site of a home originally built and named by Ogden Haggerty, "Strong Wind" was for four years home to the Whitneys, who gave the land for October Mountain State Forest. But it paled in comparison to the new Morgan home of "15 bedrooms, 13 bathrooms, and 17 fireplaces." Built perhaps too quickly, the brickwork has sadly decomposed.

Sarah Morgan died soon after it was completed, and the building passed through a number of owners, both private and institutional, until a proposed nursing home threatened "structure-cide" by wrecking ball in 1990. In 1997, local residents joined to form the Ventfort Hall Association and, with a loan from the National Trust for Historic Preservation, purchased the building and the remaining 11.7 acres of grounds. Further state grants and private funds began the daunting preservation work—on the interior, with the skilled assistance of joiner Michael Costerisan, who meticulously pieced together tattered paneling. With none of the original furnishings available, to become a period museum will require a lot more money and a lot more time.

LIBRARIES

Berkshire Athenaeum
413-499-9480
www.pittsfieldlibrary.org
One Wendell Avenue, Pittsfield, MA 01201
The former Berkshire Athenaeum is a 19th-century specimen of the Venetian Gothic style, constructed next to the courthouse on Pittsfield's handsome Park Square. Built of Berkshire deep-blue dolomite (a limestone) from Great Barrington, along with red sandstone from Longmeadow, Massachusetts, and red granite from Missouri, this Athenaeum, once Berkshire's central library, now serves as Pittsfield's courts and registry of deeds.

The new Athenaeum is the three-level brick and glass facility next door featuring a tall and airy reading room with natural clerestory lighting. An outdoor reading terrace serves adults and another serves children. Parking is limited.

There is an outstanding dance collection, a Local Authors' Room, and a Local History Room. The jewel of the Athenaeum is its Herman Melville Room: a trove of Melville memorabilia, from carved scrimshaw depicting the terror of the Great White Whale to first editions of the author's works. Here are *Moby-Dicks* in Japanese; autographed letters from Melville; photos of his Pittsfield farm, Arrowhead (described under "Historic Homes," above), and the desk on which he wrote his last, haunting work, *Billy Budd*.

Chapin Library of Rare Books
413-597-2462
chapin.williams.edu
Chapin Library, Williams College, 26 Hopkins Hall Drive, Williamstown, MA 01267
On the 2nd floor of Stetson Hall, Williams College
Chapin Library has one of the most well-rounded collections of rare books and manuscripts anywhere. On permanent display are the four founding documents of this country: *The Declaration*

of Independence, originally owned by a member of the Continental Congress; *The Articles of Confederation and Perpetual Union; The Constitution of the United States*, annotated by George Mason; and two copies of the *Bill of Rights*. The library also owns General Greene's handwritten order for boats to cross the Delaware. Every July Fourth, actors from the Williamstown Theatre Festival read the Declaration and the British Reply.

In 1923 Alfred Clark Chapin—Williams class of 1869 and mayor of Brooklyn—presented his alma mater with his magnificent library of first editions and manuscripts, specializing in historic literary and artistic master works. Other alumni have subsequently given their collections.

The literary holdings include a Shakespeare First Folio and first editions of Pope, Swift, Fielding, Defoe, Richardson, Sterne, Johnson, Scott, Byron, Burns, Browning, Keats, Shelley, Thackeray, and Dickens. There is also a fine T. S. Eliot collection. Representing American literature are first editions by such writers as Crane, Melville, Whitman, and Faulkner. Tycho Brahe's *Astronomia* (1602), Harvey's *Anatomical Exercitations* (1653), Darwin's *Origins of the Species* (1859), and a double elephant folio of Audubon's *Birds of America* represent scientific endeavors.

Lenox Library

413-637-0197
www.lenoxlib.org
18 Main Street, Lenox, MA 01240

Built in 1815 as the Berkshire County Courthouse, when Lenox was still the "shire town," this classic Greek-Revival building became the Lenox Library Association in 1873. It is listed on the National Register of Historic Places.

Readers can enjoy the main reading room, with its lofty illuminated ceiling and its amazing array of periodicals, or the outdoor reading park. This is Old World reading at its best. A solid collection of about 75,000 volumes, plus a music room, are available to the public. There is a closed collection of historical memorabilia, too, including the sled from the incident on which Edith Wharton based her novella *Ethan Frome*.

Recent renovations have increased space for young people and computers, and uncovered the domed ceiling that arched over the original courtroom.

Milne Public Library

413-458-5369
www.milnelibrary.org
1095 Main Street, Williamstown, MA 01267

Williamstown is proud that a treasured resource has a roomy home—a former school with ample parking. With strong holdings of children's books, fiction, local history, videos, and popular music, the public library complements the Sawyer Library (below). Comfortable areas for reading and a helpful staff. A former tenant, the Williamstown Historical Museum, is moving to the Little Red Schoolhouse in South Williamstown. The library exhibits area artists and offers frequent programs.

North Adams Public Library

413-662-3133
www.NAPLibrary.com
74 Church Street, North Adams, MA 01247

Sanford Blackinton built a marvelous mansion in 1867. Although the first mayor of North Adams, Albert C. Houghton, purchased it and donated it to the city for a library in 1896, no fundamental changes were made to the building until 2004, when it was totally refurbished and expanded to create a modern library that nevertheless meticulously maintained the aura of the original. As former librarian Marcia Gross says, the library "is the community's living room." Private citizens who raised over $1 million of the $4.3 million are honored in the brick walkways and via a stained glass window. Furthermore, this green building manufactures much of its electricity through solar panels on the roof and is largely heated and cooled through geothermal wells, so that its utility costs are minimal. An elegant setting for an up-to-date, working library.

Sawyer Library

413-597-2501
sawyerlibrary.williams.edu
26 Hopkins Hall Drive, Williamstown, MA 01267
Center of Williams College campus

Added on to the old Stetson, the new Sawyer—with 900,000-plus volumes, 1,600 periodicals in paper, 10,000-plus electronic texts, 500,000 micro texts, 29,000 sound recordings (including the Paul Whiteman Collection), 9,000 videos, and 430,000 Federal documents—is an unmatched resource. Here we find a wide array of the latest periodicals, shelves of newly released books, and a library staff as helpful as they come. The public may use the facility, the stacks are open, and Sawyer is a pleasant place in which to work. The Schow Science Library, in the science quadrangle across Route 2, is state of the art; all titles are included in Francis, the online catalog.

Simon's Rock Library

413-528-7370
simons-rock.edu/student-life/
campus-experience/alumni-library/
84 Alford Road, Simon's Rock, Great Barrington, MA 01230

The Simon's Rock Library is one of the best in South County, the staff always attentive to one's research needs. The college it serves may be small, but this library's holdings are exceedingly well chosen. It is open to visitors and to all Berkshire County residents who obtain a library card. This is a library of half a dozen rooms on two floors in three interconnected pagoda-style buildings—all in a sylvan setting. With large skylights, the reading rooms are highly recommended for naturally lit, wet-weather browsing. Fascinating art exhibits almost always grace the library's sky-lighted gallery.

Stockbridge Library and Historical Room

413-298-5501
stockbridgelibrary.org
Mail: PO Box 119, Stockbridge, MA 01262
Main Street (Route 7)

Parts of the Stockbridge Library date to 1864, and the reading room is one of the most felicitous anywhere—tall, stately, and obviously from another era. The children's collection is also first-rate.

Called *W-nahk-ta-kook* ("Great Meadow") by the Mohican Indians who settled there, the town of Stockbridge was incorporated by the English in 1739. The colonial charter made the town Indian property, a mission, and so it was known as "Indian Town." The history of this great meadow and its town is displayed and explained in the Stockbridge Historical Room, a small museum in the basement of the library. Here are Indian artifacts, photos from the mid-1800s onward, memorabilia from many famous residents and visitors to the village, and other intriguing historical bits that illuminate Stockbridge's present.

MUSEUMS

The Berkshire Museum

413-443-7171
www.berkshiremuseum.org
39 South Street (Route 7), Pittsfield, MA 01201

Three museums in one, the Berkshire Museum presents strong collections of art, science, and regional history as well as an exciting calendar of lectures, films, concerts, classes, and field trips.

Founded in 1903 by Dalton paper maker and philanthropist Zenas Crane, the museum shows Hudson River School paintings, the Proctor Shell Collection, and the Cohn Collection of Minerals. Changing exhibits are featured throughout the year. The collections are far ranging: 19th-century glass made in the towns of Berkshire and Cheshire and pre-Christian glass bottles from Egypt; exhibits of shells and aquatic life, fossils, mushrooms, reptiles, and amphibians. The Bird Room has a special section on Berkshire birds; the owl exhibit especially captivates. The Berkshire Backyard presents native mammal specimens. A collection of beautiful dioramas by Louis Paul Jonas, Sr., shows the animals of the world in one-tenth scale. An aquarium holds more than 100 species, featuring a hands-on exhibit for children called "Touch of the Sea." The Feigenbaum Hall of Innovation highlights technical inventions made in the Berkshires.

The exhibits and numerous programs demonstrate that the museum is committed to families and community. The life-size stegosaurus (named Wally) on the museum's front lawn is a community landmark. The Museum Theater, a 300-seat facility, is site for lectures, plays, concerts, and the Little Cinema's admirable program of feature films.

Upstairs, works of Copley, Stuart, and Peale represent American portraiture. The Hudson River School appears in works by Cole, Inness, and others. A European gallery is devoted to the work of such English portrait painters as West and Reynolds, plus European works by masters spanning the 15th to 18th centuries. In the museum's center is the lofty and skylighted Ellen Crane Memorial Room, devoted to American and European sculpture from the 19th and 20th centuries.

Sterling and Francine Clark Art Institute

413-458-2303, 413-458-9545
www.clarkart.edu
225 South Street, Williamstown, MA 01267
One mile south of the junction of Routes 7 and 2

Sterling Clark acquired his first Renoir in 1916. By the time he was finished collecting, he owned 36. He and his French wife, Francine, bought what they liked—the basis of this fine collection reflects their personal taste. Included with Impressionists are galleries filled with 19th-century American classics—by Winslow Homer, John Singer Sargent, and Frederick Remington—and a small but impressive collection of Old Masters. Traveling exhibits of Renoir, Degas, Millet, Whistler, and Van Gogh have attracted large summer crowds.

The original 1950s building is elegant and efficient, a white Vermont-marble neoclassic structure whose interior is finished in Italian marble, plaster, and natural-finish oak. The large 1973 red-granite addition houses more galleries and a serious art library. Substantial remodeling in 1996 added more galleries, storage, and a café. Next came the Stone Hill Center, which houses exhibits and the art conservation laboratory. Completed in 2014, the Clark Center, provides additional exhibition space, while the reflecting pools reflect the ponds previously on the site. The museum shop includes an extensive collection of art books.

For most visitors, the centerpiece of the museum's collection is its gathering of French Impressionists, the Clarks' greatest artistic love. Among the standouts, besides Renoir, are works by Monet and Degas, the latter in both his racehorse and ballet dancer series. Almost every gallery has some form of natural light; many galleries offer not only splendid art on the walls, but peaceful views of the Berkshire Hills. A well-crafted and marked trail system guides the visitor outside the buildings (see Stone Hill hike, above).

The Clark is more than a painting gallery, however. As we walk among its colorful masterworks and their accompanying drawings and prints, we also see some of the collection's antique furniture and silver, masterpieces of craftsmanship. A piano as artwork may be the Clark's most controversial acquisition.

Serving as an important art education center, the Clark offers a broad spectrum of lectures open to the public, serving as classroom to a graduate program in art history run jointly with Williams College. The Clark also offers major events in connection with its exhibits: chamber music, video film programs, folk music, children's programs, and popular outdoor band concerts in the summer.

Frelinghuysen Morris House & Studio
413-637-0166
www.frelinghuysen.org
92 Hawthorne Street, Lenox, MA 01240

Anyone interested in art, architecture, or art history might be intrigued by a tour of the home and studio of George L. K. Morris and his wife, Suzy Frelinghuysen, artists and advocates of the *avant-garde*. On exhibit are his and her framed works and murals, along with a smattering of Matisse, Degas, Picasso, Braque, Leger, and Gris. A large earth mother by Gaston Lachaise reclines among the trees on the 46 wooded acres that stretch between Hawthorne Street and Route 183, adjacent to Tanglewood.

Morris built his studio on the grounds in 1930, then added the ample Corbusier-style home in 1940—to the chagrin of Berkshire's traditionally housed residents. Morris, descended from a signer of the Declaration of Independence, died in an automobile accident in 1975. Frelinhuysen, who came from a line of Dutch-Reform clergymen, college presidents, and politicians, survived the accident, living until 1988.

Hancock Shaker Village
413-443-0188, (800) 817-1137
www.hancockshakervillage.org
Mail: PO Box 927, Pittsfield, MA 01202
1843 West Housatonic Street,
Pittsfield, MA 01201
Junction of Routes 20 and 41, 6 miles west of Pittsfield.

The United Society of Believers in Christ's Second Appearing, later called Shakers, were founded in England in 1747 as a small group of religious nonconformists. Ann Lee, a young woman with strong religious convictions, became their spiritual leader. In 1774, a small group joined "Mother Ann" in sailing for the New World. They landed in New York, near Albany, where they later formed the Shaker community of Niskeyuna.

Shaker religion was a way of life. Members joined into distinct communities isolated from the outside world. Men and women held equal status in daily life and leadership positions, but the genders were separated to support the Shaker commitment to celibacy. Communities were organized into families. Members gave public confession of their sins. Ritual dancing gave rise to their name, which was originally derisive, but later adopted by the sect.

A community was established in 1790 at Hancock. Given the spiritual name of the City of Peace, it prospered for more than 150 years. Residents sought heavenly perfection, resulting in products that came to be known for their beauty. Design of clothing, furniture, implements, and buildings was strictly functional, without addition of deliberate ornamentation. Simplicity was a primary aim of both inner and outer life. Their credo: "Beauty rests on utility." Of great beauty, then, is Hancock's symbol, the stunning Round Stone Barn. As splendid as the structure is to the eye, it's even more splendid that with such efficient architecture, one farmhand at the center could easily and quickly feed an entire herd of cattle.

When the sect was at its peak in the mid-19th century, Hancock was one of 18 Shaker communities from Maine to Kentucky and had a population of about 300 members. The agricultural base of the village was augmented by cottage industries, offering such items as copperware, flat brooms, agricultural seeds, and dairy products to sell to the World's People. But as religious ferment ceased, the Shaker population at Hancock declined steadily until 1960, when the last of the Hancock Shakers moved away.

Since then, the village and its 1,200 acres of meadows and woodlands have been a living museum to accommodate visitors who want taste of the Shaker ways. The City of Peace now acts as center of re-created Shaker activities, with workshops, candlelit dinners, and evening tours.

Visitors can tour 20 original Shaker buildings to see Shaker furniture and tools, some of them attended by craftspeople working in the Shaker way: the chair maker, the blacksmith, basket makers, spinners, and weavers. Hancock's workshops teach visitors how to create Shaker chair seats, oval boxes, natural herb wreaths, and a variety of other crafts. From the gardens, both herbal and vegetable, and from any of the village workers, visitors absorb the power of Shaker simplicity.

Always a destination for families, the replica of a circa-1820 schoolhouse—complete with a teacher, in season, as well as the discovery room, and the Center for Shaker Studies, make the museum even more appealing. With a new parking lot and entrance, together with space for rotating exhibits and programs, the village nevertheless continues into the future. Enter through a new visitors' center, which features films on Shaker life. (A hike, described above, begins on Shaker land.)

Massachusetts Museum of Contemporary Art (MASS MoCA)

413-662-2111

www.massmoca.org

1040 MASS MoCA Way, North Adams, MA 01247

For 12 years, director Joe Thompson hung on by his fingernails to the idea of a big museum in an old mill—until the Massachusetts Museum of Contemporary Art (MASS MoCA) opened to critical and public success in the summer of 1999. Far more visitors than expected streamed into the "supercollider for the best of today's visual, performing, and new media arts," as Thompson defines his 13-acre, 200,000 square feet of buildings and factory campus. "Until now," he explains, "large complex art forms—exotic multimedia productions, for example, or monumental installations—have been without a public forum that is striking, properly scaled, and technically wired for cross-disciplinary collaborations."

Although the art may not be for everyone—including gigantic to minimalist works by Rauschenberg, Rosenquist, Flavin, Nauman, and Morris—visitors have responded to the gorgeous retrofitting of hanger-like spaces in this former textile mill. However, it was probably the accompanying variety of special events that made the opening summer and fall such a huge success: "Swing Shift Dance Parties," "Film Factory" with outside projection, dance performances by the Paul Taylor Dance Company and others, concerts, and a musical, "Quark Victory," put on by the Williamstown Theatre Festival. Sol LeWitt's linear designs found a place of their own. Special music festivals, such as those conducted by Bang on a Can and Wilco, attract major crowds.

North Adams, done up in banners and flowers, new streetlights, and new signage, looks, improbably, like a city being lifted up and uplifted by art. With MASS MoCA at its heart, the city itself may be the ultimate "large complex art form" on view to thousands of visitors from around the world. As the museum changes and evolves, we shall see what they shall see.

Norman Rockwell Museum

413-298-4100
www.nrm.org
Mail: PO Box 308, Stockbridge, MA 01262
9 Route 183, Stockbridge, MA 01262
0.6 mile south of Route 102

Norman Rockwell is coming to be seen more as artist than illustrator; the display of his life's work at the Norman Rockwell Museum resonates. A visit to this grand monument to his talent and insight is worth the crush of bus passengers—or go off-season.

Set on a gracious knoll overlooking the Housatonic River in the Glendale section of Stockbridge, the $4.4-million building designed by Robert A. M. Stern has a New England town hall look to it, with slate gables, clapboard siding, and fieldstone terraces. Inside, spacious, well-lit galleries show permanent exhibits of Rockwell's paintings, while changing exhibits feature Rockwell and other illustrators.

At the core is the sky-lighted gallery where Rockwell's *Four Freedoms* hang on permanent display. Created during the Second World War, they depict what the U.S. was fighting to uphold: *Freedom of Speech; Freedom from Fear; Freedom of Worship; Freedom from Want.* These four archetypal American images constitute a shrine to America's progressive image of itself.

Rockwell's 47-year relationship with the *Saturday Evening Post* is well known; in 1963, it ended, and he signed on with *Look* and *McCall's.* His palette and cast of characters broadened. Where once he depicted white boys running from a prohibited swimming hole, now federal marshals lead a young black girl to school in Little Rock. From lovers and gossips, he moved on to Peace Corps volunteers and astronauts on the moon.

Outside stands Rockwell's studio, a 19th-century carriage house with a bucolic view of the Housatonic. Inside the studio, which was moved from Stockbridge village to its present site in 1986, we understand the light in which he loved to paint, the curious assemblage of props with which he liked to surround himself, and the modest space he felt was his "best studio yet."

The Rockwell Museum offers a variety of community-oriented programs beyond its public exhibitions, including lectures, performances, special events, and art classes.

Western Gateway Heritage State Park

413-663-6312
115 State Street, Building 4, North Adams, MA 01247-3852

Berkshire County, nestled between long ridges, had always been separated from the rest of Massachusetts. In 1851, engineers and construction workers began an assault, drilling and blasting a 4.75-mile-long tunnel through the northeastern ridge. This Hoosac Tunnel was the first major tunneling in the United States. New methods were devised over the 20-year construction, at a cost of over $20 million and more than 195 lives. The building of the tunnel and related railroad development made North Adams the largest city in Berkshire in 1900. "We hold the Western Gateway," says the North Adams seal. At the turn of the 20th century, more than half of Boston's freight came through the tunnel.

Western Gateway Heritage State Park now celebrates the former Boston and Maine Freight House and the Hoosac Tunnel, both of which are on the National Register of Historic Places. Inside, films, slide shows, and written histories of the railway and tunnel are presented. Outside are shops, the restored freight yard, the Freight Yard Pub restaurant, and the church-spired charm of North Adams. What are now the Pan Am Southern Railways freight trains continue to roll by.

Heritage State Park is also home to the North Adams Museum of History & Science (413-664-4700; www.northa dams.com/history; Building 5-A). An old-fashioned museum of 25 exhibits, discovery room, and working train models chronicles the history of and achievements related to North Adams and Northern Berkshire.

Williams College Museum of Art

413-597-2429
wcma.williams.edu
15 Lawrence Hall Drive, Suite 2, Williamstown, MA 01267
Route 2, across from Gothic chapel

One of the finest college art museums in the country, the Williams College Museum of Art is a 19th-century structure that has been strikingly revisited. Behind the original 1846 building, with its neoclassical octagonal rotunda, is an addition designed by Charles Moore that opened in 1983. Combining wit and sophistication, Moore created a versatile, multilevel exhibition space in both old and new buildings, retaining the brick wall of the former as the stunning backdrop for a multilevel stair well. His design for the building's rear facade is a continuation of his light-hearted approach, featuring his "ironic columns"—their nonfunctionality revealed by the gap near the top. Now the eyes have it in front—as a result of a searching and striking piece commissioned from Louise Bourgeois.

Inside, the museum's permanent collection contains some 11,000 objects. Complementing the Clark's collection of 19th-century European art, WCMA emphasizes early art, 20th-century art, and the art of Asia and other non-western civilizations. Thanks to a $32 million gift by the widow of American Impressionist Charles Prendergast, what was once a small, regional museum now houses the finest collection by both Charles and his talented brother, Maurice, and has become the leading center in the world for study of the Prendergasts' work.

A lively education program includes school events and other events for children. Several times a year WCMA hosts popular free "family days," when children can try a range of art projects thematically linked to the collection, guided by enthusiastic Williams students. Frequent loan exhibitions focus on a wide range of provocative subjects. Visitors should expect to be engaged, though not necessarily soothed.

Other museums ...

As of this writing, the Williamstown Historical Museum (413-458-2160) is contemplating a move from the Milne Library to the Little Red Schoolhouse, located at the junction of Routes 7 and 43 in South Williamstown. It contains memorabilia of the town, artfully displayed. Other museums in Williamstown move in other directions, such as the Hopkins Forest Museum (413-458-3080; Hopkins Memorial Forest, the Rosenberg Center, and Buxton Garden; North-west Hill Road), which offers seasonal events such as fall harvest and maple sugaring, while the museum itself exhibits old photographs, farm machinery, and tools. The 19th-century fieldstone Hopkins Observatory (413-597-2188; Main Street) projects sky shows at the Milham Planetarium and, weather permitting, offers stargazing through telescopes.

MUSIC

Aston Magna

413-528-3595, 888-492-1283 (box office)
www.astonmagna.org
323 Main Street, PO Box 28, Great Barrington, MA 01230

Of historic preservation in the Berkshires, none is more artistic than the renaissance of Baroque, Classical, and early Romantic chamber music by Aston Magna. Offering unique cross-disciplinary educational programs for professional musicians and superb concerts in the summer and at other times, Aston Magna has specialized in 17th-, 18th-, and early 19th-century music, always played on period instruments or reproductions. In recent summers, Mozart, Haydn, Bach, Handel, Vivaldi, Monteverdi, and Corelli have been played as in their own time, with festival artistic director and virtuoso violinist Daniel Stepner leading a distinguished roster of singers and instrumentalists. Participants study the temperament and cultural milieu of the age and then make music that is imbued with the period's sensibility.

Berkshire Choral Festival

413-229-1999 (box office);
administration 413-229-8526;
fax 413-229-0109
www.berkshirechoral.org

Mail: 245 North Undermountain Road, Sheffield, MA 01257

Performances: Concert Shed, Berkshire School, Route 41, Sheffield

An experiment in mixing amateur, semipro, and professional singers into a chorus culminated in a single concert. More than 30 years later, the Berkshire Choral Festival has evolved into a summer-long, professional-quality chorus—changing with each performance—that can be counted on for stirring moments, as in the *Mass in B-minor*.

Each summer now brings a five-concert Berkshire celebration featuring 200 adult, amateur voices from all over the world, powerful soloists and conductors, and the Springfield Symphony, at one of the loveliest preparatory schools in New England, The Berkshire School. These performances are also given at other venues around the world.

Berkshire Opera Festival

www.berkshireoperafestival.org.

From the website: "We are Berkshire Opera Festival (BOF), a fully producing summer festival opening in 2016. Adhering to the highest standards of artistic excellence, we are committed to restoring fully staged opera to a place of prominence in the Berkshire community. Each summer, we will present musically and dramatically compelling operatic productions, in addition to recitals and other related musical events.

We believe that opera is a living, breathing, relevant art form, and must be nurtured as such in order for it to survive and thrive. There is no substitute for experiencing the power of the live, unamplified human voice in a theater, and opera has the inherent, transformative ability to enhance one's quality of life. These are the reasons we are dedicated to bringing opera back to the Berkshires."

South Mountain Concerts

413-442-2106

www.southmountainconcerts.org

Mail: PO Box 23, Pittsfield, MA 01202

On Routes 7 & 20 about 1 mile south of Pittsfield Country Club

South Mountain's colonial-style Temple of Music, built in 1918 and the gift of Mrs. Elizabeth Sprague Coolidge, was intended to house the concerts of the Berkshire String Quartet. The acoustically splendid 450-seat auditorium, listed on the National Register of Historic Places, is set gracefully on its wooded South Mountain slope.

Distinguished performers have always made South Mountain a special place. In recent years, string quartets have led the fare—the Guarneri, the Juilliard, the Emerson, and the Tokyo String Quartets have been regular performers. Usually one concert each season features another combination, such as the Kalichstein-Loredo-Robinson Trio.

With a devoted subscription membership, South Mountain Concerts almost always sell out. Nonsubscribers should call early for seats. Fortunately, every seat is good because of the acoustics.

Unlike Tanglewood, where listening to the music is rivaled by watching the stars or basking in the sunshine, South Mountain's more limited season and number of concerts are designed for the serious music lover.

Tanglewood

Tickets/information: 888-266-1200;
concert line, 413-637-1666;
administration, 413-637-1600

www.bso.org

297 West Street, Lenox, MA 01240
On Route 183
Off-season: 617-266-1492;
301 Massachusetts Avenue, Boston,
MA 02115

Tanglewood remains *the* summer music festival in New England, an incomparable facility for all the world's musicians and music lovers. Whether you picnic on the lawn or sit closer to the Boston Symphony Orchestra in the Shed, hearing music at Tanglewood is an unparalleled experience. The powerful goodwill among musicians, students, and concertgoers alike, and the sheer fun of seeing and hearing great music made in the great outdoors makes Tanglewood the quintessential Berkshire entertainment—even if some people start repacking their picnic baskets during the Chorale in Beethoven's *Ninth*.

Tanglewood began as the Berkshire Music Festival in the summer of 1934. Members of the New York Philharmonic were bused from Manhattan to the mountains and lodged in the area's hotels for the concert series. A rousing success, it was repeated the following summer. But then the New York orchestra withdrew. As a result, Serge Koussevitzky, the Russian-born conductor of the Boston Symphony Orchestra, was wooed and won. The BSO signed on for a series of three concerts on a single August weekend in 1936.

The popularity of this series was immense, with nearly 15,000 people attending. That fall the Tappen family gave their Tanglewood estate on the Stockbridge-Lenox border to the BSO as a permanent summer home in the Berkshires. For the first two summers, concerts were held in a large canvas tent, but during one 1937 program, a tor-rential thunderstorm drowned out Wagner's "The Ride of the Valkyries" and dampened instruments, musicians, and audience alike. During intermission, an impromptu fund-raising drive raised pledges totaling $30,000 for the creation of a permanent "music pavilion." By the following summer, through the combined efforts of the distinguished architect Eliel Saarinen and Stockbridge engineer Joseph Franz, the Shed was a reality.

Sensing the opportunity and the ideal setting, Koussevitzky and the BSO added the Berkshire Music Center for advanced musicians in 1940, the only such school run by a major symphony orchestra. For the school's opening ceremony, Randall Thompson composed his haunting *Alleluia* for unaccompanied chorus, a work that made such a lasting impression that it has been performed as the school's opening music ever since.

Each summer the Tanglewood Music Center Orchestra is recreated from that year's crop of students; for their weekly concerts, this impressive group is usually led by a student conductor, but sometimes by the likes of Kurt Masur, Zubin Mehta, or André Previn. So significant is this Tanglewood education that upwards of 20 percent of the members of America's major orchestras count themselves among Tanglewood Music Center alumni. Leonard Bernstein was a graduate, as are Seiji Ozawa and Mr. Mehta.

The $10 million arched Ozawa Hall opened in the summer of 1994. Accommodating 1,200 inside and an additional 700 on nearby lawns, the new hall has sides that open, giving it flexibility and versatility as well as excellent acoustics. The hall is located on the

Highwood section of Tanglewood, now designated as the Leonard Bernstein campus.

The Music Festival has evolved into a performance center of major proportions, with an annual attendance of some 300,000 visitors. Pianists Emanuel Ax and Peter Serkin, violinist Itzhak Perlman, cellist Yo-Yo Ma, and the Juilliard String Quartet return regularly. In addition to the regular BSO concerts, Tanglewood presents weekly chamber music concerts in the smaller sheds, Prelude Concerts on Friday nights, open rehearsals on Saturday mornings, the annual Festival of Contemporary Music, the annual Jazz Festival, and almost daily concerts by gifted young musicians at the Music Center. Some student concerts are free. The Boston Pops comes to play, as well.

A favorite of each season is "Tanglewood on Parade," an amazingly varied musical day lasting some ten hours, climaxing with booming cannon shots and fireworks. But whatever the scale of the offerings, an evening at Tanglewood marks a high point in any summer.

Not content to satisfy the classical music lover, Tanglewood offers mini-festivals and series featuring contemporary, jazz, and popular music. Recent offerings in the Contemporary Music Festival have been an appropriately eclectic mix, including a performance by puppets. Artistry of an even jazzier sort is showcased during Tanglewood's annual Jazz Festival, with the likes of Branford Marsalis, Dave Brubeck, and the New Black Eagle Jazz band; and songs of a slightly different sort are featured during Tanglewood's Popular Artist Series, frequently including the always-popular James Taylor and a live broadcast of NPR's *A Prairie Home Companion*.

Other music...

In **South County**, the Berkshire Bach Society (413-528-9277; berkshirebach .org; PO Box 1002, Great Barrington, MA 01230) offers a fine series of concerts and lectures at various area churches, schools, and colleges. Bard's College at Simon's Rock (413-528-9277 84 Alford Rd., Simon's Rock, Great Barrington, MA 01230) is one of the liveliest promoters of professional music in South County. Close Encounters with Music (518-392-6677, 800-843-0778; PO Box 34, Great Barrington 01230) offers beautiful music and intriguing commentary by artistic director Yehuda Hanani and guests at Great Barrington's St. James Church and elsewhere. The Curtisville Consortium (413-637-1744; www.curtis ville.org) takes its name from the hamlet of Interlaken in Stockbridge, which was originally settled as Curtisville. The consortium is a group of Boston Symphony Orchestra musicians and guest artists who present a five-week-long series of concerts each summer at Ventfort Hall. Stockbridge Chamber Concerts (888-528-7728; P.O. 164, Stockbridge 01262) offers a summer series in Searles Castle.

In **Central County**, chamber music can also be enjoyed at the Richmond Performance Series (413-698-2837; PO Box 199, Richmond 01254). Each of these concerts—performed at the Richmond Congregational Church, Route 41, and other venues—features professional symphony orchestra veterans making intimate music in special settings. Berkshire Community College (413-499-4660; www.berkshirecc.edu; 1350 West Street, Pittsfield 01201) offers concerts year-round. The Berkshire Lyric Theatre (413-499-0258; www.berkshirelyricinfo.org; PO Box 347, Pittsfield 01202) plays at Lenox Town Hall and in Central and South County churches. The Berkshire Concert Choir (413-442-6120; www.berkshireconcertchoir.org; PO Box 452, Pittsfield, MA 01202-0452), under the direction of John Cheney, presents sacred and secular music in two concerts each year, one in December and one in May.

In **North County**, Williams College alone offers enough music to keep anyone humming, with four classical Thompson visiting performances, a world-music series, and performances by Williams faculty. The Berkshire Symphony, part professional and part student, and Williams Choral Society, both under the auspices of the Williams Department of Music, generally present three concerts apiece during the academic year. The student Jazz Ensemble, Kusika, the Zambezi Marimba Band, and close harmony groups too numerous to name provide musical saturation of high quality (24-hour Concertline: 413-597-2736).

Elsewhere in Williamstown, the Clark Art Institute (413-458-2303; www.clarkart.edu, 225 South Street, Williamstown, MA 01267) presents free band music outdoors in the summer and a variety of concerts indoors. The Northern Berkshire Chorale, a citizens' group, offers a concert spring and fall. Over in North Adams, Massachusetts College of Liberal Arts (413-662-5000) sponsors the Smith House Concert Series (413-662-5201), usually professional musicians with local connections.

THEATRE

Barrington Stage Company
413-236-8888
www.barringtonstageco.org
Berkshire Music Hall, 30 Union Street, Pittsfield, MA 01201

Julianne Boyd, artistic director of the Barrington Stage Company, is a whiz at detecting the enduring in what might seem the old soft shoe, e.g. the 2002 production that took *South Pacific* into the 21st century. Or consider what really got BSC under way in 1995: *Lady Day at Emerson's Bar & Grill*, starring Gail Nelson as blues singer Billie Holiday, playing to sell-outs at restaurants. In between, *Mac and Mabel* had a highly successful run on the main stage, while *St. Nicholas* and *Grease* flourished on Stage II. Perhaps the greatest hit so far, however, has been 2004's *The 27th Annual Putnam County Spelling Bee*, which enjoyed considerable success on Broadway after opening in Berkshire County. *The Man of La Mancha* was a recent success. Barrington runs Kids-Act, training ten-to-seventeen-year-olds, summer and fall, and has opened StudioSpace for intimate productions.

In 2005, BSC purchased the old Berkshire Music Hall and adjoining administrative building, allowing it to move from summer use of a high school stage in Sheffield to year-round occupancy in a former theater and movie house in Pittsfield.

Berkshire Theatre Group
Box office 413-997-4444;
administration 413-298-5536.
www.berkshiretheatregroup.org
Stockbridge Campus Ticket Office:
83 East Main Street, Stockbridge, MA 01262
On Route 102

In 1887, architect Stanford White completed his design for the Stockbridge Casino Company, created for the "establishment and maintenance of a place for a reading room, library and social meeting." Forty years later, when the structure had fallen into disuse, Mabel Choate, daughter of Ambassador Joseph H. Choate of Stockbridge, gave the Casino to the Three Arts Society. That group, in turn, moved it to its present site at the foot of Yale Hill, renting it to Alexander Kirkland and F. Cowles Strickland, who opened the Berkshire Playhouse in 1928. The building is now on the National Register of Historic Places.

Since that time, the playhouse—later renamed Berkshire Theatre Festival, now Berkshire Theatre Group—has been in the forefront of American summer theater. Major works by nearly every American playwright of note have been performed here, including Lillian Hellmann, Tennessee Williams, Eugene O'Neill, and Thornton Wilder. The playhouse produced Wilder's *Our Town* and *The Skin of Our Teeth,* with Wilder himself in featured roles.

Berkshire Theatre Group was created in 2010 by the merger of two of Berkshire County's oldest cultural organizations: Berkshire Theatre Festival in Stockbridge and The Colonial Theatre, built in 1903 in Pittsfield. One of the largest arts organizations in the area, BTG oversees the development, production and presentation of theatre, music and the performing arts on multiple stages.

The campus in Stockbridge, which is home to Berkshire Theatre Festival, presents work at two venues: The Fitzpatrick Main Stage and The Unicorn Theatre. The Fitzpatrick Main Stage is in the Casino building, producing classical theatre and world premieres each summer, such as *The Bells Are Ringing* and *Deathtrap.* The Unicorn Theatre, a theatrical jewel, is the home for new and emerging artists, and challenging and thoughtful work. The Colonial is located in downtown Pittsfield, providing year-round performances. The educational aspect, called "The BTF Plays," reaches out to local schools.

Shakespeare & Company
413-637-3353
www.shakespeare.org
70 Kemble Street, Lenox, MA 01240

Shakespeare is revitalized onstage in Lenox, having moved uptown to Springlawn. Under the powerful artistic guidance of English actor/ director Tina Packer, Shakespeare & Company, which celebrated its 25th anniversary in 2002, brought new light, feeling, and clarity to Shakespeare, making the works more accessible. Shakespeare & Company brings its much-anticipated, collaborative projects to area schools in the winter, spreading the wonder of the Bard even farther.

Part of the dramatic impact derives from the actors' ability to treat the audience as their alter ego, always privy to secrets of the drama. The plays are staged all around the seating area; intimacy with the action is inevitable, with stage and lighting design creating magical effects.

As *New York Times* critic Ben Brantley wrote of the company's performance of *A Midsummer Night's Dream*: "The overall result is vulgar, over scaled and loud. And it works. . . . There are few productions of Shakespearean comedy in which the meaning of every joke (whether intended by

Shakespeare or not) reads so clearly, and the audience was responsive to each one."

While Shakespeare & Company attends to its namesake, it has also produced Edith Wharton-oriented plays and contemporary plays. Under the aegis of its Arden Institute, the company has toured, offering free workshops and demonstrations. It also runs programs for young actors. Shakespeare & Company is a "must see" for locals and visitors alike.

Williamstown Theatre Festival & '62 Center for Theatre and Dance

413-597-3400; administration 413-458-3200; fax 413-458-3147
www.WTFestival.org
1000 Main Street, PO Box 517,
Williamstown, MA 01267

For former Producer Michael Ritchie, the challenge was not to be "the best summer theater but the best theater in America." Williamstown Theatre Festival took a giant step in that direction in the summer of 1999, exciting the theater world with Academy Award winner Gwyneth Paltrow in *As You Like It,* followed by an extraordinary production of Arthur Miller's *The Price*. More recently, *The Unknown Soldier* was a critical hit. Stellar WTF plays regularly move on to Boston or Broadway. In 2002, WTF received a regional Tony Award for 48 years of sustained excellence, the first summer theater in the nation to be so recognized. Newer producers have a solid base on which to build.

Each summer, in addition to full-scale productions with first-rate sets and costumes on the Main Stage at the sparkling '62 Center for Theatre and Dance, WTF offers other more intimate theater experiences. These are mounted at the smaller Downstage, dubbed "Nikos Stage" in the summer. Late-night musical cabarets provide surprise cameo appearances by Main Stage celebrities like inveterate songster and raconteur Dick Cavett. Catch Staged Readings; Free Theater, usually outdoors on Poker Flats field; Act I Performance Projects by the WTF young actor training ensemble; and the Greylock Theatre Project, which connects economically disadvantaged young people from North Adams with professional theater artists.

It's no mistake, then, that *Newsweek* ranked WTF as "the best of all American summer theaters" with "the cream of America's acting crop." And in its new facility, the sky's the limit!

The '62 Center, meanwhile, carries on a full program of student and professional theater and dance during the fall, winter, and spring, both student and visiting professional productions (413-597-2425; 62center.williams.edu; '62 Center for Theatre and Dance, 1000 Main Street, Williamstown, MA 01267).

Other theatre . . .

In **South County**, the biggest little theater is Mixed Company (413-528-2320; at the Granary, 37 Rosseter Street, Great Barrington, MA 01230), where fall-off-the-seat comedy alternates with moving drama. Under the direction of playwright Joan Ackermann, Mixed Company has built a solid following, often leading to competition for the theater's few dozen seats. Ackermann's award-winning *Zara Spook and Other Lures* premiered here, as did her droll *Bed and Breakfast,* in which she played an addled

Mrs. Digby. The Desisto Estate Cabaret (413-298-4032; DeSisto School, Route 183, Stockbridge, MA 01230) hosts dinner theater some evenings in the summer, cabaret performances Friday and Saturday following dinner, and additional cabaret after some Friday and all Saturday Tanglewood concerts. The venerable Mahaiwe Theater in Great Barrington (413-528-0100; www .mahaiwe.org; 14 Castle Street, Great Barrington, MA 01230) has reopened as a performing arts center, with a full schedule of local and touring talent.

The *Central County* theater scene has never been livelier. The Berkshire Community College Players regularly appear at the Robert Boland Theater at BCC (413-499-4660 when performances are staged; 1350 West Street, Pittsfield 01201). The Town Players (413-443-9279; www.townplayers.org; Whitney Center for the Arts, 42 Wendell Ave., Pittsfield, MA 01201). More than 90 year old, the players present a fall, winter and spring production, with occasional special shows, usually at the Whitney Center on Wendell Street. The News in Revue (866-811-4111) performs political satire during the summer at the Mountainside Playhouse at Bousquets.

North County is especially theatrical, including the Starlight Stage Youth Theatre (413-458-4246; starlightstage youththeatre.com; 57 Linden Street, Williamstown 01267), a hands-on theater experience for youth from eight years to 18, performs summers at the First Congregational Church. In the fall and winter the Williams Theatre Department picks up any slack (413-597-2425; 62center.williams.edu; '62 Center for Theatre and Dance, 1000 Main Street, Williamstown 01267). It stages impressive revivals and new plays. The drama department at Massachusetts College of Liberal Arts (413-662-5000) presents additional performances.

BOOTS, BOOKS, MAPS, PACKS

Stores throughout the county sell items useful to hikers: for example, ice cream cones. Nevertheless certain kinds of stores are of particular value.

SPORTING GOODS

South County

Gerry Cosby & Co., 413-229-6600; www. cosbysports.com; 103 S. Undermountain Road, Sheffield, MA 01257.
Housatonic River Outfitters, Inc., 413-528-8811, fax 413-528-5054; www .dryflies.com; 684 South Main Street, Great Barrington 01230

Central County

Arcadian Shop, 413-637-3010; www. arcadian.com; 91 Pittsfield-Lenox Road, Route 7/20, PO Box 1637, Lenox, MA 01240
Dave's Sporting Goods, 413-442-2960; davessporting.com; 1164 North Street, Route 7, Pittsfield, MA 01201
Dick's Sporting Goods, 413-395-0870; dickssportinggoods; 635 Merrill Road, Pittsfield, MA 01201
Dick Moon Sporting Goods, 413-442-8281; fax 413-448-2718; 114 Fenn Street, Pittsfield 01201
Eastern Mountain Sports, 413-445-4967; www.ems.com; Berkshire Mall, Old State Road and Route 8, Lanesborough, MA 01237
Plaine's Bike Snowboard Ski Shop, 413-499-0294; 55 West Housatonic Street, Pittsfield, MA 01201

North County

Berkshire Outfitters, 413-743-5900; fax 413-743-3359; www.berkshireoutfitters.com; Route 8 Grove Street, Adams, MA 01220

Williams College Bookstore, 413-458-8071, bookstore.williams.edu, 81 Spring Street, Williamstown, MA 01267

Nature's Closet, 413-458-7909, 61 Spring Street, Williamstown, MA 01267

BOOKS

South County

The Bookloft, 413-528-1521; www.thebookloft.com; 332 Stockbridge Road, Great Barrington, MA 01230

Yellow House Books, 413-528-8227; www.yellowhousebooks.com; 252 Main Street, Great Barrington 01230

Central County

Barnes & Noble, 413-496-9051; Berkshire Crossing Mall, 555 Hubbard Avenue, Pittsfield, MA 01201

The Bookstore and Get Lit Wine Bar, 413-637-3390; 11 Housatonic Street, Lenox, MA 01240

Waldenbooks, 413-499-0115; Berkshire Mall, Lanesborough, MA 01237.

North County

Water Street Books, 413-458-8071; www.waterstreet.bkstr.com; 26 Water Street, Williamstown, MA 01267—moving to Spring Street in 2016.

Bibliography

Appalachian Trail Guide to Massachusetts-Connecticut. P.O. 807, Harpers Ferry, WV, 25425-0807, 1988.

Binzen, William. *The Berkshires* (a book of photographs). Chester, CT: Globe Pequot Press, 1986.

Brady and White. *Fifty Hikes in Massachusetts.* Woodstock, VT: Backcountry Publications, 1983.

Burns and Stevens, updated by Leah Katzelnick. *Most Excellent Majesty: A History of Mount Greylock.* Pittsfield, MA: Berkshire Natural Resources Council, 2009.

Cuyler, Lewis. *Bike Rides in the Berkshire Hills.* Lee, MA: Berkshire House Publishers, 1990.

Drew, Bernard. *A History of Notchview.* Gt. Barrington, MA: Attic Revivals Press, 1986.

Federal Writers Project. *The Berkshire Hills.* Reprinted by Northeastern University Press, 1987.

Griswold, Whit. *Berkshire Trails for Walking and Ski Touring.* The East Woods Press, 1986.

Ryan, Christopher J. *Guide to the Taconic Trail System.* Amherst, MA: New England Cartographics, 1989.

Stevens, Lauren R. *The Berkshire Book: A Complete Guide* (8th edition). Woodstock, VT: The Countryman Press, 2006.

Taconic Hiking Club. *Guide to the Taconic Crest Trail.* Troy, NY, 1988.

Thoreau, Henry David. *A Week on the Concord and Merrimack Rivers.* Boston: Houghton Mifflin Co., 1893.

Williams Outing Club. *Northern Berkshire Outdoor Guide.* Williams College, 1999.

Index

Berkshire Regional Transit Authority, 20, 158, 179
Berkshire School, 18, 54, 263
Berkshire Visitors Bureau, 21
Berkshires: natural history of, 26; settlement of, 27
Berlin Mountain, 193
Berlin Pass, 196
Bernard Farm Trail, 192
Berry Pond, 116
Berry, William, 116
Bessemer process, 174
biking, 16, 88, 155, 158, 196
Birch Brook, 211
birch, 27, 51, 215; and Bellows Pipe Trail, 192; and Mount Greylock, 153; and Lenox, 112; and the Lulu Brook Trail, 118; and Nan Path, 203; and Three Trails, 90
birds, 48, 83, 153, 257. *See also birds by name*
Birnie, Alexander, 98
blazes, 16
blueberry: and Alander, 50; and Berlin Mountain, 195, 196; and Mount Everett, 57; and Jones' Nose, 162; and Pine Cobble, 216; and Rounds' Rock, 162; and Snow Hole, 209
Bluebird Trail, 109
Bob Quay Bridge, 186
bobcat, 136, 153
bobolinks, 48
Bog-Trotting for Orchids (Niles), 206
bogs: and Bear Mountain, 40; and Bradley Farm Trail, 161; and Cheshire Harbor, 178; and Clam River, 65; and Diane's Trail, 70; and the Dome, 217, 221; and Greylock, 153; and Hopper Trail, 182, 183; and Money Brook, 188; and Notchview, 136; and Saddle Ball, 153; and Snow Hole, 212; and Tannery Falls, 229
Bond shelter, 54, 58

Borland Trail, 46
"born free and equal" clause, 46
Boulders, the, 131
Boy Scouts, 145
Brackett, Joseph, 142
Bradley Farm Trail, 153, 159
Bradley, Ephraim, 159
Bradley, William, 159
Broad Brook Trail, 216, 217, 221
Brom, 46
Brook & Berry Trail, 161
Brooks, Robert R. R., 200
Bryant, William Cullen, 83, 241, 250
Budd, Arthur D., 136
Bullard Woods, 104
"Butter Bates," 139
Buxton Gardens, 209
Buxton School, 17, 201

C
Campbell Falls, 43
Campground Trails, 153, 165
Canoe Meadows, 112, 127
cascades, 37, 40, 42, 83, 116, 222. *See also* waterfalls
Cascades, the, 222
Catskills: and Alander, 49; and Berlin Mountain, 196; and Berry Pond, 120; and Elbow Trail, 57; and Lenox, 111; and Mount Greylock, 150; and Three Trails, 88
CCC. *See* Civilian Conservation Corps
Charcoal Trail, 91
charcoal-burning sites, 91, 142, 146, 147, 174
Chef's Hat, the, 207
cherry, 161
Cheshire Harbor, 176
Cheshire Harbor Trail, 179
chipmunks, 153
Circuit Trail, 138, 140
Circular Trail, 174
Civilian Conservation Corps, 15, 17, 96

Greylock Glenn, 178
Griffin, Edward Dorr, 180
grouse, 153
Guilder Hollow, 58
Guilder Pond, 56, 57
gypsy moth, 96

H

Hairpin Turn, 221, 225, 229
Haley Farm, 188
Haley Farm Trail, 165, 172, 174, 182, 186
Hancock Shaker Village, 142, 243, 258
hares, 153, 157
Harrison, Almond, 180
Hatch, Olivia Stokes, 91
hawks, 48, 136, 153, 228
Hawthorne, Nathaniel: and "Little Red House" replica, 243; and Bellows Pipe Trail, 191; and Berkshire culture, 241; and Berkshires, 28; and Mount Greylock, 151, 191; and Monument Mountain, 83; and Saddle Mountain, 150
Heaphy, Harry W., 18
Hemlock Brook, 193, 194, 196
hemlock: and Alander, 51, 53; and Bear Mountain, 40; and Berlin Mountain, 195, 196; and Campbell Falls, 44; and Charcoal Trail, 91; and the Cascades, 224; and Deer Hill Trail, 153, 167; and Dunbar Brook, 232, 235; and Fitch Trail, 200; and Jambs Trail, 140; and Jug End, 61; and Lenox, 111; and Money Brook Trail, 188; and Monument Mountain, 83; and Mount Everett, 56; and Mount Greylock, 153; and Nan Path, 203; and Ramblewild, 148; and Roaring Brook Trail, 175; and Ross Brook, 230; and Shaker Mountain, 146; and Snow Hole,

211; and Stevens Glen, 122; and Tannery Falls, 230; and Three Trails, 89; and Wahconah Falls, 134
hepatica, 51
hickory, shagbark, 146
hobblebush, 175, 196
Holmes, Oliver Wendell, 83, 127
honeysuckle, 127
Honwee Trail, 118
Hoosac Range Trail, 225
Hoosac Valley, view of, 225, 213, 228
Hoosic River Watershed Association, 155
Hopkins Forest, 209
Hopper, 153, 171, 185, 187
Hopper Trail, 165, 168, 180
Housatonic Flats Reserve, 77
Housatonic River, 40, 45
Housatonic River Walk, 68, 69
Housatonic Valley, 40
Housatonic Valley Association, 113
Hume Brook, 140
hunting, 24
Hurlburt's Hill, 48
Hurricane Diane, and York Lake, 63
Hyde, C. E., 212

I

Ice Glen Trail, 88
Indian Monument Trail, 83
Inner Hopper, 187

J

Jambs Brook, 141
Jensen, Peter, 9, 100, 113, 225
Jimapco Map C12, Berkshire County, MA, 18
John D. Kennedy Park, 104
Jones' Nose, 152, 162, 164, 178
Judge's Hill, 136
Jug End, 58
Jug End State Reservation and Wildlife Management Area, 58
"Jungle, the," 157